Economics, Rational Choice and Normative Philosophy

Following Amartya Sen's insistence on expanding the framework of rational choice theory by taking into account 'non-utility information', economists, political scientists and philosophers have recently concentrated their efforts on analysing the issues related to rights, freedom, diversity intentions and equality. Thomas Boylan and Ruvin Gekker have gathered essays that reflect this trend.

The particular themes addressed in this volume include the measurement of diversity and freedom, formal analysis of individual rights and intentions, judgment aggregation under constraints and strategic manipulation in fuzzy environments. Some chapters in the volume also deal with philosophical aspects of normative social choice.

This book will be of great interest to students engaged in social choice, public choice and normative philosophy.

Thomas A. Boylan is a Personal Professor of Economics in the Department of Economics at the National University of Ireland, Galway.

Ruvin Gekker is a Lecturer in Economics in the Department of Economics at the National University of Ireland, Galway.

Routledge Frontiers of Political Economy

Economics, Rational Choice and Normative Philosophy

Edited by Thomas A. Boylan and Ruvin Gekker

Routledge
Taylor & Francis Group

LONDON AND NEW YORK

First published 2009
by Routledge
2 Park Square, Milton Park, Abingdon, Oxon OX14 4RN

Simultaneously published in the USA and Canada
by Routledge
270 Madison Ave, New York, NY 10016

Routledge is an imprint of the Taylor & Francis Group, an informa business

© 2009 Editorial matter and selection, Thomas A. Boylan and Ruvin
Gekker; individual chapters, the contributors

Typeset in Times New Roman by Prepress Projects Ltd, Perth, UK
Printed and bound in Great Britain by TJI Digital, Padstow, Cornwall

British Library Cataloguing in Publication Data
A catalogue record for this book is available from the British Library

Library of Congress Cataloging in Publication Data
Economics, rational choice, and normative philosophy / edited by Thomas
A. Boylan and Ruvin Gekker.
p. cm.
Includes bibliographical references and index.
1. Economics. 2. Philosophy. 3. Rational choice theory. I. Boylan, Thomas
A. II. Gekker, Ruvin.
HB72.E277 2009
330.01–dc22
2008021536

ISBN10: 0–415–43580–3 (hbk)
ISBN10: 0–203–88764–6 (ebk)

ISBN13: 978–0–415–43580–2 (hbk)
ISBN13: 978–0–203–88764–6 (ebk)

Contents

Contributors

Nicholas Baigent, Graz University, Austria

Thomas A. Boylan, National University of Ireland, Galway

Matthew Braham, University of Groningen, Netherlands

Boudewijn de Bruin, University of Groningen, Netherlands

Franz Dietrich, Maastricht University, Netherlands

Ruvin Gekker, National University of Ireland, Galway

Nicolas Gravel, University of the Mediterranean and IDEP-GREQAM, Marseilles, France

Manfred J. Holler, University of Hamburg, Germany

Christian List, London School of Economics, UK

Paschal F. O'Gorman, National University of Ireland, Galway

Gerald Pech, American University, Bulgaria

Juan Perote-Peña, University of Zaragoza, Spain

Ashley Piggins, National University of Ireland, Galway

Olivier Roy, University of Amsterdam, Netherlands

Martin van Hees, University of Groningen, Netherlands

Preface

This book is based on the International Workshop that was held at the National University of Ireland, Galway, in August 2005. The theme of the workshop, 'Rational Choice and Normative Philosophy', was designed to further foster a close collaboration between economists, philosophers and political scientists working in normative social choice. The organizers were fortunate to attract some leading experts in normative social choice who contributed their papers to this volume.

The chapters in this book explore a number of issues pioneered recently by Amartya Sen in his critique of rational choice theory. The first issue relates to an examination of how individual rights or liberties affect collective decision-making. The problem was demonstrated by Sen's theorem on the impossibility of a Paretian liberal and has produced an enormous response not only by economists but also by philosophers. In particular, Robert Nozick has argued that rights do not establish an ordering of social states but instead divide them into classes or serve as a constraint. Subsequently Peter Gardenfors, Wulf Gaertner, Persanta Pattonaik and Kotaro Suzumura among others have developed Nozick's insights into analysis of individual rights by suggesting a game-theoretic approach to the study of rights and liberties.

Another issue that was explored by rational choice theorists, and again was influenced by Amartya Sen's work, is the measurement of freedom and diversity. The typical problem here is to determine how the various sets of options that might be available to an agent could be compared in terms of the amount of freedom or diversity they offer. The starting point is to formulate certain conditions or axioms that are imposed on possible freedom or diversity measures. This axiomatic method allows us to assess various measures of freedom and diversity on the basis of their underlying assumptions.

Recently the problem of judgment aggregation has attracted a lot of attention from rational choice theorists. A collective decision here is presented not as one choice between various alternatives but instead as many decisions on interconnected propositions. This model of judgment aggregation is quite general and it allows us to represent beliefs, desires, acts and other propositional attitudes. The model of judgment aggregation is also very close to real decision-making situations.

In organizing an international workshop and presenting its contents in a book we have incurred many debts of gratitude. We would like to thank the Department of Economics and the Faculty of Commerce at the National University of Ireland, Galway, who helped us with the costs of organizing this workshop. We also would like to thank all the participants in the workshop for very stimulating discussions that have helped to revise the conference papers. Special thanks for their help in organizing this workshop are due to Imelda Howley and Claire Noone. However, we would like to single out Martin van Hees, who was instrumental in shaping the idea of this workshop and also provided invaluable help in organizing it.

Claire Noone provided her customary indispensable support on the final stages of preparation of the manuscript. Without her help we would not have been able to cope with the deadlines.

Last, but not least, we would like to express our gratitude to the staff of Routledge, as always, for their professionalism and efficiency in handling our manuscript. In particular, we would like to thank Terry Clague not only for commissioning this volume, but also for his patience and understanding in the face of a protracted delay in delivering the final manuscript for reasons that were outside our control. For this we are most grateful. We would also like to thank Sarah Hastings for her outstanding efforts in coordinating and expediting the publication of this book.

Introduction

In the last three decades some new approaches to the study of rights, freedom, diversity, norms and intentions among others have evolved. These approaches have their origin in rational choice theory. Rational choice theory covers a wide variety of disciplines among which particularly helpful for our purposes are social choice theory, game theory and individual decision theory. Amartya Sen was particularly influential in his critique of traditional models of rational choice theory. Since the 1970s the traditional models of rational choice theory not only were expanded to include welfare consequences but also took into account 'non-utility information' referring to rights, freedom, diversity and equality.

The present collection of papers is based on the workshop 'Rational choice and normative philosophy' which was held in August of 2005 at the National University of Ireland, Galway. The workshop attracted a number of leading experts in normative social choice and philosophy from the Netherlands, France, Germany, the United Kingdom and Ireland. The participants focused their attention on the formal analysis of issues related to rights, norms, variety and freedom, intentions and responsibility among others and also on the philosophical aspects of those issues. The chapters in the book are grouped into three sets. The chapters in Part I provide a formal analysis of such aspects of normative social choice as diversity, individual rights, internalized norms and intentions. The three chapters in Part II discuss issues related to constraints in judgment aggregation, the strategic manipulation in fuzzy environments and the rationality of legal order. Finally, the chapters in Part III deal with some philosophical aspects of normative social and public choice.

Part I opens with N. Gravel's chapter 'What is Diversity?' The chapter surveys many contributions to the formal analysis of diversity. The author strives to keep the formalism to a minimum and he provides some informal discussion of the results and the assumptions or axioms. Specifically, he starts with a (finite) set X of objects which are clearly identified. Then the problem of diversity evaluation is to provide a ranking of a binary relation $\geq$, with asymmetric and symmetric factors $>$ and $\sim$, defined on subsets of X. Denote by $P(X)$ the set of all non-empty subsets of X. Then for any A, B in $P(X)$, $A \geq B$ means 'A offers at least as much diversity as B', $A > B$ means 'A offers strictly more diversity than B' and $A \sim B$ means 'A offers the same diversity as B'.

Typically, the researchers in the field assume that the diversity ranking is reflexive, complete and transitive. Since X is finite, we know that the diversity ordering can be represented by a numerical diversity index. This numerical index can be thought of as 'measuring' the diversity of various sets. However, some other assumptions (axioms) relating to the axiomatic ranking of sets in terms of their diversity could be imposed. Many axioms introduced in the second section were already discussed in the context of the axiomatic ranking of freedom. The list would include weak and strong monotonicity axioms (Axioms 1.1 and 1.2). In terms of diversity these axioms simply say that the addition of objects to a set never reduces (strictly increases, respectively, in the case of Axiom 1.2) diversity. Similarly to the axiomatic analysis of freedom, we can assume that singleton sets provide no diversity at all. Axiom 1.3, indifference between non-diverse situations, says precisely this. This axiom is satisfied by most indices used in biology to measure biodiversity. It is also satisfied by all approaches viewing the diversity of a set as a result of the aggregation of the pairwise dissimilarities of its elements. Another group of axioms introduced by Gravel, the so-called independence axioms, compare sets of objects to the extent to which the contribution of objects to diversity should depend on the set to which they are added or subtracted.

Using these axioms, the author establishes a very general characterization result of diversity rankings. He refers to them as additive rankings and he shows that the cardinality ranking that compares sets on the basis of their number of elements represents a special case of additive rankings. There exists an extensive discussion of cardinality ranking in the context of axiomatic ranking of freedom (see among others Pattanaik and Xu 1990; Jones and Sugden 1982; Barberà, Bossert and Pattanaik 2004).

In his third section, Gravel examines a wide class of diversity base rankings in biology that is associated with Renyi's generalized entropy measure. He notes that the properties that characterize the generalized entropy family of rankings have been identified in completely different contexts of income inequality measurement by Shorrocks (1984). It is interesting to point out that the axioms used by Shorrocks clearly illustrate the limitations of generalized entropy as a method for evaluating diversity.

The author then evaluates an approach to the ranking of sets in terms of their diversity initiated by Weitzman (1992). Weitzman uses a distance function in this recursive method. A distance function (or metric function) d is a mapping from a Cartesian product of X into non-negative reals. It associates with every ordered pair (x,y) from X, a non-negative number $d(x,y)$ interpreted as the distance that separated x from y. Typically it is required that d must be symmetric, normal (that is, $d(x,x)=0$) and that it also satisfies another property of triangle inequality (which could be problematic in the context of diversity evaluation). Using such a distance function Weitzman proposed to compare sets on the bases of the sum of these smallest non-zero minimal distances.

Sets with larger sums are considered more diverse than those with smaller sums. Hence Weitzman's definition of diversity was in effect an aggregation of dissimilarities. The procedure was sequential, combining sequential selecting of the objects associated with the minimal distance and an additive procedure of summing these minimal distances. According to Gravel, the fundamental difficulty associated with Weitzman's approach is his assumption of a cardinally meaningful distance function. Is it possible to view diversity as an aggregation of dissimilarities between the objects and yet to reject the requirement that these dissimilarities can be measured cardinally? The positive answer is provided by Bervoets and Gravel (2007).

An ordinal notion of dissimilarity is formalized by a quaternary relation Q an X. The statement $(x,y)\,Q\,(w,z)$ can be interpreted as 'x is at least as dissimilar to y as w is to z'. Asymmetric ('strictly more dissimilar') and symmetric ('equally similar') factors of Q can be defined in the usual manner. They are denoted by Q_A and Q_S respectively. To motivate this interpretation, the authors assume that, for all distinct objects x and y from X, both $(x,y)\,Q_A\,(x,x)$ and $(x,x)\,Q_S\,(y,y)$ hold. Further it is assumed that Q is symmetric, that is, $(x,y)\,Q\,(y,x)$ holds for every x and y and that a binary relation on the Cartesian product of X is reflexive, complete and transitive. Furthermore, Bervoets and Gravel introduce three more principles (axioms): weak monotonicity, dissimilarity monotonicity and robustness of domination. The third principle (robustness of domination) requires the domination of a set by another one to be robust to the addition of options when the options added are themselves dominated in terms of diversity. It turns out that a ranking of sets that satisfies the principles of weak monotonicity, dissimilarity monotonicity and robustness of domination compares sets on the basis of their two most dissimilar objects, that is, we can say that a set A is at least as diverse as set B if the two most dissimilar objects in A are at least as dissimilar as the two most dissimilar object to B. The authors refer to this ranking as the 'maxi-max' criterion.

Finally, Gravel examines a new approach to the definition of diversity introduced recently by Nehring and Puppe (2002). They propose to define the diversity of a set as the sum of the values of the attributes realized by the objects in the set. Hence this approach relies on the categorization of the objects into a certain number of attributes and may lead to the conclusion that some singleton sets could have more diversity than sets containing multiplicity of objects, contrary to Axiom 3. This might happen simply because the value of the attributes in the single object could be larger than the value of the attributes realized in the collection of many objects. Therefore, this approach, according to Gravel, evaluates not so much the diversity of a set but rather the attributes possessed by the objects.

Given the current state of the field, the author prefers the approach that defines the diversity as an aggregation of ordinal information about pairwise dissimilarities between objects expressed by a quaternary relation. This approach seems to raise fewer objections than other approaches to diversity such as the generalized entropy approach or the approach initiated by Weitzman that defines diversity as an aggregation of cardinally meaningful information about the pairwise dissimilarity objects expressed by a distance function.

The next chapter, 'Intentions, Decisions and Rationality' by M. van Hees and O. Roy, proposes to extend the traditional decision-theoretic model by including 'action intentions'. Action intentions refer to the future performance of some actions, for example the intention 'to take the plane to London'. These intentions can be distinguished from 'outcome intentions', which refer to the intention to bring about some future states of affairs, for example 'to be in London next month'. The philosophical theory that motivates the authors' formal modelling is Bratman's planning theory of intentions. This theory describes plans as special sets of intentions. They have an internal hierarchical structure. On top of the structure are general intentions, such as going to London, and then come increasingly more precise intentions, such as going by plane, departure time etc. Rational plans (which are partial) in this planning theory of intentions are regulated by norms of consistency, that is, they should not contain inconsistent intentions. This requirement is called endogenous consistency. The plan to achieve a certain goal must be supplied with intentions to undertake appropriate means. This requirement for plan completion is called means–end consistency.

The authors choose to formalize intentions by working with sequential or extensive models of decision theory (see Osborne and Rubinstein 1994 or Aliprantis and Chakrabarti 2000). They argue that the intentions of ideal agents (perfectly rational and capable of representing and solving any decision problem) can be viewed as plans of action. The authors restrict their attention to intentions that do not have autonomous effects. Later on they show that some difficulties may arise when intentions with autonomous effects are introduced in decision theory.

Formally, van Hees and Roy assume that the agent comes with both outcome and action intentions, that is, with a decision tree T they associate an intention structure I consisting of sets of outcomes and a collection of (perhaps partial) plans of actions. The authors want to impose some constraints on these sets in order to capture the familiar consistency requirements of the planning theory of intentions. These are captured in Postulates 2.1 and 2.2, so-called postulates of endogenous consistency of outcome intentions and endogenous consistency of action intentions, respectively. Postulate 2.1 says that the set of outcome intentions is closed under intersection and that the agent intends at least something and does not intend to do the impossible. Postulate 2.2 precludes the agent from having two action intentions that are not executable in a single run. Postulate 2.3, means–end consistency, connects the action intentions to the outcome intentions, saying that there should be at least one partial plan of action that ensures the agent will obtain some outcome (if the plan is enacted). Postulate 2.4, actions intentions for ideal agents, simply requires that intentions of ideal agents reduce to plans of actions. Although intentions reduce to plans of actions to the ideal agent, van Hees and Roy show that intentions can be useful 'to break ties' between equally desirable strategies. To establish this result they need yet another Postulate, 2.5, intentions and expected payoff compatibility, which establishes that certain intentions will not be formed given the preferences of the agent. Specifically, the result says that for any decision tree T and intention structure I satisfying Postulates 2.1–2.5, there exists one and only one plan that coincides with all (partial or non-partial) plans in the collection of plans of actions and also maximizes expected value. The result also confirms what philosophers of actions have been claiming all along, namely, intentions are key anchors to one person in sequential decision-making.

The authors also show that the formation of intentions might have some autonomous consequences and it may present some additional modelling problems. They illustrate these problems by using the famous 'Toxin Puzzle' introduced by Kavka (1983). In order to analyze the Toxin Puzzle, van Hees and Roy extend their framework by allowing the formation of an intention to perform some action and hence in effect introducing the second-order intentions. They impose the following Postulate 2.6, consistency between first- and second-order intentions, that says that an agent who has a second-order intention to perform the action a also has a first-order intention to do so. Then van Hees and Roy produce an impossibility result that illustrates a clash between Postulates 2.5 and 2.6 and is not bound to the scenario of the Toxin Puzzle.

In his chapter 'Waiving and Exercising Rights in the Theory of Social Situations', R. Gekker suggests an analysis of individual rights within the framework of the theory of social situations. The original formulation of individual rights by A. Sen (1970) within social choice theory simply restricts social choice based on an individual's preferences over two social states that differ only with respect to the individual's recognized personal sphere (RPS). Gaertner, Pattanaik and Suzumura (1992), utilizing Gibbard's example, have pointed out some intuitive problems with Sen's original formulation of individual rights. Instead they have suggested that each individual should be able to determine a certain aspect of any social state provided that an aspect is within that individual's RPS. Then according to them the game-form formulation of individual rights should adequately capture this intuition. Since the publication of their paper in 1992, the focus of researchers in the field has shifted from producing impossibility/possibility results to discussing an issue of adequacy/inadequacy of different formulations of individual rights.

The author's proposal was motivated by Gardenfors's (1981) suggestion that an individual right can be described as a possibility for an individual i to restrict the set of social states X to a subset Y of X. A right system is defined by Gardenfors as a set of pairs (i, Y). Gardenfors then imposes various conditions on the right system. For example, he requires that different individuals should not have conflicting rights. However, the analysis of individual rights in the situations where these rights are conflicting is the most interesting. For example, how should we resolve the conflict of individual rights when the right to smoke for one individual may conflict with the right of another individual to clean air? Another of Gardenfors's conditions on combination of rights allows him to ignore the sequential aspect of moves in a game and to identify the set of strategies available to an individual with the set of rights assigned to him or her.

The author, following the lead of Gardenfors, proposes to analyse individual rights within the framework of the theory of social situations. Similarly to Gardenfors's formulation of individual rights, he distinguishes between having a right and exercising that right. Unlike Gardenfors, however, Gekker does not impose any restrictions on individual rights, that is, he allows individuals to have conflicting rights and he also allows them to exercise their rights sequentially. Using the flexibility of the theory of social situations, the author utilizes different rights-exercising protocols to analyse individual rights. For example, the first rights-exercising protocol prohibits both sequential rights exercising and the formation of coalitions. The second rights-exercising protocol allows individuals to exercise their rights sequentially but prohibits the formation of coalitions. Finally, the third rights-exercising protocol allows both the formation of coalitions and sequential rights exercising. Using familiar examples from the literature on individual rights, the author illustrates how the difference in the rights-exercising protocols affects exercising or waiving individual rights in each case.

Part II opens with the chapter 'Social Choice, Fuzzy Preferences and Manipulations' by J. Perota-Peña and A. Piggins. The authors examine the nature of social choice, which is based on fuzzy individual preferences. A fuzzy binary relation R defined on X is characterized by a function F_R from a Cartesian product of X into the closed interval $[0.1]$. F_R (x, y) can be interpreted as the degree of confidence that 'x is at least as good as y'. Semantically it can also be interpreted as the degree of truth of the sentence 'x is at least as good as y.' In social choice theory fuzzy relations are used to represent vague preferences. Now, if individuals have fuzzy preferences, how do they make their choices? Would the classical impossibility result in social choice theory continue to hold when individuals have fuzzy preferences?

In their chapter the authors produce a positive answer to this question. They establish a version of the classical Gibbard–Satterthwaite theorem in the context of fuzzy preferences and exact social choice functions. The exact social choice functions combine non-empty subsets of the set of alternatives with a fuzzy preference profile, thereby producing a social choice. Perota-Peña and Piggins prove that any exact social choice function that has 'minimal links' to a fuzzy social welfare function is dictatorial provided that this fuzzy social welfare function (or fuzzy aggregation rule) is strategy-proof and not constant. The authors then examine the question of what can be responsible for this impossibility result.

The requirement of the fuzzy aggregation that it should not be constant is not particularly strong. In fact, it is similar to the standard condition of non-imposition in social choice theory. Assumption of strategy-proof ness is rather standard and is not controversial. The most contentious assumption is that of transitivity of fuzzy preferences. In the chapter the authors assume that their fuzzy preferences (individual and social) satisfy 'max–min' transitivity. Although this assumption is somewhat controversial, Perote-Peña and Piggins believe that even this condition should not be simply dismissed since there exists no experimental evidence showing that people with fuzzy preferences violate max–min transitivity. Hence their impossibility result can serve as a useful benchmark for future work in this area.

In their chapter 'Judgment Aggregation under Constraints', F. Dietrich and C. List focus on the role that constraints play in judgment aggregation problems. These decision problems are modelled using propositions in a language of propositional or predicate logic, each proposition to be accepted or rejected, and constraints can also be modelled as propositions with which the decisions should be logically consistent. For instance, suppose a three-member court has to make a collective judgement on three connected propositions:

x: The defendant did action *A*.
y: The defendant had a contractual obligation not to do action *A*.
z: The defendant is liable for breach of contract.

Assume further that the law imposes the constraint that action and obligation (the two premises *x* and *y*) are both necessary and sufficient for liability (the conclusion *z*), that is, *z* if and only if *x* and *y* (symbolically, $z <=> x \wedge y$). It is then possible that the majority judgments on the two premises *x* and *y* could conflict with the majority judgment on the conclusion *z*, relative to that constraint. This might happen if the first judge holds both *x* and *y* true, the second judge holds *x* true but *y* false, and the third judge holds *y* true but *x* false. Now, if each judge would respect the constraint that *z* if and only if *x* and *y*, then the majority judgments in support of *x* and *y* and against *z* would violate the given constraint. Another example is modelling judgments on ranking propositions in the form 'option *x* is better than option *y*'. These propositions should be consistent with the transitivity or acyclicity constraints. In biology, judgments on whether two organisms fall into the same species are often constrained by the assumption that belonging to the same species is an equivalence relation. In their chapter the authors make constraints explicit in judgment aggregation, and they review some general impossibility results in the light of explicit constraints.

In his chapter 'Rationality and the Legal Order', G. Pech develops a positive analysis of the legal system based on the constitution. The constitution has two elements: (1) the government must not seize property from its proper owner; (2) if a property right has been violated, the proper owner has a claim to restitution. (1) might be seen as guaranteeing non-arbitrariness in the exercise of governmental power, and (2) imposes some negative commitment preventing a lawfully acting government from illegal redistribution of property rights.

The author examines the consequences of the legal order in its application to property rights. Specifically, in his model there is a chain of successive governments with an exogenously fixed lifespan. The government is only interested in its tax revenue. However, it can also win some political support by redistributing property among its supporters. Pech solves the problem of the missing enforcer by delegating the enforcement of the rule compliance by the present government to its successor government. A constitutional successor government, though, is prevented from honouring illegal redistributions of property. The author then establishes when it is optimal for the future government to act constitutionally. Specifically, under certainty he finds that both defection and non-defection could be equilibria of the game. However, he does provide some conditions under which the only trembling-hand perfect equilibrium of this game is the one in which every government chooses to be legitimate with a probability approaching 1. That is, under trembling-hand perfection no government can rule out the possibility that it might be succeeded by constitutional government and, if the punishment that a constitutional government imposes under the rule of law is sufficiently great, a defecting government will put the greatest possible weight on the possibility that it will be succeeded by a constitutional government.

The author then discusses various simplifying assumptions of his modelling. In particular, he points out that he does not model political constraints resulting from a re-election objective. As a result, the distribution of property rights is given together with the constitution and hence the focus on a deterministic constitution might ignore the possibility of constitutional reforms. Although the author believes that such constitutional reforms could be incorporated in his model, he recognizes that there are some important issues that might arise from the possibility of allowing competing concepts of a legal order.

The chapters contained in Part III address rather different philosophical aspects of rationality and normative social choice. The first chapter in this section, by Matthew Braham and Manfred Holler, provides an interesting and innovative analysis of the difficult problem of ascribing responsibility in the context of collective action. Entitled 'Distributing Causal Responsibility in Collectivities,' it provides an extremely valuable and much needed synthesis 'of the literature on causality, power and responsibility in collectivities', which it places in a formal structure. The authors argue that the conventional approach of allocating responsibility is inappropriate in the context of collective action. Central to their critique of the conventional approach is the fact that, in so far as the 'many hands problem' exists in terms of identifying causal contributions to collective actions, it does only 'on account of a deeply rooted and pervasive conception of social causality'. This conception of social causality is one that attempts to identify at least one person who can be said to have with his or her 'own hands' achieved the collective outcome. It is, as the authors describe it, a conception of 'cause' as 'authorship'.

Within the formal structure which Braham and Holler introduce, this conception is characterized as that of 'strong necessity' or, as further elaborated by them, represents the application of the canonical counterfactual 'but-for test'. In legal terminology, it is the concept of cause as *sine qua non* – 'making a difference'. Braham and Holler argue, however, that there is an alternative conception of cause, what they term 'weak necessity/strong sufficiency,' which is available in the philosophical and legal literature. This alternative conception has entered the academic discourse under the acronyms of NESS (necessary element of a sufficient set) or INUS (insufficient but necessary part of a condition which is itself unnecessary but sufficient for the result). This, as the authors point out, 'is a weaker conception that embeds the "but-for" test in a set theoretic framework'. The chapter goes on to argue (1) that the 'many hands problem' is in fact a case of causal over-determination, and (2) that the INUS/NESS formulations were designed precisely to cover the case of causal over-determination, and that it is more appropriate to apply the INUS/NESS conception of cause than the more conventional 'but-for' conception when trying to identify causal responsibility in collectivities. In as much as the 'many hands problem' concerns the identification of causal contributions, the authors argue that 'the NESS/INUS conception of cause defuses the problem'.

The problem or 'responsibility paradox' addressed in this chapter is of fundamental theoretical and practical importance, as it does indeed, as the authors point out, lie at the very root of individual accountability in public life. Surprisingly, however, 'little effort has been devoted to meeting it head on' and, apart from some notable exceptions, the literature on responsibility in collectivities in general assumed the 'many hands problems' as being *prima facie* true, but then attempted to step around the problem of invoking the concept of collective responsibility, i.e. the idea that it is the collectivity that is answerable for causal responsibility and, if any responsibility is to devolve to its individual members, this is by virtue of association or membership only. The extended chapter by Braham and Holler, apart from being a masterly synthesis of the topic, delivers a number of important results, which may be summarized briefly here, and include the following. First, they have shown that it is possible to reconcile the role of individual acts with over-determined outcomes, thus strengthening earlier work that causal responsibility in a collective context is 'not necessarily nondistributive', certainly for the class of outcomes that can be modelled in a game-theoretic framework. Second, the class of outcomes for which causal responsibility is necessarily distributive is large. Third, the NESS test outlines a framework for quantifying judgments on responsibility in situations of collective action. Fourth, they demonstrate that, through a detailed analysis of the NESS test, a person can be held causally responsible for an outcome, notwithstanding the fact that the person is 'not directly indispensable' for the outcome under investigation, but in addition can be deemed to be so even if he or she is totally powerless to prevent the outcome in question. Finally, the authors argue that, by defusing the 'many hands problem', one of the traditional justifications for a theory of collective responsibility is undermined, or in the authors' words 'evaporates'. These are interesting and important results that clearly warrant further analysis along with providing a serious stimulus to new lines of research.

In the second contribution to Part III, Boudewijn de Bruin, in a succinct and focused chapter, addresses the topic of 'The Logic of Valuing'. The aim of the chapter is an analysis of the logical form of valuing. A distinction is drawn between the valuing of a concept or property, which is held to be a universal statement with respect to logical form, and the valuing of an object, which is an existential statement with respect to logical form. A correct analysis of the logical form of valuing, de Bruin argues, contains doxastic operators. Deploying these components in his analysis, de Bruin generates an interesting interaction between uniform and non-uniform quantification on the one hand, and *de dicto* and *de re* beliefs on the other. Applying the differences between these conceptions of quantification and beliefs, de Bruin generates a two-dimensional typology of six types of valuing. While adopting a doxastic perspective on valuing, de Bruin's analysis remains, he argues, 'neutral with respect to many issues from meta-ethics'. Nor is the analysis particularly narrow. Although de Bruin selected, for the sake of argument, concepts and objects to be the bearers of value in this offering, the same structural observations can be made, he argues, 'if you attach value to events, propositions, or even to possible worlds'. The analysis is applied to a particular area, i.e. political freedom, and de Bruin draws a distinction between the received view, which argues that the value of freedom lies in the domain of specific things one is free to do, and recent work that argues, in contrast, that freedom has an irreducible, non-specific value also (Carter 1999). Here de Bruin demonstrates that underlying their debate between the received view and its critics is a dispute about logical form, with the received view adhering to non-uniform *de dicto* beliefs about freedom as a concept, whereas the critics hold uniform half *de dicto* and half *de re* beliefs about freedom as an object.

In the final chapter, 'Holistic Defenses of Rational Choice Theory: A Critique of Davidson and Pettit', Boylan and O'Gorman engage the implications of the turn to holism, under the influence of the later Wittgenstein, in the work of Quine and Davidson. These philosophers developed holistic approaches to philosophy of language in general and to philosophy of mind in particular. This holistic approach was in response to a rejection in large parts of the philosophical community of logical atomism on the one hand and methodological individualism on the other. Because of both the historical and philosophical links of the concept of rationality in mainstream economics, as embedded in *Homo economicus*, to both logical atomism and methodological individualism, a new philosophical rationale in defense of *Homo economicus* had to be brought forward that was compatible with the newly emergent holistic framework. Donald Davidson was among the first to engage this challenge and developed a novel defence of *Homo economicus* within the holistic framework. More recently, and within the spirit of the holistic linguistic turn, Philip Pettit, in what he terms 'a conciliationist position', attempts to reconcile *Homo economicus* with the common-sense belief that *Homo economicus* principles are in fact not used by ordinary people in the activity of their decision-making within the specificity of their own unique cultural settings, which Pettit refers to as 'cultural framing'.

Building on their earlier work of developing a Wittgensteinian approach to rationality, and in particular its implications for mainstream economics, Boylan and O'Gorman critically engage both the contributions of Davidson and Pettit, accepting fully the commitment to the paradigm of holism on the part of these philosophers. Arising from their critique they argue, contrary to the assumption of Davidson and Pettit, that rationality is not rule-governed in the sense of being defined by a finite set of precise rules or algorithms. In the spirit of the later Wittgenstein, and invoking van Fraassen's provocative but engaging phrase that rationality is 'bridled irrationality' and that this irrationality is constrained in different ways in different contexts or 'language-games' to use Wittgenstein's phrase. Within this Wittgensteinian framework, rationality is a family resemblance concept and has no common essence. Following from this the authors argue for an empirical rather than an a priori approach to economic rationality. In this context they suggest an alternative approach, which they term the socio-historical learning feedback model of rationality.

The principal conclusions that Boylan and O'Gorman derive from their examination of Davidson's and Pettit's contributions are as follows. First, contrary to Davidson's holistic defense of *Homo economicus*, which presupposes that there is an essential core to human rationality that is rule-governed, they argue that human rationality is historically situated, specifically contextualized and dynamic in nature with no common core. Contra Pettit, they highlight an ambiguity of his 'conciliationist' position: on one reading the principles of *Homo economicus* are fundamental, whereas on another reading they clearly are not. In their conception of rationality within the socio-historical learning feedback model, they eschew an a priori prescriptive approach to rationality, or indeed to the prescriptive privileging of any particular model of rationality. Rather they advocate the pursuit of detailed empirical research in different economic domains to capture the actual practice of decision-making in different sets of circumstances. If pursued, this approach challenges the economist to construct a range of models of rational decision-making, which would be evaluated on the basis of their descriptive adequacy to their specific domains.

References

Aliprantis, C. D. and Chakrabarti, S. K. (2000) *Games and Decision Making*, Oxford: Oxford University Press.

Barberà, S., Bossert, W. and Pattanaik, P. K. (2004) 'Ranking sets of objects', in S. Barberà, P. Hammond and C. Seidl (eds), *Handbook of Utility Theory*, Vol. 2: Extensions, Dordrecht: Kluwer.

Bervoets, S. and Gravel, N. (2007) 'Appraising diversity with an ordinal notion of similarity: an axiomatic approach', *Mathematical Social Sciences*, 53: 259–273.

Carter, I. (1999) *A Measure of Freedom*, Oxford: Oxford University Press.

Gaertner, W., Pattanaik, P. K. and Suzumura, K. (1992) 'Individual rights revisited', *Economica*, 59: 161–177.

Gardenfors, P. (1981) 'Rights, games and social choice', *Nous*, 15: 341-56.

Jones, P. and Sugden, R. (1982) 'Evaluating choices', *International Journal of Law and Economics*, 2: 47–65.

Kavka, G. S. (1983) 'The toxin puzzle', *Analysis*, 43: 33–36.

Nehring, K. and Puppe, C. (2002) 'A theory of diversity', *Econometrica*, 70: 1155–1190.

Osbourne, M. J. and Rubinstein, A. (1994) *A Course in Game Theory*, Cambridge, M.A.: MIT Press.

Pattanaik, P. K. and Xu, Y. (1990) 'On ranking opportunity set in terms of freedom of choice', *Recherches Economiques de Louvain*, 56: 383–390.

Shorrocks, A. F. (1984) 'Inequality decomposition by population subgroups', *Econometrica*, 52: 1369–1386.

Sen, A. (1970) 'The impossibility of a Paretian liberal', *Journal of Political Economy*, 78: 152–157.

Weitzman, M. L. (1992) 'On diversity,' *Quarterly Journal of Economics*, 107: 363–406.

Part I

Diversity, rights, norms and intentions

1 What is diversity?[1]

Nicolas Gravel

Introduction

Diversity is an issue that is attracting increasing attention in various spheres. The governments of more than 150 countries have ratified the Rio convention of 1992, which requires them to adopt economically costly policies aiming at the conservation of biological diversity (article 1 of the Rio convention). More recently, UNESCO has approved, in October 2005, the convention on the promotion and protection of diversity of cultural expressions. This convention has been invoked by the representatives of many countries in the negotiations at the World Trade Organization (WTO) in order to remove certain cultural goods from the scope of free trade agreements. In economics, there is a long-standing tradition of research in industrial organization that is concerned with product diversity and how it can be promoted by various forms of market competitions (Dixit and Stiglitz 1977) is a classical analysis of this topic. Diversity appears also to be an important aspect of the freedom of choice that individuals may have in different situations (Barberà, Bossert and Pattanaik 2004; Sugden 1998) according to surveys of the literature on the measurement of freedom of choice. More colloquially, one finds a significant concern in popular discussions about the diversity of opinions expressed in the media or in the political arena. But what is diversity? Would the killing of 500,000 flies of a specific species have the same impact on the reduction of biological diversity as the elimination of the last 6,000 remaining tigers on earth? Is the diversity of opinions expressed in the written press greater in France than in the US? Is the choice of models of cars offered more diverse at General Motors than at Volkswagen? In order to put the Rio or the UNESCO convention into force, or to study the impact of concentration of the media industry on the diversity of opinions expressed in the media, it is of some importance to have available clear yet accurate answers to questions such as these. I propose in this chapter to critically examine some of the approaches that have been proposed in various disciplines – biology and economics for the most part – for answering such questions.

It could of course be argued, without playing on words, that the diversity of contexts to which these questions refer is such that they cannot be handled by a single concept. The biodiversity of an ecosystem is not the same thing as the diversity of opinions found in the media and the two types of situation require completely different notions.

The discussion of this chapter will certainly give some credence to this view by illustrating, on several occasions, how the relative merits of the various proposed approaches to diversity appraisal are dependent upon the context. Yet the point of view that is taken herein is that, different as they are, all problems of diversity appraisal share a common formal structure that will be the main object of analysis. At the most abstract level, the formal structure is very simple. A universe of objects (e.g. living organisms, opinions, car models, cultures, etc.) is given to the diversity appraiser, and various subsets of these objects (ecosystems, newspapers, car retailers, countries) are to be compared on the basis of their diversity. The general question examined is: how can one make these comparisons?

It should be noticed that this very way of addressing the problem limits somehow the kind of issues handled by the approaches covered herein. An important limitation has to do with uncertainty. The consequences on biodiversity, however defined, of many human decisions, deforestations, carbon emissions, etc. are uncertain. So are the consequences, on cultural diversity (however defined), of allowing WTO to treat 'cultural goods' as standard freely tradable goods. Hence a question that could be asked, but that will not be asked herein, is: how should one rank decisions with uncertain consequences in terms of diversity?

Answering such a question is obviously a more ambitious task than answering the previous question. If we know how to rank all decisions that have uncertain consequences in terms of diversity, then we know how to rank the subclass of these decisions that have certain consequences; but the converse is obviously false. Some important contributions to the literature on diversity appraisal, notably those of Weitzman (1992, 1993, 1998) and Nehring and Puppe (2002), have proposed answers to this broader question that contain therefore also answers to the first question. However, in discussing these answers, attention will be limited to aspects that concern the narrow problem at hand. To a large extent, this choice of narrowing the discussion to the issue of 'what is diversity', rather than to that of 'how to rank decisions that have (possibly uncertain) consequences on diversity' is motivated by a prosaic consideration of time and space. Yet this choice also reflects a sentiment that diversity is a delicate notion that remains poorly understood. For this reason, progress in understanding this notion is more likely to come from a narrow focus on its very meaning in some ideally simple situations than from a mixing of it with other complex notions such as uncertainty.

In making diversity comparisons of different sets of objects, it is important to be explicit about the exact information that is assumed to be available on the objects and to be useful for diversity appraisal. All approaches for evaluating diversity differ in the kind of information that they assume and on the role played by the information. For example, in the context of biological diversity, the elements of the ecosystems are very often assumed to be living organisms grouped into species. This grouping obviously plays a crucial role in the appraisal of diversity commonly done by biologists. In other theories of diversity appraisal, especially those developed in economics following Weitzman (1992), a primitive notion of dissimilarity between objects is assumed to play a role. The precision of the information conveyed by the underlying notion of dissimilarity differs across theories. In papers such as those by Bossert, Pattanaik and Xu (2003), Van Hees (2004) and Weitzman (1992, 1993, 1998), this information takes the form of a cardinally meaningful numerical distance between the objects. In other approaches, such as those considered in Bervoets and Gravel (2007), Nehring (1997) and Pattanaik and Xu (2000), the information on dissimilarity is assumed instead to be only qualitative or ordinal in nature. Finally, in the approach developed by Nehring and Puppe (2002) (see also Nehring and Puppe 2003), it is information on the valuation of various attributes of the objects that plays a key role in appraising diversity.

It could be argued that the relevant information for evaluating diversity, and more generally the evaluation of diversity itself, should depend upon the final objective reached by this evaluation. Why is one interested in evaluating diversity? Why is diversity important? The answer to these questions is likely to depend upon the context in which the evaluation is performed. The reasons for being interested in biodiversity are certainly different from those that justify an interest in the promotion of cultural diversity, or a concern for product diversity. Should the reasons that motivate an interest for a measurable phenomenon affect the way by which the measurement of this phenomenon is to be performed?

Opinions on this matter differ. In the context of freedom appraisal, some authors, such as Carter (1999) or Van Hees (1997), have argued that the reasons for being interested in a phenomenon such as freedom of choice – what they call the value of freedom – should not affect the definition, and therefore the measurement, of the phenomenon. A phenomenon can be defined and appraised irrespective of the role played by the phenomenon in the theory used by the appraiser. On the other hand it is quite possible to hold the converse view that the definition and appraisal of a phenomenon depends totally upon the consequences that this phenomenon is expected to have or upon the reasons for being interested in it. After all, the precise measurement of temperature in physics is entirely motivated by the role played by temperature (as measuring the speed of movement in particles) in the physical theory and does not attempt to measure an *a priori* notion of temperature that is independent from this role.

Although I tend to sympathize somewhat with this latter view, this survey will not discuss the reasons for developing an interest in diversity appraisal. Here again, my reluctance to examine this complex issue is the result of a mixture of prosaic considerations of time and space as well as a more substantial belief that the reasons for developing a concern for diversity are not clearly understood. Human sciences and even, for that matter, biology do not seem to have developed a theoretical apparatus in which the notion of diversity could play a role as precise as the one played by temperature in physics.

As mentioned above, the proposed survey will focus on the formal structure of the various existing proposals for defining diversity. Yet the presentation of this formal structure is intended to be non-technical. This means that the formalism will be kept to a minimum and that the properties and results will be stated as heuristically as possible. In particular, I shall not provide detailed proofs of the results even though I will, on occasion, provide indicative comments about how such a detailed proof can be constructed from various results in the literature.

Specifically, the presentation is organized as follows. In the next section, the formal framework is introduced, and some principles for diversity appraisal, as well as their implications, are examined in the case where no information on the objects – other than their existence – is provided. The third section examines the approaches developed in biology where the objects are partitioned into categories (species) and where the diversity of a set is assumed to be measured by some generalized entropy. The approaches that base diversity appraisal on the aggregation of an *a priori* notion of dissimilarity between objects are considered in the fourth section, and the fifth discusses the multi-attributes approach. Finally I provide some elements of conclusion.

Comparing sets of objects: general principles

The framework

At the centre of any exercise in diversity evaluation is a (typically finite) set X of objects. While the objects in X can be *a priori* anything (living organisms, products, opinions, cultural expressions, etc.), they need to be clearly identified at the outset. This identification is not always made in the literature, and is not always easy to make in practice. For instance, in the case of biodiversity appraisal, there is sometime some ambiguity whether the living individual or the species should be treated as the unit of analysis. This choice has obviously some impact for the formal analysis. Suppose we have an ecosystem in which there are 10,000 trees of a species A and 5,000 tree of a species B. If the tree is taken as the unit of analysis, this ecosystem has 15,000 elements; if we take species to be the unit of analysis, it has only two elements. Furthermore, most indicators used by biologists to evaluate diversity use information on the relative frequency of living individuals belonging to each species. Here again, the way in which this information can be handled in the formal analysis will depend upon the unit of analysis chosen. If species is the unit of analysis, then some extra (non-set-theoretic) information need to be included (e.g. the set has two species, species 1 comes with frequency 2/3 and species 2 with frequency 1/3). If the living individual is the unit of analysis, then information on the relative frequency is provided, more parsimoniously, by a partition of the set of individuals into two (species) groups.

Given this clear identification of the objects, the problem of diversity evaluation is that of providing a ranking, denoted $\geq$, with asymmetric and symmetric factors > and ~, of the various sets of objects in X. In this setting, $A \geq B$ means 'set A offers at least as much diversity as set B', $A > B$ means 'set A offers strictly more diversity than set B' and $A \sim B$ means 'set A offers the same diversity as set B'. Without any reason for excluding certain sets of objects *a priori*, it is typically assumed that every non-empty subset of X can be considered for diversity appraisal. I denote by $P(X)$ the set of all non-empty subsets of X.

The diversity ranking is always assumed to be reflexive (any set is at least as diverse as itself) and transitive (*A* is at least as diverse as *C* if *A* is at least as diverse as *B*, which is itself at least as diverse as *C*). Also, all rankings considered in the literature and used in practice are complete in the sense of being capable of comparing any pairs of sets in terms of their diversity. Although completeness is quite convenient for applications (funding agencies do not usually like answers like 'we don't know whether or not biodiversity of this particular ecosystem has been reduced or increased in the last 15 years'), it is probably the least desirable of these requirements. Yet it is fair to say that no attractive diversity ranking that is incomplete has emerged so far. A reflexive, transitive and complete ranking is called an ordering. I will also often assume that the ranking of sets is non-trivial in the sense that it does not consider all sets to be equivalent in terms of diversity.

If the diversity ranking $\geq$ is an ordering, and the number of possible sets is finite, we know that $\geq$ can be represented by a numerical diversity index $I_d: P(X) \rightarrow$ R in such a way that $I_d(A) \geq I_d(B)$ if and only if A $\geq$ B. The index I_d can therefore be thought of as 'measuring' the diversity of various sets even though the usual ordinal caveat applies to this measurement: it is unique up to a monotonic transformation.

Which principles could plausibly underlie a ranking (or an ordinal diversity index) of sets on the basis of their diversity? Without further information on the structure of the objects themselves (i.e. their dissimilarities, the attributes that they possess, etc.), the list of these principles is likely to be rather small. Yet it is not empty. It is therefore instructive to go through this list and to examine some of these principles as well as the rankings to which they naturally lead. Although most of the principles and rankings discussed in this section have been proposed in other contexts than diversity appraisal, they do have a bearing on the problem at hand when properly reinterpreted.

Monotonicity

A first well-known category of principles concerns the monotonicity of a diversity criterion with respect to the addition of objects: diversity is never reduced when objects are added to a set. This principle can be expressed axiomatically as follows.

Axiom 1.1 (monotonicity). For all distinct sets *A* and *B* in *P(X)*, $A \supset B \Rightarrow A \geq B$.

Although this principle looks quite reasonable for diversity appraisal, its general acceptance depends upon the interpretation given to the objects. In the context of biodiversity appraisal, if the elements of the sets are assumed to be species, then this axiom is quite reasonable: adding a species does not reduce diversity and eliminating a species never increases diversity. On the other hand, if the elements of the set are living individuals, then it is easy to think of plausible conceptions of diversity that violate this principle. For example, it is not uncommon in biology (see below) to measure the diversity of an ecosystem by the Shannon (1948) entropy defined on the relative frequencies of the various species present in the ecosystem. This measure violates monotonicity if the objects of the set are assumed to be living individuals. Suppose in effect a world in which the population of living individuals is equally split between species 1 and 2. The addition to such a world of living individuals of species 1 will increase the ratio of individuals from species 1 over those of species 2 and will therefore reduce the entropy of the ecosystem.

Yet it is fair to say that many criteria proposed to evaluate diversity satisfy monotonicity. It could even be argued that monotonicity is, in fact, a weak requirement, compatible with very coarse rankings such as the trivial one that considers all sets to be equally diverse. It is therefore not rare to see notions of diversity that satisfy stronger versions of the same idea.

The strongest of all these versions is certainly the following requirement of strong monotonicity according to which the addition of objects in a set strictly increases diversity.

Axiom 1.2 (strong monotonicity). For all distinct sets A and B, $A \supset B \Rightarrow A > B$.

This property appears also somewhat natural in the context of biodiversity appraisal if, as in the previous discussion, objects in X are interpreted as species rather than individual organisms. After all it is not absurd to postulate that the elimination of a species from an ecosystem reduces this ecosystem's diversity. A similar kind of consideration seems to hold for other instances of diversity measurement (such as products diversity or, more generally, the diversity of choices offered to a decision maker). Yet, as will be seen below, there are several plausible conceptions of diversity that violate this strong monotonicity principle while satisfying the weak version of it. The reason these conceptions of diversity violate this principle is that they base diversity appraisal on richer information than what is considered here. For example, in the penultimate section, some attention will be devoted to approaches that view the diversity of a set as the sum of the values of the attributes realized by the objects in the set. In this setting, an object contributes to the diversity of a set only if it possesses an attribute not possessed by the other objects in the set. Unless all objects possess a unique attribute that is not possessed by the others, it is clear that such an approach will violate strong monotonicity while satisfying weak monotonicity (adding objects never hurts).

Monotonicity properties provide a natural 'direction', so to speak, in which it makes sense to talk about diversity improvement, or deterioration. This leads naturally to the question of defining a set of minimal, or zero, diversity. Singletons are natural candidates for this purpose. A car dealer that offers only one model of car is clearly not diverse. Nor is an ecosystem in which only one species is represented, or a newspaper in which only one opinion is reflected. Yet there are as many singletons as there are objects. How should a plausible diversity ranking compare different singletons?

One answer to this question, proposed by Pattanaik and Xu (1990) in their influential contribution on freedom appraisal, would be to consider them as equally 'non-diverse'. This answer is contained in the following axiom.

Axiom 1.3 (indifference between non-diverse situations). For all distinct objects x and y, $\{x\} \sim \{y\}$.

This answer is certainly consistent. The principle of indifference between non-diverse situations is actually satisfied by most indices used by biologists to measure biodiversity, irrespective of the fact that the objects in the sets represent species or individual organisms. This axiom is also satisfied by all approaches that view the diversity of a set as resulting from the aggregation of the pairwise dissimilarities of its elements (as there is not much dissimilarity between an object and itself). On the other hand, conceptions of diversity that focus on the attributes of the objects rather than on the objects themselves have no reason to respect this principle. After all should an ecosystem with only protozoans be considered as diverse as one populated only by humans?

Independence

Another category of principles that have been invoked for comparing sets of objects concerns the extent to which the contribution of objects to diversity should depend upon the set in which they are added or subtracted.

> An angel is more valuable than a stone. It does not follow, however, that two angels are more valuable than one angel and a stone.
>
> (Thomas Aquinas, *Summa contra Gentiles*, III, quoted in Nehring and Puppe 2002)

Thus spoke Thomas Aquinas, who seemed to believe that the contribution of an angel to diversity was dependent upon the set to which the angel was added. And Thomas was probably right on this. An essential feature, it seems, of diversity appraisal is that the contribution of an object to the diversity of a set depends upon the objects already present in the set. Eliminating a species of fly does not have the same impact on biodiversity in a situation where there are thousands of different species of fly as in a situation where there are only 10. A particular right-wing opinion contributes less to diversity of opinions when it is added to a right-wing journal than when it is added to a left-wing journal.

Yet the issue of dependency of the contributions of objects with respect to the sets to which they are added or subtracted is delicate. After all, one of the most widely used measure of biodiversity, species counting, assumes that the contribution of a species to the diversity of an ecosystem is one no matter what the ecosystem is. It is therefore of some interest to clarify the notion of dependence, or independence, involved.

Following the work of de Finetti (1937), qualitative probability theorists such as Kraft, Pratt and Seidenberg (1959; see also Fishburn 1969) have identified, in a somewhat different context, an axiom that describes quite compactly the property involved. A good starting point for understanding this axiom is through the notion of a bilateral transfer of objects from a set A to a set B. To remain in the realm of biodiversity applied to objects interpreted as species, suppose that a species initially presented in ecosystem B and absent from ecosystem A is removed from B and added to A (for instance all bears from Slovenia are transferred to the French Pyrenees). How should a plausible ranking of sets on the basis of their diversity record such a transfer? Specifically, is it possible that this transfer increases diversity in one set without reducing that in the other?

Anyone believing that the contribution of an object to diversity is independent of the set to which the object belongs should be inclined to answer negatively to this question. If the object involved in the transfer contributes to diversity in a way that is independent of the set, the transfer of the object from one set to another is bound to have opposite effects in the two sets. There are really only three possibilities here. The object contributes positively to diversity, in which case the transfer increases diversity in the receiving set and reduces that of the donating set, or it contributes negatively to diversity, in which case the reverse conclusion holds, or it does not contribute at all to diversity, in which case no change in the diversity of the two sets is recorded. Any other possibility would be indicative of a contribution to diversity that depends upon the set (for instance the transfer does not reduce the diversity of the donating set but strictly increases diversity in the receiving set).

One can now take a step further and consider transferring objects across sets in a sequential manner: first transferring an object from a set A to a set B, and then transferring an object from a set C (not necessarily distinct from A or B) to some set D (again not necessarily distinct from A or B) and so on, a finite number of times. Can such a finite sequence of transfers increases the diversity in one set without reducing that in at least one other set? Even though the intuition here is less straightforward than in the elementary case of a transfer of one object between two sets, the answer to this question should be negative for someone who believes in the set-independence of the contribution of objects to diversity. Moving around objects across a given list of sets cannot strictly increase the diversity in some sets without reducing that of some other set if the contribution of any object to diversity is set-independent. This general principle can be stated formally as follows.

Axiom 1.4 (general independence). For any two lists of k sets $(A_1, A_2, \ldots, A_k)$ and $(B_1, B_2, \ldots, B_k)$ (for $k = 2, \ldots$), if the list $(A_1, A_2, \ldots, A_k)$ is the result of performing a finite sequence of transfers of objects between sets in the list $(B_1, B_2, \ldots, B_k)$, then if $A_h > B_h$ for some $h \in \{1, \ldots, k\}$, one must have $B_j > A_j$ for some $j \in \{1, \ldots, k\}$.

As will be seen shortly, this axiom captures this notion of independence in a very exhaustive way, since it identifies all complete and reflexive diversity rankings that compare sets on the basis of the sum of the 'contributions' to diversity of their elements, with the elements' 'contributions' being measured by some function that does not depend upon the sets. It is actually quite a demanding axiom that implies other notions of independence discussed in the literature.

One of them is that considered in Pattanaik and Xu (1990), which asserts that adding or subtracting the same objects to two sets does not affect their ranking.

Axiom 1.5 (Pattanaik and Xu's independence). For any sets A, B and C such that $A \cap C = B \cap C = \varnothing$, $A \succeq B \Leftrightarrow A \cup C \succeq B \cup C$.

It can easily be seen (see, for example, Gravel, Laslier and Trannoy 1998) that general independence implies Pattanaik and Xu's independence but that the converse does not hold.

But there is another interesting direction in which the notion of independence can be weakened. For the discussion so far has concerned the extent to which the contribution of an object to the diversity of a set should depend upon the set. Yet one could also consider a (much weaker) notion of independence that would require only the contribution of an object to the diversity of a set to be independent from the other objects already present in the set. Coming back to the earlier example, suppose that it is recognized that adding new bears in the French Pyrenees (say by transferring them from Slovenia) increases the diversity of the French Pyreneans ecosystem. Should this verdict be maintained if the last remaining 42 couples of eagles that inhabit the French Pyrenees (according to recent accounts) were to be eliminated? An 'independentist' would undoubtedly answer yes to such a question. If the presence of bears increases biodiversity in the French Pyrenees with eagles, it should also increase biodiversity in the French Pyrenees without eagles. But saying this is obviously not to say that the contribution of bears to diversity should be the same in every set. For instance, it is quite possible to hold this statement while believing that the transfer of bears from Slovenia to France has no impact on the diversity in Slovenia (say because there are sufficient numbers of bears there).

This property of limited independence has been called contraction consistency by Nehring and Puppe (1999) and Puppe (1998) and is equivalent, at least for rankings of sets that are weakly monotonic, reflexive and transitive, to an axiom introduced by Kreps (1979; property 1.5) and analysed extensively by Nehring (1999). It is stated formally as follows.

Axiom 1.6 (contraction consistency). For all sets A and B such that $A \supset B$ and for every object x, if $A \cup \{x\} > A$, then $B \cup \{x\} > B$.

This axiom, it should be emphasized, is rather weak. It is obviously satisfied by any ranking that satisfies general independence (and also by rankings satisfying Pattanaik and Xu's independence). But contraction consistency is also trivially satisfied by any strongly monotonic ranking (contraction consistency has obviously no bite if adding objects to sets always increase diversity). The key essential feature of contraction consistency is the idea of 'decreasing contribution' of objects to diversity with respect to the size of the set: an object cannot contribute to the diversity in a set if it does not contribute to the diversity of one of its proper subsets.

Yet it is not hard to think of plausible notions of diversity that would violate contraction consistency. This is certainly the case of notions such as those considered later in this chapter which attach importance to the underlying 'dissimilarity' between the objects. To take a simple example, suppose that we are interested in comparing the diversity of meals offered in various restaurants. Consider first a (rather carnivorous) restaurant offering to its clients only chicken and lamb dishes. It would not be absurd to consider that adding to this restaurant a beef dish does not increase significantly the diversity of plates. This could be so because the dissimilarity between beef and chicken or between beef and lamb may be judged lower than the existing dissimilarity between lamb and chicken. Yet it would not be absurd either to consider that adding the same beef dish to a restaurant offering initially chicken, lamb and paneer (an Indian vegetarian delicacy) would increase the diversity of meals offered at this restaurant. Again this could happen simply because the dissimilarity between beef and paneer may appear much larger than any existing dissimilarity between lamb and chicken, paneer and chicken or paneer and lamb (after all, many Indian gourmets consider beef to be a rather extravagant kind of food, especially as compared with paneer).

Some implications of the principles

The properties just discussed are actually quite exhaustive in terms of the kind of diversity rankings that they allow. Consider first the property of general independence. As it turns out, this axiom characterizes all reflexive and transitive rankings of sets that result from the comparisons of the sum of 'contributions' of their elements, with the contributions measured by numbers pre-assigned to every object of the universe. If the ranking of sets is further required to be monotonic, the contribution of objects to diversity is constrained to be non-negative. If the ranking of sets is required to be strictly monotonic, then the contributions have to be strictly positive.

This result is stated formally as follows.

Theorem 1.1. Let $\geq$ be a reflexive and complete diversity ranking of $P(X)$. Then $\geq$ satisfies general independence if and only if there exists some function $c : X \rightarrow R$ that assigns to each object x its numerical contribution $c(x)$ such that, for all sets A and B, $A \geq B$ if and only if:

$$\sum_{a \in A} c(a) \geq \sum_{b \in B} c(b)$$

Moreover, if $\geq$ is weakly (resp. strongly) monotonic, $c(x) \geq 0$ (resp. > 0) for every object x.

Proof. The main part of the proof consists in showing that an axiom formally equivalent to general independence, and called additivity by Fishburn (1970), implies the additive representation. This proof, which rides on the theorem of the alternative, can be found in Kraft, Pratt and Seidenberg (1959) or Fishburn (1970). The equivalence between the current formulation in terms of sequence of transfers and of additivity is proved in Gravel, Laslier and Trannoy (1998: lemma 1). Yet the proof in Gravel, Laslier and Trannoy (1998) uses a slightly different kind of transfer from what has been (informally) discussed here since it allows for transferring objects from singleton to other sets. It is possible to prove a variant of lemma 1 in Gravel, Laslier and Trannoy (1998) with the transfers discussed herein if some care is taken with the treatment of singletons. Details of the construction are omitted. ∎

Let me refer to the rankings characterized by Theorem 1.1 as additive rankings. An important special case of additive rankings is the cardinality ranking that compares sets on the basis of their number of elements (for instance the number of species if species are interpreted as being the objects). This ranking has been the object of extensive discussions in the literature on freedom of choice, where it received a nice axiomatic characterization by Pattanaik and Xu (1990; see also Jones and Sugden 1982; Suppes 1987). The cardinality ranking differs from other additive rankings by assigning the same numerical contribution to diversity to all objects. Although this 'equal treatment' property may look arbitrary – there is little reason after all to consider that a specific species of flies contributes the same way to biodiversity as a chimpanzee – it may equally well be seen as an appropriate assumption to make in the abstract setting considered in this section where no information is assumed to be available on the nature of the objects. Without any reason for treating different objects differently, why distinguish between them?

This non-distinction between objects is clearly at the heart of the axiom of indifference between non-diverse situations. Quite obviously, this axiom suffices to select, in the class of non-trivial, monotonic, complete and reflexive rankings that satisfy generalized independence, the cardinality ranking. Let me state this fact formally as follows.

Proposition 1.1. Let $\geq$ be a reflexive, complete, monotonic and non-trivial diversity ranking of $P(X)$. Then $\geq$ satisfies general independence and indifference with respect to non-diverse situations if and only if it is the cardinality ranking.

Proof. From Theorem 1.1, a reflexive, complete and monotonic diversity ranking satisfies general independence if and only if there exists a function c that assigns a non-negative numerical contribution $c(x)$ to every object x in X such that $A \geq B$ if and only if:

$$\sum_{a\in A} c(a) \geq \sum_{b\in B} c(b)$$

For this ranking to satisfy indifference with respect to non-diverse situations, we must have $c(x)=c(y)$ for all objects x and y. As non-triviality precludes the case where $c(x)=c(y)=0$ for every x and y, we must conclude that $c(x)=c(y)>0$ for every x and y. ∎

It is probably worth comparing the characterization of the cardinality ranking provided by this proposition with the widely discussed one of Pattanaik and Xu (1990). Both characterizations share in common the principle of indifference between singletons. Yet Pattanaik and Xu require the ranking to be transitive (but not necessarily complete) whereas Proposition 1.1 only requires it to be complete (but not necessarily transitive). Proposition 1.1 requires the ranking to be non-trivial and monotonic whereas Pattanaik and Xu require it to satisfy the 'preference for choice over non-choice' principle according to which a set made of two distinct objects should be ranked above any of the two singletons made of one of the two objects. On the other hand, the above proposition rides on the general independence principle whereas Pattanaik and Xu obtain cardinality out of their own (much weaker) independence condition.

This last state of affairs is actually an interesting logical fact. Without indifference between non-diverse situations, the class of strictly monotonic rankings satisfying Pattanaik and Xu's independence is larger than the additive class (as shown in Kraft, Pratt and Seidenberg 1959, there are non-additive strictly monotonic rankings that satisfy Pattanaik and Xu's independence). The fact that the addition of indifference between non-diverse situations is capable of shrinking the (large) class of strictly monotonic rankings satisfying Pattanaik and Xu's independence up to the unique cardinality ranking is somewhat surprising.

Any additive ranking has the property that it can be thought of as measuring the diversity of a set by summing the numerical contributions of all its elements. Hence such a ranking can be viewed as resulting from a two-step procedure:

1 measuring the numerical contribution of every object in the universe by a numerical function c;
2 comparing sets on the basis of the sum of the contributions of their elements as measured by the function c.

A disputable feature of this approach is that the contribution made by an object to the diversity is borne by the object itself and not by some more fundamental attributes that the object may have. Yet there are many contexts in which it is the attributes of the objects, rather than the objects themselves, that are contributing to diversity. Industrial organization and the characteristics-based or hedonic approach to product differentiation developed by Lancaster (1966) and Rosen (1974) have made economists aware that differentiated products such as cars, televisions, etc. are best seen as vectors in a space of more fundamental characteristics. If one adopts the characteristics-based view of products differentiation, it becomes clear that the appraisal of diversity in, say, different car retailers should depend upon the characteristics possessed by the cars and not so much upon the cars themselves. In recent years, Nehring and Puppe (2002; see also Nehring and Puppe 2003) have forcefully defended the view that attributes, rather than objects, should be the ultimate contributors to diversity.

Of course the abstract framework considered in this section does not provide information on the attributes possessed by the objects. A natural, if not formal, way to define attributes in this setting would be to view them as sets of objects. Each such set would be interpreted to be the list of all those objects possessing the attribute considered. A surprising consequence of the principle of contraction consistency is that, along with monotonicity, it characterizes all rankings that can be thought of as comparing sets on the basis of the sum of the values of the attributes that are *realized* in the sets for some family of attributes, and for some function that values the contribution of the attributes. Put differently, when imposed on an ordering, the properties of monotonicity and contraction consistency imply the existence of a family of attributes and a numerical function that values these attributes in such a way that the ranking of sets can be viewed as resulting from the comparisons of the sum of the values of the attributes that are realized in the sets.

This result, first proved by Kreps (1979), and reinterpreted, in terms of attribute weighting, by Nehring (1999) and Nehring and Puppe (2002) on the basis of results developed in Chateauneuf and Jaffray (1989), is stated formally as follows:

Theorem 1.2. An ordering $\geq$ on all sets in $P(X)$ satisfies weak monotonicity and contraction consistency if and only if there exists an attribute valuation function λ that assigns a non-negative value $\lambda(S)$ to any subset S of X ($\lambda(S)$ is zero if S does not correspond to an attribute or, equivalently in this theory, if it corresponds to an attribute that is not valued) such that, for every two sets A and B, $A \geq B$ if and only if

$$\sum_{C:C \cap A \neq \varnothing} \lambda(C) \geq \sum_{D:D \cap B \neq \varnothing} \lambda(D)$$

Proof. As noticed above, a complete, reflexive and transitive diversity ranking $\geq$ can be numerically represented by a diversity indicator $I_d : P(X) \rightarrow R$. There is actually a wide range of such diversity indicators as any increasing transformation of a diversity indicator is also a diversity indicator. As any set function, a diversity indicator has a *conjugate Möbius inverse* (see, for example, Nehring 1999: section 3; Nehring and Puppe 2002: fact 2.1) $\lambda : P(X) \rightarrow R$ defined, for every B, by:

$$\lambda(B) = \sum_{S \subset B} (-1)^{\#(B \backslash S)+1} I_d(X \backslash S) \tag{1.1}$$

and satisfying, for every set A, the equality:

$$I_d(A) = \sum_{S: S \cap A \neq \varnothing} \lambda(S) \tag{1.2}$$

In view of this last equality, the only thing that needs to be shown is the existence of a diversity indicator that admits a non-negative conjugate Möbius inverse for every set other than X. This non-negative conjugate Möbius inverse can be interpreted as a method for valuing the attributes (any set receiving a positive value is considered as an attribute). We don't care much about the valuation of the attribute being an object of the universe because it is an attribute that is realized in every non-empty set and therefore cannot serve for distinguishing sets. As shown by Chateauneuf and Jaffray (1989), a necessary and sufficient condition for a set function I_d to have a non-negative conjugate Möbius inverse for all sets other than X is to be weakly monotonic and *totally submodular* (see, for example, Chateauneuf and Jaffray 1989 for a definition of this property). As a numerical representation of a monotonic ranking of sets, any diversity indicator is obviously monotonic. Hence the only thing that needs to be shown is that, among all diversity indicators that numerically represent $\succeq$, there is at least one that is totally submodular. Nehring (1999) has shown that, for a monotonic ranking, the existence of a totally modular numerical representation of it amounts to requiring the ranking to satisfy the following condition, for all sets A, B and C:

$$A \succeq A \cup B \Rightarrow A \cup C \succeq A \cup B \cup C \tag{1.3}$$

Now, it is easy to verify that, for a reflexive, transitive and monotonic ranking, this condition, first formulated by Kreps (1979) is equivalent to contraction consistency. ∎

The fact that one can think of an ordering of sets as resulting from the additive valuations of attributes is, in itself, not terribly informative. For any numerical function having as domain all non-empty subsets of a finite set can be thought of, by applying Möbius inversion, as a sum of valuations of attributes, with some attributes negatively valued and others positively. The attribute valuation function provided by the Möbius inversion formula is constructed in a mechanical manner from the numerical representation of the diversity ranking itself. For this reason, it depends crucially upon this numerical representation.

More substantial information is obtained from the fact that, if the ordering satisfies contraction consistency and weak monotonicity, there exists at least one numerical representation of the ranking for which Möbius inversion provides a non-negative valuation of all attributes other than the universe. Yet it is important, here again, to notice the dependency of the valuations of the attribute with respect to the particular diversity index used to represent the ranking. Different families of attributes and different valuations of them will obtain as one changes from one numerical representation of the same diversity ranking to another. This is a problem for the interpretation of this theorem as providing an argument in favour of a multi-attributes approach to diversity measurement. For it is somewhat bizarre for the attributes that are considered relevant for appraising diversity as per a given ranking to be dependent upon the numerical representation of the ranking – that the attribute of, say, being a mammal be valued positively and largely for one representation of the ranking while being given no weight at all for other representations of the same ranking. If it is believed that a diversity ranking of sets can be thought of as aggregating the values of the attributes realized in the sets, the attributes concerned and their relative importance should be independent from the particular numerical representation of the ranking.

An example may perhaps be useful for understanding this point. Suppose one is interested in ranking subsets of the set {*lizard, shark, whale*} using the following ordering ≥:

$$\{lizard, shark, whale\} > \{shark, whale\} \sim \{lizard, whale\} >$$
$$\{whale\} > \{lizard, shark\} > \{shark\} \sim \{lizard\} \tag{1.4}$$

It is easy to verify that this ordering satisfies contraction consistency and weak monotonicity. Yet the valuation of attributes revealed by this ranking is far from clear. If we except the trivial attribute 'being an object in the universe' (represented by X), the possible attributes here are 'fish', 'reptile' and 'mammal', represented respectively by the singletons {*shark*}, {*lizard*} and {*whale*} as well as 'ocean-living' ({*shark, whale*}), 'air-breathing' ({*lizard, whale*}) and 'cold-blooded' ({*lizard, shark*}). The problem is that the diversity ranking provided by the ordering of sets of this example does not tell us much about the valuation of these various attributes. The only obvious thing that can be said from looking at the ranking is that a positive value is attached to singleton attributes, e.g. 'fish', 'mammal' and 'reptile' (because the triplet X is ranked strictly above any ecosystem consisting of pairs of animals). The valuation of the other attributes will depend crucially upon the particular diversity index used.

For instance, if one represents the ranking by the diversity index I_d defined by

$$I_d(\{lizard, shark, whale\}) = 4$$
$$I_d(\{shark, whale\}) = I_d(\{lizard, whale\}) = 3$$
$$I_d(\{whale\}) = 2$$
$$I_d(\{lizard, shark\}) = 1$$
$$I_d(\{lizard\}) = I_d(\{shark\}) = 0$$

then, applying the Möbius inverse formula, one obtains the following definition of the attribute valuation function λ:

$$\lambda\{lizard\} = \lambda\{shark\} = 1$$
$$\lambda(\{lizard, shark\}) = \lambda(\{lizard, whale\}) = \lambda(\{whale, shark\}) = 0$$
$$\lambda(\{whale\}) = 3$$
$$\lambda(X) = -1$$

According to this definition, the only attributes that are valued positively are 'mammal', 'fish' and 'reptile', with 'mammal' being given a greater value than 'fish' and 'reptile' and 'reptile' and 'fish' being equally valued. No values are attached to the other attributes.

Now a somewhat different story is obtained if the following numerical representation I_d of the same ranking is used instead:

$$\hat{I}_d(\{lizard, shark, whale\}) = 5$$
$$\hat{I}_d(\{shark, whale\}) = \hat{I}_d(\{lizard, whale\}) = 4$$
$$\hat{I}_d(\{whale\}) = 1$$
$$\hat{I}_d(\{lizard, shark\}) = 0$$
$$\hat{I}_d(\{lizard\}) = \hat{I}_d(\{shark\}) = -1$$

Using the Möbius inverse formula again, this diversity index provides us with the attribute valuation function $\hat{\lambda}$ defined by:

$$\hat{\lambda}(\{lizard, whale\}) = \hat{\lambda}(\{shark, whale\}) = \hat{\lambda}(\{lizard\}) = \hat{\lambda}(\{shark\}) = 1$$
$$\hat{\lambda}(\{lizard, shark\}) = 2$$
$$\hat{\lambda}(\{whale\}) = 4$$
$$\hat{\lambda}(X) = -4$$

which values positively all logically conceivable attributes (except of course the trivial attribute X). Notice also how different is the ordering of attributes in terms of the way they are valued. The fact of being cold-blooded is valued more here than the fact of being a reptile or a fish whereas the converse ranking of the attributes obtained with the index I_d.

We have examined, in this section, alternative principles that a ranking of sets of object could satisfy in order to serve as a plausible definition of diversity in a framework where no information is available on the nature of the objects. We have also summarized the main implications of these principles in terms of the rankings of objects that they allow. Two broad types of rankings have been identified in this perspective:

1   additive object-based rankings, which can be thought of as resulting from a comparison of the sum of the contributions of objects to diversity;
2   additive attribute-based rankings, which can be thought of as resulting from a comparison of the sum of the contributions of objects' attributes to diversity.

Additive object-based rankings are tightly characterized by the principle of general independence in the sense that a unique ranking of the objects on the basis of their contributions to diversity is obtained from the ranking of sets applied to singletons. On the other hand, the principle according to which each object contributes to diversity independently of the set to which it is added or subtracted does not seem to be well adapted to diversity appraisal. Additive attribute-based rankings are not tightly characterized by the principles of weak monotonicity and contraction consistency since several rankings of attributes on the basis of their contribution to diversity may come out of the same ranking of sets of objects. Yet additive attribute-based rankings are probably more suitable than their object-based counterpart to serve as plausible criteria for appraising diversity provided that some extra information on the attribute valuations is added to the model.

Diversity as generalized entropy

Biologists have been probably the first scientists to develop an interest in diversity appraisal. As typically conducted in biology, diversity appraisal interprets the objects as being species, and view ecosystems as vectors of species abundance, each component of the vector being interpreted as the number of individuals belonging to the corresponding species in the ecosystem.[2] The extra structure brought about by the grouping of living individuals into species is obviously natural in biology, even though there is some disagreement among biologists over the precise definition of what constitutes a species. A widely used criterion defines a species as a set of actually or potentially interbreeding individuals. This definition obviously applies only to organisms that reproduce sexually. Yet the reproduction criterion is important because it is through reproduction that individual organisms exchange genes and evolve over time.

In this setting, if there are m species, an ecosystem is described by a vector $x = (x_1 \ldots, x_m)$ where $x_k \geq 0$ denotes the number of individuals in the ecosystem who belong to species k. I shall assume in the discussion that x belongs to R_+^m. This means that there can be any non-negative number of individuals in any species and, therefore, that the underlying number of individuals is uncountably infinite. It is also worth noticing that this approach attaches no importance whatsoever to the diversity between individuals of the same species.

It is not rare in biology to evaluate diversity on varying sets of species. For instance, one may be interested in tree diversity, in planktonic diversity, in mammal diversity, and so on. Biologists therefore attach some importance to the fact that the diversity ranking be defined for all specifications of the set of species. I shall denote accordingly by $\geq_m$ the ranking of ecosystems based on m species (for any $m = 1, 2, \ldots$). For any vector x in R_+^m let

$$\mu(x) = \frac{\sum_{k=1}^{m} x_i}{m}$$

denote the average abundance of the ecosystem, interpreted to be the average number of living individuals that can be found in a species. For any vector x in R_+^m I also denote by $\bar{x}$ the ideally diverse ecosystem corresponding to x that is defined by $\bar{x}_k = \mu(x)$ for every k.

By far the most widely used class of diversity-based rankings of ecosystems in biology is that associated with the general entropy measure of Renyi (1961) defined over the distributions of relative frequencies of species in various sets. This class is parameterized by a real number r. For r different from 1, the ranking $\succeq_m^r$ of m-species ecosystems generated by this class is defined by:

$$x \succeq_m^r y \Leftrightarrow \left(\sum_{k=1}^{m} \left(\frac{x_k}{m\mu(x)} \right)^r \right)^{\frac{1}{1-r}} \geq \left(\sum_{k=1}^{m} \left(\frac{y_k}{m\mu(y)} \right)^r \right)^{\frac{1}{1-r}}$$

if $r \geq 0$ and by:

$$x \succeq_m^r y \Leftrightarrow -\left(\sum_{k=1}^{m} \left(\frac{x_k}{m\mu(x)} \right)^r \right)^{\frac{1}{1-r}} \geq -\left(\sum_{k=1}^{m} \left(\frac{y_k}{m\mu(y)} \right)^r \right)^{\frac{1}{1-r}} \tag{1.5}$$

if $r < 0$, whereas for $r = 1$ the ranking is defined by:[3]

$$A \succeq_m^1 B \Leftrightarrow -\sum_{k=1}^{m} \frac{x_k}{m\mu(x)} \ln \frac{x_k}{m\mu(x)} \geq -\sum_{k=1}^{m} \frac{y_k}{m\mu(y)} \ln \frac{y_k}{m\mu(y)}$$

using the convention that $0\ln0 = 0$. Posing by convention also that $0^0 = 0$, the case $r = 0$ corresponds to the widely used criterion of species counting discussed in the previous section. The (limiting) case $r = 1$ corresponds to the well-known Shannon (1948) entropy index first proposed, in the context of biodiversity measurement, by Goode (1953). Other interesting cases are $r = 2$, where the ranking is induced by the comparison of the Simpson (1949) index (also known in economics as the Herfindahl index of concentration), and r approaching infinity, where the ranking is obtained by comparing the (inverse of) the relative frequency of the most abundant species in the ecosystem. This later index is known as the Berger and Parker (1970) index of diversity.

All rankings in this family consider that an ecosystem in which all existing species are represented with the same abundance is the most diverse of all. Increasing the value of r amounts to increasing the weight given to the more abundant species in the ecosystem, with the limiting case given by the Berger and Parker (1970) index where the weight given to any species other than the most abundant one is zero. The justification given to these rankings of ecosystems by biologists (see, for instance, Magurran 1998) is a mixture of prosaic considerations of ease of calculations, and of intuitive probabilistic ideas about the appeal of having ecosystems that are 'unpredictable' in terms of the probability of success of the various species. For instance the Simpson index can be interpreted as measuring the (reciprocal of) the probability for two living individuals drawn independently at random from the ecosystem to belong to the same species. The lower the probability, the more diverse is the ecosystem. Analogously, Shannon's entropy is usually viewed in thermodynamics as a measure of 'disorder' of the system. An ecosystem that is maximally 'disordered' is this sense – that is, an ecosystem in which it is very hard *a priori* to predict which species will win the race for survival – is maximally diverse.

The properties that characterize the generalized entropy family of rankings have been identified, in the somewhat different context of income inequality measurement, by Shorrocks (1984) (see also Shorrocks 1980). It is of interest to recall here these properties because they identify clearly the limitations of generalized entropy as a method for evaluating diversity.

The first one is an axiom of symmetry. It says, in a rather disputable fashion for diversity appraisal, that 'species does not matter' and that the only things that are relevant for diversity is the ordering of the species in terms of their abundance. The fact that the more abundant species is chimpanzees or mosquitoes has no bearing whatsoever on our evaluation of biodiversity. This axiom is stated as follows.

Axiom 1.7 (symmetry between species). For every number m of species, for all ecosystems x and y in R_+^m, if x is a permutation of y, then $x \sim^m y$.

The second axiom is also somewhat problematic for diversity appraisal. For it says, in contradiction with the principle of weak monotonicity, that it is only the relative abundance that matters and that increasing uniformly the population size of each species in an ecosystem has no effect whatsoever on diversity. A world in which each species has 10 individuals is just as diverse as a world in which each species has 1 million individuals.

Axiom 1.8 (scale invariance). For every number m of species, and for any ecosystem x in R_+^m $tx \sim^m x$ for every real number t.

The third axiom captures the 'equalizing' feature of diversity as appraised by generalized entropy rankings. It says that reducing disparities in abundance in an ecosystem is, ceteris paribus, a good thing for diversity. Specifically, any change that would lead to the elimination of a certain number of individuals in an abundant species and to an increase in the same number of individuals in a less abundant species would be worth doing from the view point of diversity if the change does not affect the ranking of the two species in terms of their abundance.

Axiom 1.9 (abundance equalization). For every number m of species, and for all ecosystems x and y in R_+^m, if there exists two species h and k such that $x_i = y_i$ for all i other than h and k and for which one has

$$x_h = y_h + \Delta < y_k - \Delta = x_k$$

for some strictly positive real number Δ, then A > B.

The last substantive axiom that characterizes generalized entropy rankings reflects the concern for convenience in applications alluded to above. It is common for biodiversity appraisal to be made separately and sequentially on various subsets of species. For example, in examining the biodiversity of a particular forest, some biologists will focus on the different species of trees, while others will be interested in species of fungus and others will investigate mammals and birds. Yet it is of practical importance that these various appraisals of diversity be made in a consistent fashion with each other. Suppose we first appraise the diversity of trees in a forest, and we then appraise the diversity of fungus in this forest. How can one obtain, from these two separate evaluations, an overall appraisal of the diversity of this forest in terms of both fungus and trees? It would be nice if, for instance, the overall evaluation could be obtained in a simple fashion from the two 'sub-evaluations' made in isolation, rather than requiring a new appraisal of diversity in the large population made of both fungus and trees. A simple and convenient way of proceeding would be to write the overall diversity as the sum of the diversity of fungus, the diversity of trees and the diversity of the 'aggregate' ecosystem made only of the average abundance of the species of fungus and the average abundance of the species of trees. Using the terminology of Shorrocks (1984), I call 'decomposable' a diversity indicator that satisfies this property.

In the ordinal setting considered herein, this property is expressed as the requirement that, among all numerical indicators that represent the diversity ranking, there is at least one that is decomposable.

Axiom 1.10 (decomposable representability). There exist functions I_d^m from R_+^m to R representing numerically the ranking $\succeq_m$ for every m such that, for any $x \in R_+^{m_1}$ and $y \in R_+^{m_2}$ one has:

$$I_d^{m_1+m_2}(x,y) = I_d^{m_1}(x) + I_d^{m_2}(y) + I_d^{m_1+m_2}(\bar{x}, \bar{y})$$

for every number of species m_1 and m_2, where the vector (x,y) is defined by $(x,y) = (x_1, \ldots, x_{m_1}, \ldots, y_{m_2})$.

The attractiveness of this property is, of course, a pure matter of computational convenience. It is convenient, in evaluating the diversity of fungus and trees, to rely only on the (presumably) known diversity of fungus, the (presumably) known diversity of trees and the easy-to-calculate diversity of the simple ecosystem in which all fungus species have their average abundance and all tree species have their average abundance. But apart from this convenience there is nothing intrinsically appealing in this property.

A powerful result, due to Shorrocks (1984), shows that any continuous ordering[4] of ecosystems in R_+^m, for any m, satisfying decomposable representability, abundance equalization, scale invariance and symmetry between species can be thought as resulting from the comparison of generalized entropy, as calculated by the entropy formula defined above for some value of r, with the exception of $r=0$. This result is expressed in the following theorem.

Theorem 1.3. An infinite list $\succeq_m$ for $m=1, \ldots$, of continuous orderings of ecosystems (each involving m species) satisfies symmetry between species, scale invariance, abundance equalization and decomposable representability if and only there exists a real number r different from zero such that, for any m, and for every two ecosystems x and y, one has

$$x \succeq_m y \Leftrightarrow \left(\sum_{k=1}^m \left(\frac{x_k}{m\mu(x)} \right)^r \right)^{\frac{1}{1-r}} \geq \left(\sum_{k=1}^m \left(\frac{y_k}{m\mu(y)} \right)^r \right)^{\frac{1}{1-r}}$$

if r is different from 1 and

$$x \succeq_m y \Leftrightarrow \sum_{k=1}^m \frac{x_k}{m\mu(x)} \ln \frac{x_k}{m\mu(x)} \geq -\sum_{k=1}^m \frac{y_k}{m\mu(y)} \ln \frac{y_k}{m\mu(y)}$$

otherwise.

Proof. By Debreu's (1954) theorem, any continuous ordering $\succeq_m$ on R_+^m, can be represented numerically by a continuous function $I : R_+^m \to R$. Given symmetry and abundance equalization, this function satisfies $I(\bar{x}) \geq I(x)$ for all x in R_+^m. Hence this function is just like (the inverse of) an inequality index as defined in Shorrocks (1984). Given decomposable representability, it satisfies all axioms of an inequality index considered in Shorrocks (1984). For this reason, the analysis of Shorrocks (1984) applies and, by virtue of theorem 5 of his paper, there exists a real number r and a numerical representation I^m_d of the ordering $\succeq_m$ such that:

$$\frac{1}{m} \frac{1}{r(1-r)} \sum_{k=1}^m \left(\frac{x_k}{\mu(x)} \right)^r \quad \text{if } r \neq 0,1$$

$$I_d^m(x) = \frac{-1}{m}\sum_{k=1}^{m}\frac{x_k}{\mu(x)}\ln\left(\frac{x_k}{\mu(x)}\right) \text{ if } r = 1 \tag{1.6}$$

$$\frac{-1}{m}\sum_{k=1}^{m}\ln\left(\frac{x_k}{\mu(x)}\right) \text{ if } r = 0$$

Yet it is clear that, for $r < 0$, the ranking of vectors induced by the function

$$\frac{1}{m}\frac{1}{r(1-r)}\sum_{k=1}^{m}\left(\frac{x_k}{\mu(x)}\right)^r \tag{1.7}$$

is equivalent to the ranking induced by the function

$$-\left[\sum_{k=1}^{m}\left(\frac{x_k}{\mu(x)}\right)^r\right]^{\frac{1}{1-r}}$$

For r strictly between 0 and 1 and for r strictly greater than 1, the ranking induced by equation (1.1) is equivalent to that induced by the entropy function. The equivalence is of course trivial for $r = 1$. ∎

This theorem, which does not provide any characterization of species counting (the case $r = 0$), clearly identifies the principles that justify generalized entropy as a sensible method for appraising diversity. The most problematic of these principles is clearly symmetry across species, which neglects the varying dissimilarities that may exist between species. Yet some other principles are also open to discussion.

Scale invariance is one of them. Even if one accepts the view that equalizing the probabilities of survival across species is the best way to promote biodiversity, it is not clear that this probability of survival does not depend to some extent upon the scale of abundance of the various species. On the one hand, it is widely acknowledged that a minimal threshold of abundance within each species is required to ensure species survival. For instance, species have a much lower chance of survivals when they all contain 10 specimens than when they contain 100,000. On the other hand, there seems also to be some upper bound on the abundance that is sustainable given the limited physical resources that planet Earth has. For instance, the survival probability of mammals would certainly be challenged if the population of each species of mammal were to rise to 10 billion.

The axiom of abundance equalization can also be questioned as a fundamental principle of diversity appraisal. The axiom derives its appeal from the evolutionary context of biology in which the abundance of objects (living organisms) belonging to a particular category (species) appears to be related to the probability of survival of the category. Another evolutionary context that satisfies this feature is linguistic diversity in which the number of users of a particular language can be thought as a good indicator of the probability of survival of this language. In all such evolutionary contexts, equalizing the probabilities of survival of the different categories can be seen as a natural thing to do in an ex ante situation, provided of course that the different categories can be thought as symmetric. Yet such equalization would not be natural in non-evolutionary contexts. Consider for instance the case of products diversity. Even though a grouping of products – cars, say – into categories – such as luxury cars, sport cars, family cars, etc. – could be imagined that would play a similar role to the biological grouping of living organisms in species, there would not be much justification for imposing the axiom of abundance equalization in this context. Why would a car retailer offering an equal quantity of sport cars and family cars be considered more diverse than a retailer who, following the demand trend for the two categories of car, would offer them in different proportions?

As the symmetrical treatment of the categories provided by generalized entropy is the main weakness of this family of methods for appraising diversity, it is important to move away from this assumption. An attractive direction for making this move is to introduce explicitly some information pertaining to the underlying varying dissimilarity between the objects.

Diversity as aggregate dissimilarity

From a formal point of view, partitioning objects into various categories as done in the previous section can be seen as a (very) particular method for defining a notion of proximity, or similarity, between objects. Two objects belonging to the same category are assumed to be similar and two objects belonging to different categories are assumed to be dissimilar. Of course the notion of similarity that underlies this way of doing is rather crude: two objects can either be similar or dissimilar. They cannot have intermediate levels of dissimilarity. It is to some extent this rigidity of the notion of similarity that underlies the grouping of objects into categories that limits the interest of generalized entropy as a plausible method for appraising diversity. Would not it be possible to appraise diversity on the basis of a notion of similarity between objects that could be finer than the crude one considered thus far?

Cardinal notions of dissimilarity

In mathematics, proximity or similarity judgments are usually expressed by means of a distance, or metric, function. In the present context, a distance is a function $d : X \times X \to R_+$ that associates, to every pair (x, y) of objects in X, a (non-negative) number $d(x, y)$ interpreted as the distance that separates x from y. To motivate this interpretation, it is common to require d to be symmetric (the distance is the same in going from y to x as in going from x to y) and to satisfy the normalization property that $d(x, x) = 0$ for any object x (the distance between any object and itself is zero). It is also quite common to require a distance to satisfy the property that $d(x,y) > 0$ for every distinct objects x and y as well as the so-called 'triangle inequality' according to which $d(x,y) \leq d(x,y) + d(y,z)$ (the distance of a 'direct' trip between z and x can never exceed that of an 'indirect' trip). Yet this triangle inequality has no particular appeal here. One could very well accept for instance that the dissimilarity, in terms of modes of transportation, between a bicycle and a car be greater than the sum of dissimilarities between a bicycle and a motorcycle and between a motorcycle and a car.

Taking as given such a distance function, Weitzman (1992; see also Weitzman 1993, 1998) has proposed a recursive method for evaluating the diversity of a set based on a specific aggregation of the dissimilarities between the pairs of objects that it contains. The general idea of Weizman's method is the following. Given any set, one first calculates, for each object, the increasingly ordered vector of all distances that separate the object from the other objects in the set. This provides us with as many such ordered vectors as there are objects in the set, each vector itself having also as many components as there are objects in the set. One then compares these ordered vectors by the lexicographic criterion and selects the element in the set that corresponds to the vector that ranks last according to this criterion. There might be several such elements, in which case they will all have the same ordered vector of distances. It this is the case, any one of these elements can be selected. Once this element is selected, one records the smallest non-zero distance in its vector and removes the element from the set and redoes the procedure with the remaining elements in the set. At the end, one is left with a unique element in the set and one has obtained a finite list of smallest non-zero distance. Weitzman (1992) has proposed a comparison of sets on the basis of the sum of these smallest non-zero minimal distances, sets with larger sums being considered more diverse than those with smaller sums.

Weitzman himself has never provided axiomatic characterizations of his criterion, even though he has discussed some of its properties. The criterion does not seem completely unreasonable, be it simply because it provide the first – to my knowledge – definition of diversity as an aggregation of dissimilarities. Yet the procedure proposed is rather specific. It combines, in a rather complex way, a lexicographic procedure for selecting sequentially the objects associated with the minimal distance and an additive procedure of summing these minimal distances. One would therefore like to get a better sense of its plausibility by knowing the elementary axioms that justify this way of doing, and only this one.

The only existing – to my knowledge – axiomatic characterization of Weitzman procedure is by Bossert, Pattanaik and Xu (2003). The characterization uses three axioms and requires the set X and the distance d to allow for a sufficient richness in the ranking of alternative pairs of objects. Specifically Bossert, Pattanaik and Xu assume the set X and the distance function d to be such that, for any two non-negative real numbers s and t satisfying $s \leq t$, there exists three objects x, y and z such that $s = d(x,y) \leq d(x,z) \leq d(y,z) = t$. This assumption obviously requires the set X to contain uncountably many objects.

The first axiom considered by Bossert, Pattanaik and Xu (2003) is hardly disputable in the current context. It says that the ranking of sets consisting of one or two objects should coincide with the ranking of the corresponding pairs of elements on the basis of their distance. Formally:

> **Axiom 1.11** (dissimilarity monotonicity). For any (not necessarily distinct) objects w, x, y and z in X, $\{w,z\} \succeq \{x,y\}$ if and only if $d(w,z) \geq d(x,y)$.

Since the statement of the axiom does not require the objects w, x, y and z to be distinct, and since the distance function satisfies $d(x,y) > d(x,x) = 0$ for every distinct x and y, the axiom implies both the principle of indifference between non-diverse situations as well as Pattanaik and Xu's (1990) axiom of strict preference for choice over non-choice.

The second axiom is certainly more disputable. It captures the idea that the diversity ranking of two sets should be independent from the addition or the deletion of objects when the distances that separate the objects from the other objects in the set satisfy certain conditions. Specifically, the independence of the ranking is assumed to hold when:

1 the smallest distance that separates the added or subtracted object from the other objects in the set is smaller than the smallest distance between the other objects themselves and
2 the minimal distance between the object and the other objects in the set is the same in the two sets.

This axiom is expressed formally as follows:

> **Axiom 1.12** (minimal distance independence). For any two sets A and B, and for any two objects x and y that do not belong to A and to B respectively, if the smallest distance between x and the other objects in A is smaller than the smallest distance between all distinct objects in A, if the same is true for y with respect to B and if the smallest distance between x and the other objects in A is the same than the smallest distance between y and the other objects in B, then $A \succeq B$ if and only if $A \cup \{x\} \succeq B \cup \{y\}$.

Hence, the idea captured by this axiom is that the ranking of two sets should not depend upon the object that produces the minimal distance in the set when the minimal distance thus produced is the same. As much of the independence notions discussed earlier, this axiom has a strong additive flavour that contributes in no small part to the clearly additive feature of Weitzman's method for evaluating diversity.

The last axiom considered by Bossert, Pattanaik and Xu (2003) is certainly the most opaque of the three. It applies to pairs of objects such as $\{a,c\}$ and $\{x,y\}$ that have the property that the distance between x and y is greater than the distance between a and b. In this context, consider adding an object b to the set $\{a,c\}$, that is, 'in between' a and c in the sense that the distance that separates b from c or c from a is lower than the distance between a and c. Such an object b would be called by Weitzman (1992) a link of $\{a,c\}$ to $\{x,y\}$ if it was such that $d(x,y) = d(a,c) + \min(d(a,b),d(b,c))$. That is, b is a link of $\{a,c\}$ to $\{x,y\}$ if the minimal distance brought about by the addition of b to a and c is exactly equal to the difference in distance between x and y on the one hand and a and c on the other. The third axiom of *link indifference* introduced by Bossert, Pattanaik and Xu (2003) would require the set $\{x,y\}$ to be diversity-wise equivalent to the set $\{a,b,c\}$.

> **Axiom 1.13** (link indifference). For all objects a, b, c, x and y in X such that $x \neq y$ and a, b and c are pairwise distinct, if $\{x,y\} > \{a,c\}$ and if b is such that $\max\{d(a,b),d(b,c)\} \leq d(a,c)$ and $d(a,c) + \min\{d(a,b),d(b,c)\} = d(x,y)$, then $\{x,y\} \sim \{a,b,c\}$.

The opacity of this axiom is impressive. And there is no reason really, either practical or philosophical, to adhere to it. Supposed we are interested in appraising the diversity of modes of transportation and that we are told that the distance between riding a bike (a) and riding a motorcycle (c) is 6 and that the distance between walking (x) and driving a car (y) is 10. Suppose that we know that the distance between riding a motorcycle and skateboarding (b) is 6 and that the distance between skateboarding and riding a bike is 4. Why should we deduce from this information than the set $\{x,y\}$ offers exactly the same diversity as the set $\{a,b,c\}$?

Yet this axiom of link indifference is inextricably connected to Weitzman's method for evaluating diversity. For Bossert, Pattanaik and Xu (2003) have shown the following.

> **Theorem 1.4.** If X and d have the richness defined above, then $\geq$ is an ordering defined over all finite subsets of X satisfying dissimilarity monotonicity, minimal distance independence and link indifference if and only if it ranks sets by the Weitzman procedure.

The lack of appeal of the axiom of link indifference, to mention just this one, sheds serious doubts on the appeal of the Weitzman procedure as a sensible method for making diversity appraisal. We do not have, at the present moment, any reason for appraising diversity in the particular way proposed by Weitzman.

Moreover Weitzman's approach suffers from a more fundamental interpretative difficulty. It assumes the existence of a cardinally meaningful distance function.[5] That is, it requires from the diversity appraiser an *a priori* capacity to formulate statements such as 'the dissimilarity between walking and driving a car is twice that between riding a bicycle and riding a motorcycle'. Such a capacity is clearly assumed in the very formulation of the axiom of link indifference. Yet it is far from obvious that this capacity exists, even for an appraiser working in the very developed and sophisticated context of biological diversity. Whereas it seems reasonable to believe that many biologists would agree, say on the basis of a taxonomic or phylogenetic criterion, to say that a bee and a wasp are more similar than a chimpanzee and a protozoan, it is more doubtful to think that they would agree on saying that the dissimilarity between a chimpanzee and a protozoan is exactly 10 times that between a bee and a wasp. Would it not be possible to view diversity as an aggregation of the underlying dissimilarities between the objects without going as far as requiring these dissimilarities to be measured cardinally by a distance function?

Ordinal notions of dissimilarity

An obvious alternative to a cardinal measure of dissimilarity is an ordinal, or qualitative, one, which enables the formulation of statements like 'w is more dissimilar to z than x is to y' but does not enable a further quantification of these statements. In particular, statements like 'the dissimilarity between w and z is twice that between x and y' have no meaning in an ordinal theory of dissimilarity.

A simple ordinal notion of dissimilarity is the crude one implicitly assumed in the partitioning of living organisms in species performed in biology: two objects are either similar (say if they belong to the same species) or dissimilar (if they belong to different species), with no other intermediate possibilities. Assuming the existence of such a dichotomous ordinal notion of dissimilarity, Pattanaik and Xu (2000) have proposed an axiomatic characterization, which shall not be detailed here, of a particular criterion for comparing sets on the basis of their diversity. According to their criterion, the diversity of a set can be defined by the number of elements in the smallest partition of the set into subsets of similar objects. Applied to the biodiversity context, in which the objects are living organisms, and in which living organisms are similar if and only if they belong to the same species, the Pattanaik and Xu criterion amounts to evaluating diversity by counting the number of species.

Although the species counting criterion has already been characterized above in a framework where the objects were interpreted as species (and not as objects), the characterization proposed by Pattanaik and Xu (2000) is significantly different. This re-emphasizes the importance of specifying properly the nature of the objects that are involved in appraising diversity. If objects are interpreted as species right from the beginning, the characterization of the criterion of species counting is obtained quite straightforwardly from the principles of general independence and indifference between non-diverse situations. If objects are interpreted as living individuals, and are grouped into species on the basis of a dichotomous notion of similarity (living individuals are similar if and only if they belong to the same species), then the principles that characterize the criterion of species counting are quite different. If one wants to introduce a finer, but yet ordinal, notion of dissimilarity into the picture, it is important to go beyond the dichotomous notion of dissimilarity considered in Pattanaik and Xu (2000).

A general way to describe an ordinal notion of dissimilarity is through the formalism of a quaternary relation Q on X, which can, alternatively, be viewed as a binary relation on the Cartesian product $X \times X$ In this light, the statement

$(w,z)\,Q(x,y)$ is interpreted as meaning w is at least as dissimilar to z as x is to y. Asymmetric (strictly more dissimilar than) and symmetric (equally similar) factors of Q can also be defined in the usual fashion and are denoted Q_A and Q_S respectively. To motivate this interpretation further, it is natural to assume that, for all distinct objects x and $y \in X$ both $(x,y)\,Q_A(x,x)$ and $(x,x)\,Q_S(y,y)$ hold (that is, two distinct objects are always strictly more dissimilar than either of the two objects in isolation, and pairs of identical objects are just equally similar). We assume also that Q is symmetric in the sense that $(x,y)\,Q(y,x)$ holds for all objects x and y and, as a binary relation on $X \times X$, is reflexive, complete and transitive. All these properties of Q would clearly hold true if, like Van Hees (2004) or Weitzman (1992), we would accept to go as far as measuring the dissimilarity by a (cardinally significant) distance function (as distances are conventionally assumed to be symmetric and to satisfy $d(x,y) > d(x,x) = 0$ for all distinct x and y). Conversely, any Q satisfying these properties can be represented numerically by a distance function, which can even be chosen in such a way that it satisfies the triangle inequality.[6] Obviously no cardinal significance is attached to a distance function representing a particular quaternary relation, as any monotonic transformation of such a distance function is also a numerical representation of the quaternary relation. In particular, a property such as link indifference, which requires that meaning be attached to distance summations, cannot be formulated here because the value of a sum is not preserved if a monotonic transformation is applied to the terms of the sum.

What properties can a ranking of sets of objects be required to satisfy in such a setting?

A principle that is difficult to avoid here is dissimilarity monotonicity, according to which the information on the underlying dissimilarities between the objects is the only datum that should be used for ranking singletons and pairs. This principle has been formulated above in terms of a distance function. Yet it is clearly ordinal in nature in the sense that, if holds for a particular distance function, it holds also for all monotonic transformation of this distance function. Another highly plausible principle is weak monotonicity.

A third principle has been proposed by Bervoets and Gravel (2007). This principle, to be referred to as robustness of domination, requires roughly the domination of a set by another to be robust to the addition, in the dominated set, of options when the options added are themselves dominated in terms of diversity. Specifically, the principle requires that, if adding separately objects taken from some sets C and D to a set B is insufficient to reverse the domination of the set B by some other set A, then adding jointly the objects in C and D to B should also be insufficient to reverse the domination if the added objects are themselves considered less diverse than those contained in A. I formulate this robustness of domination principle as follows.

Axiom 1.14 (robustness of domination). For every set of objects A, B, C and D such that $B \cap C = B \cap C = C \cap D = \varnothing$ if $A \geq (B \cup C)$, $A \geq (B \cup D)$, and $A \geq (C \cup D)$, then $A \geq (B \cup C \cup D)$, and if $A > (B \cup C)$, $A > (B \cup D)$ and $A > (C \cup D)$, then $A > (B \cup C \cup D)$.

A ranking of sets that satisfies the principles of dissimilarity monotonicity, weak monotonicity and robustness of domination is that which compares sets on the basis of their two most dissimilar objects: set A is at least as diverse as set B if the two most dissimilar objects in A are at least as dissimilar as the two most dissimilar objects in B. Let me refer to this ranking as to the 'maxi-max' criterion. Such a ranking is certainly extreme in that it only focuses on the two most dissimilar objects to appraise the diversity of a set. For example, in a biological context, with the objects interpreted as living organisms, and using the crude ordinal notion of dissimilarity according to which two living organisms are either similar (if they belong to the same species) or dissimilar (if they belong to different species), the maxi-max ranking would consider all ecosystems in which at least two species are represented to be equally diverse, and will consider any such ecosystem to be more diverse than an ecosystem with only one species represented, irrespective of the number of individuals in each species. Obviously finer rankings could be obtained from the maxi-max criterion if finer notions of dissimilarity were used. Yet it is clear that the maxi-max ranking is rather coarse in that it refuses to recognize any contribution to diversity brought about by pairs of objects that are not maximally dissimilar.

The maxi-max ranking, it should be mentioned, violates all independence principles discussed earlier, including of course contraction consistency. This can be seen easily from the restaurant example considered earlier. Suppose, plausibly, that the notion of meals dissimilarities that applies to this example is given by:

$$(beef,paneer)\,Q_A\,(lamb,paneer)\,Q_A\,(chicken,paneer)\,Q_A\,(lamb,chicken)$$
$$Q_S\,(beef,chicken)\,\,Q_A\,(lamb,beef)$$

In that case, the maxi-max criterion would consider that adding a beef meal to a restaurant offering lamb and chicken dishes does not enlarge diversity because it does not affect the dissimilarity of the two most dissimilar meals (which would still be lamb and chicken, or the equally dissimilar beef and chicken). On the other hand, and contrary to the requirement of contraction consistency, adding beef to a restaurant offering chicken, lamb and paneer dishes enlarges diversity as appraised by the maxi-max criterion because such addition increases the dissimilarity of the two most dissimilar dishes (lamb and paneer before the introduction of beef, beef and paneer after the introduction of beef).

Are there other rankings of sets than the maxi-max that satisfy the three principles of dissimilarity monotonicity, weak monotonicity and robustness of domination? The answer to this question is, unfortunately, negative, as the following theorem has been proved in Bervoets and Gravel (2007).

Theorem 1.5. A transitive and reflexive ranking $\geq$ of all non-empty subsets of a finite set X satisfies weak monotonicity, robustness of domination and dissimilarity monotonicity with respect to some ordinal notion of similarity Q if and only if $\geq$ is the maxi-max criterion.

A somewhat natural direction for extending the maxi-max criterion is the lexicographic one. Such an extension, called the lexi-max criterion in Bervoets and Gravel (2007), would rank sets by looking first, like the maxi-max criterion, at their two most dissimilar options. Yet, and contrary to the maxi-max criterion, in case of equal dissimilarity between the two most dissimilar options in the two sets, the lexi-max criterion would move on to the comparisons of the second most dissimilar two objects in the sets and, if a tie is also obtained there, to the third most dissimilar objects and so on. The lexi-max criterion would sequentially perform the dissimilarity comparisons from the most dissimilar to the least dissimilar pair of options until a strict ranking is obtained or, if the two sets have the same cardinality and the same dissimilarity between all their pairs of distinct objects ordered from the most dissimilar to the least dissimilar, by considering the sets as equally diverse. This lexi-max criterion satisfies strong monotonicity (if the underlying quaternary relation considers two distinct objects to be strictly more dissimilar than one object and itself) and dissimilarity monotonicity but violates robustness of domination. Axioms that characterize the lexi-max criterion have been identified in Bervoets and Gravel (2007) and will not be commented on here.

The gain in discriminatory power brought about by the lexi-max criterion, compared with the maxi-max one, is probably best seen in the simple case of the crude ordinal notion of dissimilarity underlying the partitioning of the living organisms in species. Whereas the maxi-max ranking would consider in this case all ecosystems with at least two species to be equally diverse, the lexi-max would value both the addition of individuals within existing species and the addition of individuals from other non-existing species (if there are at least two species represented). Again, more interesting ranking of sets could be obtained if the lexi-max criterion were based on a finer notion of dissimilarity.

If the gain of sensitivity with respect to less than maximally dissimilar options of a set obtained in moving from the maxi-max to the lexi-max criterion is not negligible, it is not great either. In fact, one can say that both the maxi-max and the lexi-max criteria give a veto power to the two most dissimilar options in a set. This veto power is somewhat extravagant, since it prevents any possibility of a large number of significant increases in the dissimilarities of not maximally dissimilar objects to beat an arbitrarily small reduction in the dissimilarity of the two most dissimilar objects. Would it not be possible to construct a ranking of sets based on ordinal notions of dissimilarity that allow for smoother trade-off between the various pairwise dissimilarities of the objects?

It would be nice to have a positive answer to this question. Yet such an answer is not, for the moment, available. An interesting ranking of sets that allows for trade-offs between the varying dissimilarities of the objects is one that could be thought of as defining the diversity of a set by the sum of the distances between all pairs of its elements, for some distance function representing numerically the underlying dissimilarity quaternary relation. Identifying the properties satisfied by such a ranking is clearly a worthwhile objective for future research in the area. Although any such ranking will obviously satisfy dissimilarity monotonicity and weak monotonicity, it will also have to satisfy other properties. For instance, assume that we are interested in ranking sets of transportation modes taken from the universe {*bicycle,car,motorcycle,scooter,walk*} and that the underlying dissimilarity ranking of pairs of modes of transportation is (from the more to the less dissimilar):

(*car,walk*)

(*motorcycle,walk*)

(*bicycle,car*)

(*bicycle,motorcycle*)

(*scooter,walk*)

(*bicycle,scooter*)

(*bicycle,walk*)

(*car,scooter*)

(*car,motorcycle*)

(*motorcycle,scooter*)

Consider now a diversity ranking $\geq$ of sets that generates the following comparisons between sets of modes of transportation:

$$\{motorcycle,walk\} > \{bicycle,car,motorcycle\} \qquad (1.8)$$

$$\{car,motorcycle,scooter\} > \{car,walk\} \qquad (1.9)$$

as well as the obvious rankings of pairs of mode of transportation induced by the comparisons of their dissimilarity:

$$\{bicycle,car\} > \{motorcycle,scooter\} \qquad (1.10)$$

$$\{bicycle,motorcycle\} > \{car,scooter\} \qquad (1.11)$$

$$\{car,walk\} > \{motorcycle,walk\} \qquad (1.12)$$

It is easy to see that this ranking is perfectly compatible with weak monotonic-ity and dissimilarity monotonicity. Yet such a ranking, which violates robustness of domination, can*not* be thought of as resulting from the comparisons of sums of distances representing numerically the underlying ordinal notion dissimilarity. For, if the ranking could be thought of as resulting from such sums, there would be a distance function $d: X \times X \rightarrow \mathsf{R}_+$ representing numerically the quaternary relation such that the statements (1.8) to (1.12) would write:

$$d(motorcycle,walk) > d(bicycle,car) + d(bicycle,motorcycle) + d(car,motorcycle) \tag{1.13}$$

$$d(car,motorcycle) + d(car,scooter) + d(motorcycle,scooter) > d(car,walk) \tag{1.14}$$

$$d(bicycle,car) > d(motorcycle,scooter) \tag{1.15}$$

$$d(bicycle,motorcycle) > d(car,scooter) \tag{1.16}$$

$$d(car,walk) > d(motorcycle,walk) \tag{1.17}$$

Yet summing these five inequalities and simplifying leads to:

$$d(motorcycle,walk) > d(car,walk)$$

in contradiction to statement (1.17). Identifying precisely the properties satisfied by a ranking of sets that can be thought of as resulting from a summation of distance is therefore an open, if not difficult, problem.

Although the formalism of quaternary relations appears natural for describ-ing ordinal information on dissimilarity, it is by no means the only conceivable one. The formalism of quaternary relations is natural because it represents the ordinal side of the formalism of cardinally meaningful distance functions. Any distance function generates a quaternary relation and, conversely, any quaternary relation satisfying the properties discussed above can be represented numerically by a distance function. Moving from distance functions to quaternary relations is therefore a minimal way of weakening the precision of the information assumed to be available on the underlying dissimilarities between the objects.

It is however possible to weaken the precision of this information to a more significant extent. For instance, Nehring (1997) has explored the possibility of describing the qualitative information on the object dissimilarities in terms of a ternary relation. A ternary relation enables one to express statements of 'in betweenness' between one object and two other objects. For instance, with a ternary relation, it is possible to say things such as 'y is closer to x than z is' but it is not possible to say things like 'y is closer to x than z is to w' (unless of course $w=x$). Hence the information on dissimilarity expressed by a ternary relation is significantly less precise than that expressed by a quaternary relation. Are there contexts in which the available information on the objects dissimilarity can take the form of a ternary relation but not of a quaternary relation? One such context, considered by Nehring (ibid.), is when objects are assumed to have various attributes. In such a framework, the attributes of the objects naturally define a ternary notion of similarity between them in the following way: y is closer to x than to z if all attributes possessed by both x and z are also possessed by y. Yet such a framework does not generate naturally a notion of similarity that takes the form of a quaternary relation. Nehring has proved interesting results on the duality that exists between a ternary relation satisfying certain properties and a family of subsets of X, interpreted as attributes.

The duality is clear at an abstract level. For any statement of the type 'y is closer to x than to z', I can define a family of sets (attributes) such that, every time a set in this family contains x and z, it also contains y. Applied, with some care, to all triples of objects over which the ternary relation tells something, this leads to the definition of a family of subsets that can be interpreted as a 'multi-attributes' representation of the ternary relation. Conversely, a family of subsets (attributes) of X induces a ternary relation by considering that y is closer to x than to z if any set in the family containing x and z also contains y. The results of Nehring (1997) state that some properties of the ternary relation, such as reflexivity, symmetry and transitivity could be translated into properties of the family of attributes and vice versa.

Yet it is fair to say that the interest of expressing judgments about objects' dissimilarity in the form of a ternary, rather than a quaternary, relation is derived from some underlying attribute structure, rather than being intrinsic. Without assuming an attribute structure, it may seem rather unusual to express judgments of dissimilarity between objects only in the terms of statements involving triples of objects. Why should I be able to compare the similarity between a trout and a salmon with that between a salmon and a shark but unable to compare the dissimilarity between a trout and a salmon with that between a shark and a whale?

Diversity as the valuation of realized attributes

In recent years, Nehring and Puppe (2002; see also 2003) have forcefully argued in favour of defining the diversity of a set as the sum of the values of the attributes realized by the objects in the set. As discussed earlier, this approach rides on the categorization of the objects into a certain number of attributes (being a mammal, being an ocean-living animal, being an air-breathing animal, having a specific ancestor, etc.). These attributes are naturally modelled as sets of objects having the considered attributes. Hence, an *attributes structure* is a collection, A say, of subsets of X. As discussed above, Nehring and Puppe have proposed to rank all sets A and B by

$$A \succeq B \Leftrightarrow \sum_{C \in A: A \cap C \neq \varnothing} \lambda(C) \geq \sum_{D \in A: B \cap D \neq \varnothing} \lambda(D) \tag{1.18}$$

for some family A of attributes and some non-negative valuation function $\lambda: P(X) \to R_+$ of the attributes. By Theorem 1.2, any ordering satisfying contraction consistency and weak monotonicity can be viewed as being generated by a valuation function λ assigning positive values to attributes in some family.[7] Yet, as also discussed, this result cannot really be seen as a justification for measuring diversity by the above formula. For there are typically different families of relevant attributes and different attribute valuation functions that can rationalize, in the sense of this formula, a given ordering of sets satisfying contraction consistency and weak monotonicity. When confronted with this wealth of attributes structures and valuation functions, which one should the diversity appraiser choose? Much more information is therefore required on the diversity ordering of sets to define the family of attributes and the valuation function underlying the above formula uniquely.

Leaving this issue aside, an important contribution of Nehring and Puppe (2002) was to examine the implications, for the form of the diversity indicator corresponding to this formula, of various assumptions that can be made about the structure of the family A of attributes. Quite clearly, if this family is very large (for instance any set of objects is a positively valued attribute), the multi-attributes approach to diversity evaluation is likely to be rather cumbersome to apply. At the other extreme, if the family of attributes is only made of singletons (each object is itself an attribute and does not have any other attribute than itself), the ranking induced by the above formula becomes a member of the additive family of rankings discussed above (with each object being valued by a non-negative number).

Most of the properties of λ considered in Nehring and Puppe (2002) are expressed in terms of the (pseudo-)distance function δ induced by the difference in diversity, as measured by the diversity indicator corresponding to the above formula, between pairs and singleton. That is, for a given family A of attributes and a value function λ generating the above formula, define

$$I_d(S) = \sum_{A \in A: A \cap S \neq \phi} \lambda(A) \tag{1.19}$$

for every set S and

$$\delta(x, y) = I_d(\{x, y\}) - I_d(\{y\}) = \sum_{\{C \in A: x \cap C \text{ and } y \notin C\}} \lambda(C)$$

for every two objects x and y. Hence, when appraised by the function δ, the distance of x from y is defined as the gain of diversity brought about by the addition of x to y. This distance can be defined as the sum of the values of all attributes that are possessed by x and not possessed by y. Although the function δ just defined is non-negative and satisfies $\delta(x,x)=0$, it is not necessarily symmetric. There is indeed no reason for the gain in dissimilarity brought about by adding x to y to be the same as the gain in dissimilarity brought about from adding y to x. Hence δ is not really a distance function and is sometimes referred to as a pseudo-distance.[8] The pseudo-distance δ will be a distance, and therefore symmetric, if and only if $I_A(\{x\})=I_A(\{y\})$ for all objects x and y. This case is *a priori* unlikely in a multi-attributes framework. Why would the sum of the values of all attributes possessed by an object be the same for all objects?

A structure of attributes that plays a role in biology is that described by Nehring and Puppe (2002) under the heading of taxonomic hierarchy. This structure is what underlies the grouping of individual organisms into species, themselves grouped into genera, which can be grouped into families and so on. This sequential grouping of attributes imposes a hierarchical structure on the family of attributes in the sense that if two sets of attributes have a non-empty intersection, then one set must be a subset of the other (for example the set of chimpanzees is a subset of the set of primates). Nehring and Puppe (2002) have shown (theorem 3.1) that requiring the family A of attributes to have a hierarchical structure is equivalent, within the framework of diversity appraisal provided by the above formula, to requiring the diversity indicator I_d to satisfy, for every set S, and every object x, the condition:

$$I_d(S \cup \{x\}) - I_d(S) = \min_{y \in S} \delta(x, y) \qquad (1.20)$$

Hence, hierarchical families of attribute have the property that the diversity of sets, provided that it is appraised by the above formula, can be seen as resulting from a sequential aggregation of the (pseudo-)distance between its elements. This sequential aggregation is, actually, quite reminiscent of Weitzman's method discussed in the preceding section.

Another structure that can be imposed on the family of attributes is to be made of sets that are interval with respect to some underlying ordering of the universal set of objects. For instance one could think of objects as political opinions which are completely ranked on a left–right scale, or as animals ranked in terms of their average mass, or life expectancy. In this setting, an attribute is an interval with respect to the ordering if, any time it contains two objects, it also contains all objects that are 'between' those two objects for the given ordering. Examples of such an interval attribute in the context of political opinions expressed on a left–right scale would be 'being leftist' (as defined with respect to some 'centre') or 'being more right-wing than some reference point'. On the other hand the attribute 'being extremist', in the sense of being either far to the right or far to the left, would not be part of an interval attribute structure in such a setting.

Another result of Nehring and Puppe's theorem 3.2 is that requiring the structure of attributes to be made of intervals with respect to an ordering of objects is equivalent, again in the approach to diversity appraisal provided by the above formula, to requiring the function I_d to write:

$$I_d(\{x_1, x_2, ..., x_m\}) = I_d(x_1) + \sum_{i=2}^{m} \delta(x_i, x_{i-1})$$

for every objects x_1, ..., x_m increasingly ordered by the underlying ordering of objects. Here again, it happens to be possible to express, within the realm of the multi-attributes approach to diversity associated with the above formula, diversity judgments as aggregations of pairwise dissimilarities between the objects as measured by the pseudo-distance δ.

Obviously, this possibility of expressing diversity comparisons as aggregations of pairwise dissimilarities measured by the (pseudo-)distance function δ is closely related to the assumptions made in the underlying attributes structure (for instance the fact that they are taxonomic hierarchies or intervals). Other attribute structures may not lead to an appraisal of diversity as aggregation of dissimilarities. For instance, Nehring and Puppe (2002) have shown that, if the attributes can be described by a vector of zeros and ones, each component being interpreted as a dichotomous indicator of whether or not the object possesses a property, then the diversity of a set can*not* be expressed as an aggregation of the pairwise dissimilarities, as appraised by δ, between its elements. Attributes that have this 'zero–one' structure, which can be geometrically depicted as a hypercube of length 1, are not rare in economic theory of differentiated products. In the hedonic housing price literature for instance, initiated by the work of Rosen (1974), attributes of housing are very often described by 0–1 variables: it has a main exposition to the south or not, it has an equipped kitchen or not, etc.

Nehring and Puppe (2002) have identified a property of the attributes structure that is necessary and sufficient for the value of the diversity indicator I_d, to depend only upon the information on the pairwise dissimilarities between the elements (in the sense that two sets that generate the same list of (pseudo-)distances between their elements as measured by δ should be considered equivalent). The property of the attribute structure identified by Nehring and Puppe (2002) is the absence of triples of objects that have the properties that each subset of the triple possesses an attribute of its own. Consider for instance the interval attribute structure discussed above in the context of the political left–right scale. Take any set of three political opinions in this framework. The three elements of this set can by definition be ordered on the left–right scale. No matter what are the interval attributes that have been defined, it is clear that the two 'extreme' political opinions of the triple cannot have an attribute that the 'central' opinion does not have if the attributes are intervals. Hence, in the interval attribute structure, no triple of objects has the property that a specific attribute can be assigned to each of its subsets. As shown by Nehring and Puppe (2002: theorem 4.1), this property happens to be necessary and sufficient for the ability to express diversity judgments, as per the indicator I_d defined by (divindic), as aggregation of pairwise dissimilarity as measured by δ.

Although it is beyond the scope of this survey to provide a detailed description of all the results contained in Nehring and Puppe (2002), there are two comments that are worth making about the multi-attributes approach to diversity appraisal proposed by these authors.

First, in its current state of development, it requires, on the part of the appraiser, some information both on the relevant attributes to be considered and on the (cardinally meaningful) valuation function of these attributes. As discussed above, this information is required because it cannot be obtained uniquely from the mere property of the ranking of sets, even if one accepts the axioms of contraction consistency and weak monotonicity. For many practical problems of diversity appraisal, this information is likely to be difficult to obtain.

Second, from a more philosophical point of view, and except for some degenerate cases, the additive multi-attribute approach described in this section is bound to lead to the conclusion that some singletons will have more diversity than sets containing many objects. Although there is no formal problem with this, it is a feature of the approach that may hurt several intuitions about the very meaning of diversity. How can one object be more diverse than several objects? The answer to this question is of course straightforward within the multi-attribute approach. A single object will be more diverse than a collection of many objects if the attributes possessed by the single object have a larger value than the attributes that are realized in the collection of many objects. This answer suggests, however, that, in the multi-attributes approach, it is not so much the diversity of a set that is evaluated but rather the attributes possessed by the objects. Are the two notions – set diversity and attributes possessed by the objects – synonymous? I remain unconvinced that the answer to this question should always be positive.

Conclusion

What can be concluded from the attempts, summarized in this chapter, to define diversity? Besides the general principles mentioned in the second section, we have compared the following four categories of approach:

1 the biologically inspired approach, which defines diversity as generalized entropy;
2 the approaches that define diversity as an aggregation of cardinally meaningful information about the pairwise dissimilarities of objects conveyed by a distance function;
3 the approaches that define diversity as an aggregation of an ordinal information about pairwise dissimilarities between objects conveyed by a quaternary relation;
4 the approaches that define the diversity of a set as a sum of the values of the attributes that are realized by the objects in the set.

Given the current state of justification and elaboration of all these approaches, I would feel inclined to give my preference to approach 3. The generalized entropy approach to diversity appraisal suffers clearly from the fact that it treats all species symmetrically. Yet it seems that an essential ingredient of any plausible notion of diversity is that it should not treat grouping objects as being symmetric and should account for the varying dissimilarities that exist between objects.

The approaches 2, 3 and 4 can be viewed as alternative ways of introducing this dissimilarity. Approach 2, which requires the diversity appraiser to have available a cardinally meaningful distance function, strikes me as being very demanding from an informational point of view, even for a discipline as sophisticated and developed as biology. Since judgments about the proximity between the objects are likely to be difficult to make, it appears safer to require them to take the milder form of an ordinal ranking of the various pairs of objects in terms of their proximity, and to base the diversity evaluation on the information conveyed by this ordinal ranking.

The multi-attributes approach is also a promising way for apprehending diversity. Yet, as it has been developed so far, it requires a rather demanding selection of the relevant attributes of the objects as well as the evaluation of each of these attributes by a cardinally meaningful valuation function. Of course, Theorem 1.2 of this chapter tells us that such an attribute structure, as well as the valuation function, can be revealed from the ranking on the sole basis that it satisfies the properties of weak monotonicity and contraction consistency. But there are many collections of attributes, and many rankings of these attributes by a valuation function, that can be revealed by a given ordering. Without a criterion for selecting the 'right' collection of attributes, and the 'right' valuation function, the ordinal representation theorem cannot, by itself, provide a justification for the multi-attribute approach. Given our current state of knowledge, the only available way to apply the additive multi-attributes approach to diversity is to select both the family of relevant attributes and the valuation function of the attributes. The informational burden put on the diversity appraiser for making this selection is, in my view, quite significant.

The logical independence between the additive multi-attributes approach of Nehring and Puppe (2002) on the one hand and the aggregation of ordinal dissimilarity approach on the other is worth noticing. For some structure of the attributes, and as shown by Nehring and Puppe, it is impossible to view diversity appraisal as resulting from the aggregation of pairwise dissimilarities. Conversely, there are diversity rankings of sets resulting from the aggregation of an ordinal notion of pairwise dissimilarities that violate the property of contraction consistency and, for this reason, cannot be thought of as resulting from comparing the sum of the values of attributes. The somewhat radical difference between these two approaches makes the choice between them difficult. In my view, the small amount information required by an approach based on the aggregation of an ordinal notion of dissimilarity represents a clear advantage.

Of course, this ordinal dissimilarity approach needs to be further developed. The rankings to which it has led so far, that is, the maxi-max and the lexi-max criteria, are far too extreme. It is therefore important to develop other criteria for ranking sets based on an ordinal notion of pairwise dissimilarities. A priority for future research in the area would be to explore other approaches for defining diversity than those, considered in approaches 2 and 3, of defining diversity as aggregate pairwise dissimilarity. Suppose that we are interested in comparing the diversity of car models offered by various retailers and that we adopt the hedonic perspective of viewing a car as a combination of values taken by, say, k characteristics (such as size, degree of comfort, speed, fuel consumption, etc.) that are numerically measurable. This amounts to thinking of a model of a car as a point in R^k and to a car retailer as a (finite) set of points in R^k. A reasonably natural notion of dissimilarity between cars in this perspective could be given by the ranking of pairs of points (cars) induced by the comparisons of the Euclidian distances between them. Furthermore, an equally plausible notion of diversity of car retailers in this setting could be given by the ranking of set of points (retailers) induced by the comparison of the dimension of the subspace spanned by these sets of points. Yet it is clear that this dimension can not be deduced from the information of the distance between these points alone.[9] It would therefore be nice to find the axiomatic properties of a ranking of sets that would characterize the fact that this ranking could be thought of as resulting from the aggregation of the pairwise dissimilarity of its elements for some underlying dissimilarity quaternary relation.

Notes

1 This survey owes much to the discussions I have had on this subject with Jean-François Laslier and to my collaboration with Sebastian Bervoets. The survey has also greatly benefited from the comments of Clemens Puppe and Klaus Nehring. The usual disclaimer of course applies fully.

2 As mentioned earlier, an alternative would be to view objects as being individuals, partitioned into a number of different species. Everything that will be said in this section could be also said in this alternative framework, albeit at some extra cost in terms of notation.

3 Applying de L'Hospital's rule, it is immediate to see that, if $p_1, \ldots p_m$ are any m non-negative numbers summing to 1, the limit of the expression

$$\frac{1}{1-r} \ln(\sum_{i=1}^{l} p_i^r) \text{ as } r \text{ tends to 1 is } -\sum_{i=1}^{l} p_i \ln p_i$$

4 Continuity of an ordering on R_+^m, is defined in the standard way (see, for instance, Debreu 1954) by the requirement that the no-better-than and the no-worse-than sets be closed in R_+^m.

5 Another paper that addresses the issue of diversity measurement in terms of a cardinal notion of dissimilarity is Van Hees (2004).

6 See Suppes *et al.* (1989: 162) theorem 1 for a proof of this somewhat surprising fact that any quaternary relation satisfying the aforementioned properties can be represented numerically by a distance function satisfying the triangle inequality.

7 In Nehring and Puppe (2002), the axiomatic justification given to this formula is a bit different because it is derived within a framework in which one is interested in ranking *lotteries* whose consequences are sets of objects rather than *sets of objects*. As argued in the introduction, I have decided in this survey to stick to the basic question of what diversity is rather than that of how to rank decisions with uncertain consequences on diversity. Theorem 1.2 is the analogue of theorem 2.1 in Nehring and Puppe (2002) in a framework without uncertainty.

8 It is, on the other hand, easy to verify that δ satisfies the triangle inequality.

9 I am indebted to Jean-François Laslier for the mathematical backbone of this example. Notice that this example is valid no matter what is the distance notion used. One cannot recover the dimension of the subspace spanned by using only information on the pairwise distance between these points no matter what this distance is.

References

Barberà, S., Bossert, W. and Pattanaik, P. K. (2004) 'Ranking sets of objects', in S. Barberà, P. Hammond and C. Seidl (eds), *Handbook of Utility Theory*, Vol. 2: *Extensions*, Dordrecht: Kluwer.

Berger, W. H. and Parker, F. L. (1970) 'Diversity of planktonic foraminifera in deep sea sediments', *Science*, 168: 1345–1347.

Bervoets, S. and Gravel, N. (2007) 'Appraising diversity with an ordinal notion of similarity: an axiomatic approach', *Mathematical Social Sciences*, 53: 259–273.

Bossert, W., Pattanaik, P. K. and Xu, Y. (2003) 'Similarity of options and the measurement of diversity', *Journal of Theoretical Politics*, 15: 405–421.

Carter, I. (1999) *A Measure of Freedom*, Oxford: Oxford University Press,

Chateauneuf, A. and Jaffray, J.-Y. (1989) 'Some characterizations of lower probabilities and other monotone capacities through the use of Möbius inversion', *Mathematical Social Sciences*, 17: 263–283.

Debreu, G. (1954) 'Representation of a preference ordering by a numerical function', in R. L. D. R. M. Thrall and C. H. Coombs (eds), *Decision Processes*, New York: Wiley.

De Finetti, B. (1937) 'La prévision: Ses lois logiques, ses sources subjectives', *Annales de l'Institut Henri Poincaré*, 7: 1–68.

Dixit, A. and Stiglitz, J. (1977) 'Monopolistic competition and optimum product diversity', *American Economic Review*, 67: 297–308.

Fishburn, P. (1969) 'Weak qualitative probability on finite sets', *Annals of Mathematical Statistics*, 40: 2118–2126.

—— (1970) *Utility Theory for Decision Making*, New York: John Wiley.

Good, I. J. (1953) 'The population frequencies of species and the estimation of population parameters', *Biometrika*, 40: 237–264.

Gravel, N., Laslier, J.-F. and Trannoy, A. (1998) 'Individual freedom of choice in a social setting', in J.-F. Laslier, M. Fleurbaey, N. Gravel and A. Trannoy (eds), *Freedom in Economics: New Perspectives in Normative Analysis*, London: Routledge.

Jones, P. and Sugden, R. (1982) 'Evaluating choices', *International Journal of Law and Economics*, 2: 47–65.

Kraft, C. H., Pratt, J. W. and Seidenberg, A. (1959) 'Intuitive probability on finite sets', *Annals of Mathematical Statistics*, 30: 408–419.

Kreps, D. M. (1979) 'A representation theorem for "preference for flexibility"', *Econometrica*, 47: 565–577.

Lancaster, K. (1966) 'A new approach to consumer theory', *Journal of Political Economy*, 74: 132–157.

Magurran, A. E. (1998) *Ecological Diversity and its Measurement*, Princeton, NJ: Princeton University Press.

Nehring, K. (1997) *A theory of qualitative similarity*, University of California Davis, Department of Economics, Working Paper No. 97-10.

—— (1999) 'Preference for flexibility in a Savagian framework', *Econometrica*, 67: 101–119.

Nehring, K. and Puppe, C. (1999) 'On the multi-preferences approach to evaluating opportunities', *Social Choice and Welfare*, 16: 41–63.

—— (2002) 'A theory of diversity', *Econometrica*, 70: 1155–1190.

—— (2003) 'Diversity and dissimilarity in lines and hierarchies', *Mathematical Social Sciences*, 45: 167–183.

Pattanaik, P. K. and Xu, Y. (1990) 'On ranking opportunity sets in terms of freedom of choice', *Recherches Economiques de Louvain*, 56: 383–390.

—— (2000) 'On diversity and freedom of choice', *Mathematical Social Sciences*, 40: 123–130.

Puppe, C. (1998) 'Individual freedom and social choice', in J. Laslier, M. Fleurbaey, N. Gravel and A. Trannoy (eds), *Freedom in Economics: New Perspectives in Normative Analysis*, London: Routlege.

Renyi, A. (1961) 'On measures of entropy and information', in J. Neyman (ed.), *Proceedings of the Fourth Berkeley Symposium on Mathematical Statistics and Probability*, Vol. 1, Berkeley: University of California Press.

Rosen, S. (1974) 'Hedonic prices and implicit markets: product differentiation in pure competition', *Journal of Political Economy*, 82: 34–55.

Shannon, C. E. (1948) 'A mathematical theory of communication', *Bell System Technical Journal*, 27: 379–423.

Shorrocks, A. F. (1980) 'The class of additively decomposable inequality measures', *Econometrica*, 48: 613–626.

—— (1984) 'Inequality decomposition by population subgroups', *Econometrica*, 52: 1369–1386.

Simpson, E. H. (1949) 'Measurement of diversity', *Nature*, 163: 688.

Sugden, R. (1998) 'The metric of opportunity', *Economics and Philosophy*, 14: 307–337.

Suppes, P. (1987) 'Maximizing freedom of decision: an axiomatic approach', in G. Feiwel (ed.), *Arrow and the Foundations of the Theory of Economic Policy*, New York: New York University Press.

Suppes, P., Krantz, D. H., Luce, R. D. and Tversky, A. (1989) *Foundations of Measurement*, Vol. 2: *Geometrical, Threshold and Probabilistic Representations*, New York: Academic Press.

Van Hees, M. (1997) 'On the analysis of negative freedom', *Theory and Decision*, 45: 175–197.

—— (2004) 'Freedom of choice and diversity of options: some difficulties', *Social Choice and Welfare*, 22: 253–266.

Weitzman, M. L. (1992) 'On diversity', *Quarterly Journal of Economics*, 107: 363–406.

—— (1993) 'What to preserve? An application of diversity theory to crane conservation', *Quarterly Journal of Economics*, 108: 157–183.

—— (1998) 'The Noah's ark problem', *Econometrica*, 66: 1279–1298.

2 Intentions, decisions and rationality

Martin van Hees and Olivier Roy

Introduction

Rational agents, as conceived in decision and game theory (Myerson 1991; Osborne and Rubinstein 1994), are agents who choose the actions they believe to be the best means to achieve their preferred ends. But human beings are also *planning* agents. That is, we have the capacity to 'settle *in advance* on more or less complex plans concerning the future, and then [let] these plans *guide our later conduct*' (Bratman 1987). Do decision-theoretical models do sufficient justice to this planning aspect of human agency? In particular, can one account within a decision-theoretical framework for the fact that planning agents can commit themselves by forming intentions? In van Hees and Roy (2007) we addressed this question for one particular kind of intention, namely the intention to bring about some future states of affairs, or what we now call 'outcome intentions'. These intentions, for example, the intention 'to be in France next week', can be distinguished from 'action intentions', which refer to the future performance of some actions, for example, the intention 'to take the plane to France'. We argued that outcome intentions can be fruitfully incorporated within a decision-theoretical framework, and presented conditions under which rationality with respect to intentions is compatible with the standard payoff-maximizing notion of rationality.

This chapter presents a further extension of the decision-theoretical model that now also includes action intentions. First we introduce the philosophical theory of intentions that motivates our investigation, followed by a fairly standard decision theoretic model. Next we propose a way to introduce action intentions in this model. We explain why – assuming that such intentions do not have autonomous consequences – they reduce to something that is already modelled. We nevertheless show that intentions can be useful as 'tie breakers' between equally desirable plans of actions. From the subsequent section on, we concentrate on intentions with autonomous consequences. We first look at a case where different intentions may lead to the same outcome, while nevertheless influencing the payoffs. We argue that the standard decision theoretic framework falls short of accounting for such cases and present a counterfactual extension that fixes this deficiency. Then we turn to the famous 'Toxin Puzzle' (Kavka 1983), in which it is rational to form a certain intention to act but not to *perform* that very act. We argue that decision theory cannot account for this particular type of autonomous effect either, and propose a second modification to cope with it. This extension allows us to capture the tension that, in our view, forms the heart of the toxin puzzle, i.e. the tension between, on the one hand, a consistency requirement between intentions and actions and, on the other, the assumption of payoff maximization. The final section provides a brief conclusion.

All of the analysis is performed under the umbrella of fully idealized agency. We think that the non-ideal case is also very interesting, but we do not investigate it here. The reader may consult Sen (1977), McClennen (1990) and Gauthier (1997), in which intentions for non-ideal agents are considered more thoroughly.

Intentions to act

Michael Bratman (1987, 1999, 2006a) famously argued for the importance of intentions and plans in rational decision-making in the development of his 'planning theory of intentions'.[1] This theory describes the functions of *future-directed* intentions, that is, intentions that are formed some time before their achievement. It is common in the philosophy of action to distinguish between these intentions and intentions *in action* or *tryings* (Searle 1983). Whereas the former are acquired before the action takes place, the latter form the 'mental component' of intentional actions (O'Shaughnessy 1973).

In the planning theory of intentions, 'plans' are special sets of intentions. They have an internal *hierarchical structure*. On 'top' are general intentions, for example going to Paris, beneath which come increasingly more precise intentions, for example going by train, departing at 9.15 and so on. The intentions at the bottom of this hierarchy are the most detailed, although they need not settle every single detail. The planning theory of intentions holds that it is even counterintuitive to suppose this, particularly for agents with limited time and memory; it conceives of plans as typically *partial*. Planning agents 'cross the bridge when [they] come to it' by forming new intentions along the way (Savage 1954: 16).

The planning theory of intention sees *rational* plans as regulated by norms of consistency. First, they should not contain inconsistent intentions, as for example the intention to go to a Bob Dylan concert in Paris tomorrow evening and the intention to go to a movie the same evening in Amsterdam. We call this the requirement of *endogenous* consistency.[2] A plan to achieve a certain end should also be supplemented with intentions to undertake appropriate means. A planning agent must find a way to cross the bridge when he or she comes to it. This pressure for plan completion is called the requirement of *means–end* consistency.

One central claim of the planning theory of intentions is that rational plans are 'stable'. Once an agent has formed an intention to act in a certain way, then if nothing unforeseen happens he or she will not be disposed to reconsider it. Rather, the agent will act in order to achieve it, and take this new intention into account when planning other actions. As such, plans are 'all-purpose means' for a human agent (Bratman 2006a). They allow for a better personal coordination towards the achievement of our ends, and provide a straightforward way to avoid costly deliberations. What is more, they constitute a solid base for coordination in social contexts.

Extensive decision models

Basic definitions

Decision theory offers a huge collection of mathematical tools to analyse *rational* decision making in the face of *uncertainty*. Rationality is understood here as *instrumental*, i.e. choosing what is believed to be the best means to reach one's preferred ends. The notion of uncertainty refers both to the agent's partial control over the consequences of his or her actions and to imperfect information about the environment. For example, the consequence of an action such as buying a lottery ticket depends on the result of a random process. Similarly, the consequences of placing a bet in a horse race depend on which horse is the fastest, a fact that gamblers are typically uncertain about. 'Nature' is thus the source of uncertainty in decision theory. This should be contrasted with uncertainty that arises from the interaction with other rational agents, who form expectations about each other's behaviour. This is the subject matter of *game theory*, which we do not consider in this chapter.

Since the publications of Neumann and Morgenstern (1944) and Savage (1954), a plethora of decision-theoretical models have been proposed. We want to investigate the place of future-directed intentions to act in decision theory, so we choose to work with *extensive models*, because they make explicit the temporal structure of decision problems. A *finite decision tree* (Osborne and Rubinstein 1994), such as the one depicted in Figure 2.1, is a finite set T of finite sequences of action called *histories*. We assume that T contains the empty sequence $\varnothing$, which will be called its *root*, and that it is closed under taking subsequences. That is, if $(a_1, \ldots, a_n, a_{n+1})$ is a sequence in T then $(a_1, \ldots, a_n)$ should also be in T. Given a history $h = (a_1, \ldots, a_n)$, we denote $ha = (a_1, \ldots, a_n, a)$ the history h followed by the action a. A history h *is terminal in* T whenever it is the subsequence of no longer history $h' \in T$. The set of terminal histories in T is denoted Z.

Each non-terminal history h ends with either a *choice node* or a *chance node*. As a shorthand we often talk of the histories as being themselves nodes, i.e. the last node in the sequence. Graphically, we represent the choice nodes/histories by white circles and the chance nodes/histories by black ones. In the example shown in Figure 2.1 there are two choice nodes and one chance node. If h is a choice node, then we call the set $A(h) = \{a : ha \in T\}$ the set of *actions available at* h. In the diagram, the actions available at a choice node are arrows labeled a_1 to a_4. If h is a chance node a function δ gives a probability value to the elements of $A(h)$, which we then call the *alternatives at* h. In figures, the number neighbouring an arrow that stems from a chance node is the probability assigned by δ to that alternative. For example, in Figure 2.1, each alternative is assigned 0.5.

The real-valued payoff function $\pi : Z \rightarrow R$ gives for each terminal history the payoff that the agent receives on reaching it. In Figure 2.1, the history $(a_1, tail, a_4)$ gives a payoff of 100, for example. A *strategy* s is a function that gives, for every choice node h, an action $a \in A(h)$. When no confusion can arise, we describe a strategy – as we shall later do with plans of action – as a vector of actions. In

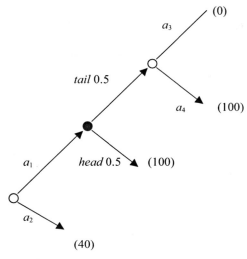

Figure 2.1 A simple decision problem.

Figure 2.1, for instance, there are four strategies: (a_1, a_3), (a_1, a_4), (a_2, a_3), (a_2, a_4). We say that a node h' is not excluded from h by the strategy s if the player can reach h' by choosing according to s from h on. Again, in our example, the history $(a_1, tail, a_3)$ can obviously be reached from the root by choosing according to (a_1, a_3), but not by choosing according to (a_2, a_3). Observe that a strategy tells the agent what to do even at histories that are not reachable by the strategy itself. In contrast, *a plan of action* is a function that assigns an action $a \in A(h)$ to each choice node h *that it does not itself exclude*.

A *partial* plan of action is a function p^1 from a *proper* subset of the set of all choice nodes to the set of actions such that there is at least one plan p that coincides with p^1 on the set of points belonging to p's domain.[3] The set of all partial plans in Figure 2.1, for instance, is $\{a_1, a_2, a_3, a_4\}$.

The set of outcomes reachable by choosing according to a strategy s, or a plan of action p, is defined as the union of the $\pi(h)$ for all terminal histories reachable from the root by s (or p). The set of outcomes reachable by a *partial* plan of action p is the union of the outcome reachable by all the plans of actions p^1 that coincide with p. We shall abuse our notation slightly and denote these sets by $\pi(p)$.

The expected value of a strategy s at the history h, denoted $EV(h, s)$, is defined inductively.

$$EV(h,s) = \begin{cases} \pi(h) & \text{If } h \text{ is a terminal history} \\ \sum_{a \in A(h)} \delta(a)EV(ha,s) & \text{If } h \text{ is a chance node} \\ EV(hs(h),s) & \text{If } h \text{ is a choice node} \end{cases}$$

One can readily calculate that in the example of Figure 2.1 the expected values of the strategies $(a_1, a_3), (a_1, a_4), (a_2, a_3), (a_2, a_4)$ are 50, 100, 40 and 40, respectively. The expected value of a plan of action p is defined only for pairs (h, p) such that p is defined on h and is computed similarly. Observe that, given this definition, a plan has exactly the same expected value as all the strategies that coincide with it. The expected value of (a_2), for example, is the same as $(a_2, a_3), (a_2, a_4)$. A strategy s is *rational at h* if and only if, for all strategies s^l: $EV(h, s) \geq EV(h, s^l)$. That is, it is rational for the agent to choose according to s at h whenever s maximizes his or her expected value at that node. We say that a strategy s is *rational for the whole decision problem T* if it is rational at the root of T. Borrowing from the game-theoretic vocabulary, we often refer to rational strategies as the solution of a decision problem. The rational strategy or the solution of our simple example is thus (a_1, a_4).[4]

Assumptions about the decision maker

Computing the solution of a decision problem is not always as easy as in Figure 2.1. If there are numerous choice nodes, interlaced with chance nodes, representing the decision tree or calculating its solution might be very tedious. Most treatments of decision theory abstract from time and complexity constraints by making two assumptions about the agent: ideal intelligence and ideal *rationality*.

The first assumption concerns the agent's representational and computational capacities. An agent 'is intelligent if he knows everything that we [the modeller] know about the [problem] and he can make any inferences about the situation that we can make' (Myerson 1991: 4). In other words, if a decision problem is representable at all and its solution computable in any sensible sense of these terms, then the agent is assumed to be capable of representing it and computing its solution. The time and energy costs of these computations are usually thereby ignored. The rationality assumption splits into two components. First, the preferences of the agents over uncertain outcomes are assumed to satisfy certain conditions, such as transitivity, completeness and what has been called the 'sure-thing principle' (Savage 1954).[5] These, together with a few others, are sufficient conditions for representing the agent's choices as a maximization of expected value (Neumann and Morgenstern 1944). In the model above we directly represented preferences in these terms. Decision-theoretical agents are also assumed to be constant and flawless maximizers, meaning that at every choice point they choose according to a rational strategy, and that they do not make mistakes, i.e. irrational choices.

Ideal decision-theoretical agents are thus perfectly rational agents who can represent any decision problem, however great, and compute without effort its rational solution. These are indeed extremely strong idealizations, and most of them are explicitly made as simplifying hypotheses. Regarding the computation cost, for example, Savage says:

> [We] deliberately pretend that consideration costs the person nothing ... It might, on the other hand be stimulating ... to think of consideration and

calculation as itself an act on which the person decides. Though I have not explored the later possibility carefully, I suspect that any attempt to do so formally leads to fruitless and endless regression.

(Savage 1954: 30)

Decision models for non-ideal or resources-bounded agents have been proposed (Simon 1982; Rubinstein 1998; Gigerenzer and Selten 2002), and intentions can be shown to be important in such cases (Hammond 1976; McClennen 1990; Gauthier 1997; van Hees and Roy 2007). As mentioned, we do not examine the non-ideal case in this chapter.

Intentions as plans of action

In this section we introduce intentions to act in the decision-theoretical framework sketched earlier. We argue that, for a large class of decision problems, the intentions of ideal agents can be viewed as plans of action, in the technical sense introduced above. This amounts to saying that intentions are already present, somehow implicitly, even though there is almost no mention of them in 'standard' decision theory. Does it therefore mean that the introduction of intentions in decision theory is a redundant enterprise? We believe not. As we show at the end of this section, intentions may help to 'break ties' between equally desirable plans. It should be kept in mind that we restrict the analysis throughout this section to intentions that do not have so-called 'autonomous effects'. As we show in the next two sections, difficulties arise when one tries to incorporate intentions that do have autonomous effects in decision theory. The conclusions of the present section thus apply only to intentions without autonomous effects.

Recall that we are interested in *future*-directed intentions, that is, intentions that are formed some time before their execution. In the decision models we use we represent this anteriority by assuming that the agent comes already equipped, so to speak, with both outcome and action intentions. We thus assign to the agent, given a decision tree T, an intention structure $I = \langle M_X, M_A \rangle$ where M_X is a collection of sets of outcomes and M_A a collection of (maybe partial) *plans of actions*. Our strategy is to impose constraints on these sets to capture the features familiar to the planning theory of intention.

The set M_X represents the outcome intentions of the agents. Each set A in M_X describes a state of affairs that the agent intends to realize. For instance, if A is a set of states of affairs in which the person is attending a Bob Dylan concert, then $A \in M_X$ represents the intention to attend a Bob Dylan concert. If B is a set of states of affairs in which the agent is in Paris, then $A \cap B \in M_X$ stands for the intention to watch a Bob Dylan concert in Paris. Borrowing directly from van Hees and Roy (2007), we assume that M_X satisfies the following constraints.

Postulate 2.1 (endogenous consistency of outcome intentions). $\varnothing \notin M_X$ and $M_X \neq \varnothing$. Furthermore, if $A, B \in M_X$, then $A \cap B \in M_X$.

This postulate prescribes that the agent does not intend to do the impossible, and that he or she at least intends something. It also enforces the set of outcome intentions to be closed under intersection.[6] The postulate implies that the agent has a 'smallest' outcome intention. That is, for some $A \in M_A$ we have $A \subseteq B$ for all $B \in M_A$. We often refer to this smallest set in what follows, denoting it by $\downarrow M_X$.

Inasmuch as $\downarrow M_X$ can be viewed as the most detailed outcome intention of the agent, or his or her 'ends', M_A can be seen as a collection of 'means' to achieve it. Each element of M_A represents a particular action intention of the agent. Clearly, it is natural to require that endogenous consistency also applies here.

Postulate 2.2 (endogenous consistency of action intentions). For all p, $p' \in M_A$, $p \cup p' \in M_A$.

The postulate precludes an agent from having two action intentions that are not executable in a single run. Suppose, for instance, that in the decision tree of Figure 2.1 the agent has the action intention $p \in M_A$, where p is defined only on $\varnothing$ and gives a_2. A partial plan p' that is defined only on $(a_1, tail)$ cannot then be an element of M_A. Observe, finally, that, given Postulate 2.2, M_A contains a 'largest' (but still maybe partial) plan of action, that is, some p that encompasses all other plans in M_A. We denote this plan by $\uparrow M_A$.

The next postulate, means–end consistency, specifies which kind of connection should hold between action and outcome intentions.

Postulate 2.3 (means–end consistency). There is some $p \in M_A$ such that $\pi(p) \subseteq \downarrow M_X$.

The postulate imposes constraints on both the outcome and the action intentions. Together with Postulate 2.1, it implies that M_A is never empty. It also aligns the action intentions to the outcome intentions, saying that there should be at least one partial plan of action that, if enacted, ensures the agent will obtain some outcome in $\downarrow M_X$. Together with Postulate 2.2, Postulate 2.3 makes the connection between action and outcome intentions even tighter, as shown in the following:

Proposition 2.1 For any I that satisfies Postulates 2.2 and 2.3, $\pi(\uparrow M_A) \subseteq \downarrow M_X$.

Proof. Take any such I. Observe that for any (maybe partial) plan of action, $p \subseteq p'$ implies that $\pi(p') \subseteq \pi(p)$. Now, because we assume that I satisfies Postulate 2.2, we know that for all $p \in M_A$, $p \subseteq \uparrow M_A$. Also, since I satisfies Postulate 2.3, we know that there is a $p \in M_A$ such that $\pi(p) \subseteq \downarrow M_X$, and thus that $\pi(\uparrow M_A) \subseteq \downarrow M_X$. ■

This is indeed a tight connection. It could be objected that it seems to exclude the possibility of *conditional* action intentions. Consider a variation of the decision problem presented in Figure 2.1 in which $\pi(a_1, tail, a_4) = 200$ instead of 100.

In this case the agent has a clear favourite outcome. Now observe that, in virtue of Postulate 2.3, the agent cannot intend to realize this outcome. That is, he or she cannot have $\downarrow M_X = \{200\}$. One fairly intuitive plan of action for reaching this outcome would, however, be a conditional one: *if* he makes it to $(a_1, tail)$, then he will act in order to get 200. Now the best he can do to reach $(a_1, tail)$ is indeed to choose a_1 and, if tails subsequently comes up, a_4. That is $\uparrow M_A = (a_1, a_4)$. But this plan is not means–end consistent since $\pi(\uparrow M_A) = \{100, 200\}$, which is not a subset of $\downarrow M_X$.

At first sight, this conclusion is rather unwelcome. After all, the conditional plan (a_1, a_4) seems perfectly reasonable. But one has to realize that the relation between M_A and M_X enforced by Postulate 2.3 goes both ways. Not only does it 'align' the means with the intended ends, it also precludes the agent from intending ends that he or she cannot force. In other words, Postulate 2.3 constrains both M_X and M_A. In the example of the previous paragraph, even though 200 is the most preferred outcome, it is not an outcome that the agent can ensure. Indeed, whereas it is perfectly reasonable to say that a person has the intention of buying a lottery ticket, it seems far less so to say that he or she has the intention of being the winner of the lottery. To paraphrase Bratman (1987), the outcome intention cannot be appropriately filled by action intentions and Postulate 2.3 thus imposes a feasibility constraint on the outcome intentions.

It should be noted that these postulates do not preclude the agent from forming action intentions for their own sake. What is more, as hinted above, $\uparrow M_A$ need not be a full plan of action. It can also be partial. As the planning theory of intentions maintains, the action intentions of the agent will typically be incomplete even when they satisfy the three postulates. Means–end consistency 'only' requires that some intended outcomes be secured, and this can leave a lot of choice nodes undecided. That is, the plan can well remain silent on what choices will be made once the outcome intentions are within reach. For agents with limited capacity, there is no doubt that this feature is an asset. They have only to make up their mind in advance on a limited number of choice points, leaving the other decisions for later. They indeed 'cross the bridge when they come to it'. But what about ideal agents? From what we said above, it should be clear that such a policy is rather pointless. They are capable of computing in advance, for any decision problem, a maximally detailed plan, and they will be willing to carry it out all the way.[7] In the famous words of Savage (1954), they are perfectly capable of pushing to its extreme the 'look before you leap' approach:

> Making an extreme idealization, ... a person has only one decision to make in his whole life. He must, namely, decide how to live, and he might in principle do once and for all.
>
> (Savage 1954: 83)

In that context, it seems to us that ideal agents have little to do with partial plans. This point has also been made by Neumann and Morgenstern (1944), who mention that the only assumption needed for agents to be able to choose full strategies 'is the intellectual one to be prepared with a rule for behaviour for all eventuality'. This, they say, 'is an innocent assumption within the confines of a mathematical analysis' (Neumann and Morgenstern 1944: 79). Whether or not one agrees with the 'innocent' character of this assumption, the point remains. For ideal agents, there is nothing that stands in the way of choosing beforehand a full plan of action. We thus think it is natural to assume that intentions of ideal agents reduce to plans of actions.

Postulate 2.4 (actions intentions for ideal agents). $\uparrow M_A$ is a plan of action.

This does not yet reduce intentions to full strategies, since strategies also provide information about the courses of action an agent would undertake in case he or she deviates from what he or she decided to do. However, as we indicated earlier, we think that this restriction is harmless in the context of decision theory with ideal agents.

But, even though intentions reduce to plans of actions for the ideal agent, we do not think they are useless additions to existing decision theoretic models. In van Hees and Roy (2007), we showed that outcome intentions can be used to 'focus' or 'break ties' between equally desirable strategies. This analysis can be carried into to the present framework. Consider the following postulate:

Postulate 2.5 (intentions and expected payoff compatibility). For all plans for action p, p' such that $EV(\varnothing, p) > EV(\varnothing, p')$: if $p \notin M_A$, then $p' \notin M_A$.

We can now easily establish the following result:[8]

Proposition 2.2 For any decision tree T and intention structure I that satisfies Postulates 2.1–2.5, there is one and only one plan that coincides with all (partial or non-partial) plans in M_A and that also maximizes expected value.

The proposition shows that the agent's intentions are compatible with expected value maximization. This is not at all surprising, being in essence what Postulate 2.6 (below) says. But note that it is also possible that a combination of intentions and traditional expected value maximization will lead to a focus on some solutions when there is more than one plan that maximizes expected value. Proposition 2.2 is thus in line with something philosophers of action have been claiming for a long time: intentions are key anchors to one-person sequential decision-making.

A limitation of the framework is, of course, its restriction to situations of *perfect information*. At any choice node the agent is aware of what happened before. Generalizing to a decision tree with imperfect information is indeed an interesting enterprise, in which the notion of exogenous consistency should play a much greater role, but we shall not pursue that route here. Instead, we argue that there are two fundamental shortcomings to the analysis presented thus far, regardless of the idealized context of a fully rational person and complete information. Both shortcomings arise from the fact that intentions can have *autonomous consequences*, that is, they may affect an agent's appraisal of the outcome *independently* of the action to which they commit.

Intentions and counterfactuals

To study the distinction between intentions and expected side effects, Michael Bratman discusses the following example:

> Both Terror Bomber and Strategic Bomber have the goal of promoting the war effort against Enemy. Each intends to pursue this goal by weakening the Enemy, and each intends to do that by dropping bombs. Terror Bomber's plan is to bomb the school in Enemy's territory, thereby killing children and terrorizing Enemy's population. Strategic Bomber's plan is ... to bomb Enemy's munitions plant. [He] also knows, however, that next to the munitions plant is a school, and that when he bombs the plant he will also destroy the school, killing the children inside.
>
> (Bratman 1987: 139)

How should we model the decision problem? Note that we have assumed thus far that an agent already has the relevant outcome and action intentions. If we make the standard assumption – as we have thus far – that a plan of action describes the available moves, then the tree is very simple (see Figure 2.2). There are only two possible plans – and also only two strategies – namely 'bomb' and 'not bomb'.

But the consequence of bombing may be different if it realizes an intention to kill the children from if it does not not. For instance, Terror Bomber might be prosecuted for war crimes if it was indeed his intention to kill the children, whereas such prosecution may be less likely for Strategic Bomber. In this scenario, the payoffs are thus dependent not only on which terminal history is reached but also on the intention with which it is reached. Be that as it may, our current model cannot distinguish between bombing with and without the intention of killing the children. For both cases we will have the same action intention set $\uparrow M_A = \{bomb\}$ and value of $\pi(bomb)$, even though the intentions and the payoffs, by assumption, are different.

Bratman argues, in essence, that Strategic Bomber does not have the intention of killing the children because, contrary to Terror Bomber, he would not adopt a new plan of action if the children were moved somewhere else, far from the munitions plant. That is, information about counterfactual events reveal the intentions of agents. We define a *counterfactual extension* of a decision problem as

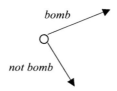

Figure 2.2 The bombing problem.

any decision tree that starts with a chance node and in which the original decision problem is one of the subtrees following that chance node. An example is given by Figure 2.3. At the first node it is determined whether the school will be deserted or not. If not, one faces the original decision problem, otherwise the counterfactual scenario arises. If we now consider this extended tree, we can assume that the plans of action of Terror and Strategic Bomber will differ. Terror Bomber's $\uparrow M_A$ will be the plan 'Only bomb when children are at school' whereas for Strategic Bomber it will be 'Always bomb'. Following Bratman's suggestion, we can use the counterfactual information carried by these plans to assign the payoff to the terminal histories.

Let ρ be a *refined payoff* function that assigns a real-valued payoff to *pairs* (h, p) in which p is a plan of action and h is a terminal history reachable from the root by p. An intention or a plan of action p has *autonomous consequences* when, for a given history h and another plan p' that coincides with p on h, $\rho(h, p) \neq \rho(h, p')$. Observe that in such a case the intention does indeed have autonomous consequences. The agent, in the course of reaching h, accomplishes the same action whether he or she follows p or p'. The agent would have acted differently only outside h, that is if things had turned out differently.

This is precisely what happens in the counterfactual version of the bombing case. The payoff ρ(Outcome 1, Always bomb) does not equal ρ(Outcome 1, Only bomb when children are at school); dropping bombs with the intention of killing the children has different consequences from dropping bombs without this intention.

Of course, the autonomous consequences of acting with a certain intention should be taken into account when the agent chooses his plan of action. We thus redefine the expected value of a plan (or a strategy) in terms of the refined payoff function ρ in a straightforward way. For all pairs (h, p) such that h is reachable from $\varnothing$ by choosing according to p:

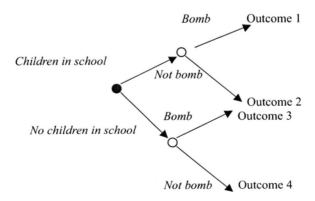

Figure 2.3 A counterfactual extension of the bombing problem.

$$EV^I(h,p) = \begin{cases} \rho(h,p) & \text{If } h \text{ is a terminal history} \\ \sum_{a \in A(h)} \delta(a)EV^I(ha,p) & \text{If } h \text{ is a chance node} \\ EV^I(hp(h),p) & \text{If } h \text{ is a choice node} \end{cases}$$

Refined payoff functions are indeed generalizations of the standard functions π. The latter are functions for which the value at a terminal history is not dependent on the plan with which it is reached. That is, any standard payoff function π can be emulated by a refined payoff function ρ for which $\rho(h, p) = \rho(h, p')$ for all terminal histories h and plans p and p' that are defined on h.

From a decision-theoretical point of view, the question, of course, is how to establish the conditions under which the agent's preferences can be represented by such a refined payoff function. After all, it may be rather difficult to determine what the appropriate counterfactual extension is. We do not address this question here. Our aim was merely to point out the necessity of such an extension of the standard decision-theoretical model if we want to take account of the fact that intentions can have autonomous effects.

The formation of intentions

Postulate 2.6 establishes a relation between a person's intentions and his preferences. It states that certain intentions will not be formed given the preferences of the agent. Apart from this postulate we have not made any further assumptions concerning the *formation* of intentions. We have modelled *acting with* a certain intention, but not the formation of intentions. Yet the possibility that the formation of intentions has autonomous consequences poses additional modelling problems that necessitate a further departure from the standard decision-theoretic framework. In particular, it poses a problem with respect to Postulate 2.6.

Our analysis is again driven by an example from the philosophical literature. In Kavka (1983), the now famous 'Toxin Puzzle' was introduced:[9]

You have just been approached by an eccentric billionaire who has offered you the following deal. He places before you a vial of toxin that, if you drink it, will make you painfully ill for a day, but will not threaten your life or have any lasting effects ... The billionaire will pay you one million dollars tomorrow morning if, at midnight tonight, you intend to drink the toxin tomorrow afternoon. He emphasizes that you need not drink the toxin to receive the money; in fact, the money will already be in your bank account hours before the time for drinking it arrives ... All you have to do is ... to intend at midnight tonight to drink the stuff tomorrow afternoon. You are perfectly free to change your mind after receiving the money and not drink the toxin. (The presence or absence of the intention is to be determined by the latest 'mind reading' brain scanner.) ... Arrangement of such as external incentives is ruled out, as are such gimmicks as hiring a hypnotist to implant the intention, forgetting the main relevant facts of the situation, and so forth.

(Kavka 1983)

This scenario involves two choice points: some time before midnight when you have to decide whether to form the intention or not, and tomorrow morning, when you have to decide whether to drink or not. The first choice point is an 'intention-formation' point. Such choice points are notably absent from the models we have used thus far. We have described agents who come 'already equipped' with some future-directed intentions; the moment of intention formation is not part of the decision problem. Even with the appropriate refined payoff function, we can model only the choice situation of a person who already has formed the intention or who did not form the intention to drink the toxin. As a consequence, the Toxin Puzzle cannot be captured in the present model.[10]

Let us therefore expand our framework by allowing for the fact that the formation of an intention to perform an action a now itself forms a possible move within the tree. In such an approach, the decision tree corresponding to the Toxin Puzzle will be as in Figure 2.4 (we assume that no drink is offered if you have not formed the intention).[11]

If the formation of intentions is itself seen as a move, then an element of M_A, say partial plan of action p, need not only describe a person's intention to perform a certain action but may also describe an intention to adopt an intention. For instance, the possible element 'drink the toxin' of M_A describes a regular action intention, viz. the intention to drink the toxin. Having 'intend to drink' in one's M_A would stand for the second-order intention of intending to form the intention to drink. The plan of action $p = $ (form the intention to drink, drink) would stand for the combination of the first- and second-order intentions, etc. Given a (partial) plan, we denote a move which consists of the formation of the intention to some action a by $\vec{a}$. Since we focus only on future-directed intentions, we assume in what follows that one can form an intention to do some a only at choice nodes h preceding (either directly or indirectly) the choice node h' at which the action can be carried out. We also avoid some technical complications by assuming that for any node h there is at most one such h' at which a can be carried out.

It is reasonable to impose the following additional requirement of endogenous consistency:

> **Postulate 2.6** (consistency between first- and second-order intentions). For all (partial) plans for action $p \in M_A$, all h, h' and all a, if $\vec{a} \in p(h)$ and $a \in A(h')$, then $a \in p(h')$.

The postulate is in line with a feature identified by the planning theory of intention: the fact that intentions are 'conduct-controlling' (Bratman 1987). It states that a person who has a second-order intention to perform the action a also has the first-order intention to do so. In other words, if a rational person intends to take up the commitment to do a (intends to intend to do a), then he cannot intend simultaneously to break that commitment at some later point in time (intend not to do a). Of course, it frequently happens that we revise our intentions when some *unforeseen events* make them unachievable. Once again, however, we refer to the assumption of ideal agency and perfect information, which rules out these possibilities.

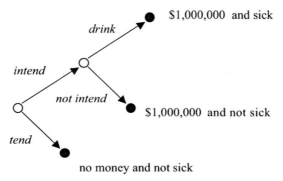

drink — $1,000,000 and sick

intend

not intend — $1,000,000 and not sick

tend

no money and not sick

Figure 2.4 The Toxin Puzzle with intentions as moves.

We can now capture explicitly the core of the tension between commitment-making and payoff maximization that is at the heart of the Toxin Puzzle. Indeed, looking again at Figure 2.4, we quickly see that Postulate 2.5 and Postulate 2.6 cannot be satisfied together. If we assume that I satisfies the former, we will have $\downarrow M_X = \{(\$1,000,000 \text{ and not sick})\}$, and thus $\uparrow M_A = (\overrightarrow{drink}, \text{ not drink})$, against Postulate 2.6. But, in turn, the only action intention consistent with Postulate 2.6 if the agent goes up at the first node is $\uparrow M_A = (\overrightarrow{drink}, \text{ drink})$, which clearly violates Postulate 2.5.

Note, however, that, in our rendition of the toxin puzzle, the crux of it is not that our (first-order) intentions may clash with our preferences, but rather that consistency between our first-order and second-order intentions clashes with our preferences. Rationality requirements that concern the structure of our intentions (Postulate 2.6) may be at odds with the rationality requirement that we maximize our utility (Postulate 2.5). Finally, we note that this tension is not bounded to the eccentric scenario of the Toxin Puzzle. The following result shows that whenever we assume that individuals can indeed decide to form intentions, if these intentions can have autonomous effects, then one can devise a payoff function such that it is never rational to follow up on the commitments that one undertook, thus violating Postulate 2.6.

Proposition 2.3 For any decision tree and any intention structure I such that for some nodes h, h' and some a, b $(a \neq b)$, $\overrightarrow{a} \in A(h)$ and $a, b \in A(h')$: there is a refined payoff function ρ such that Postulates 2.2, 2.4, 2.5 and 2.6 cannot be satisfied simultaneously.

Proof. Let h and h' be as defined, and take all plans p such that both h and h' are reachable from the root by choosing according to p. Let H_p be the set of all terminal histories reachable from h' by playing according to such p and in which $p(h') = b$. All we need is to fix $\pi(h', p') = 1$ for all $h' \in H_p$ and p' compatible with h', and $\pi(h', p') = 0$ for all other terminal histories h' and p' compatible with it. Clearly, in this decision problem no intention structure will satisfy all of the postulates. ∎

Conclusion

To summarize, we have argued in the last two sections that intentions with autonomous consequences pose difficulties that force us to go beyond traditional models of decision-making. Of course, this does not mean that all intentions require such extensions. Intentions without autonomous consequences can readily be described in terms of strategies in extensive decision problems, as we argued earlier. However, as we hope we have shown, even the incorporation of such 'standard' intentions may form an enrichment of the decision-theoretical framework.

Notes

1 Other key references include Anscombe (1957) and Harman (1986).
2 Rational intentions are also supposed to be exogenously consistent. This kind of consistency relates the agent's intentions to what he or she believes. A rational plan does not have to be feasible in the world as it actually is. It suffices that the plan is feasible in the world as the agent believes it to be. In this chapter we always deal with 'perfect information' situations, in which the agent is completely and truthfully informed. In this context, plans and intentions will always be exogenously consistent. We thus leave this constraint aside.
3 As for strategies, plans of action can be described both as vectors or as partial functions, i.e. as sets of pairs (h, a) with $a \in A(h)$. When we say that (partial or non-partial) plan p coincides with partial plan p' we mean that, viewed as sets of pairs, $p' \subseteq p$. In what follow we will also talk about union of plans of action, which should always be read as the union of such pairs.
4 Strategies are tailor-made for game-theoretic purposes. The information they carry about 'off-path' behaviour is a key input in the interactive reasoning that underlies solution concepts such as the sub-game perfect equilibrium (Selten 1975). But, in decision theory, what the agent would do were he to deviate from his own plan of action usually has no consequence, at least as long as we talk about ideal agents. The reader might already have noticed that, according to our definition, a strategy can be said to be rational even though it prescribes moves at nodes that it itself excludes. In other words, our definition of what it is for a strategy to be rational in a decision problem already ignores the 'off-path' prescriptions.
5 Transitivity states that if x is preferred to y, and y is preferred to z, then x is preferred to z. Completeness states, for any x and y, that either x is preferred to y, or y to x. Finally, the sure-thing principles stipulates that if x were preferred to y upon learning that event E occurred, and also upon learning that E did not occur, then x is preferred to y regardless of E.
6 Or that intentions are 'agglomerative' in terms of Bratman (2006b) and Velleman (2007).
7 The argument for this last point has been made by several authors in decision and game theory. See especially Myerson (1991: 11), McClennen (1990) and Gauthier (1997) for discussions of such cases.
8 The proof consists only of unpacking the definitions, and is therefore omitted.
9 See Mele (1992, 1995), and discussions in Coleman and Morris (1998).
10 The reader might wonder why, in the first place, is it so important to capture the Toxin Puzzle. For us this is because it has far more general features than Kavka's far-fetched scenario suggests. As noted in Bratman (1999: 67), the kind of autonomous effects displayed here are essential to multi-agent reciprocation problems, on which game theorists have glossed at length (Rosenthal 1982; Binmore 1996; Aumann 1998). Switching to game theory would go far beyond the scope of this chapter. But, as far

as the Toxin Puzzle is, so to speak, a one person reciprocation problem, it brings into decision theory an important aspect of planning agency.
11 This route was first explored in Verbeek (2002).

References

Anscombe, G. (1957) *Intention*, Cambridge, MA: Harvard University Press.

Aumann, R. J. (1998) 'On the centipede game', *Games and Economic Behavior*, 23: 97–105.

Binmore, K. (1996) 'A note on backward induction', *Games and Economic Behavior*, 17: 135–137.

Bratman, M. (1987) *Intentions, Plans and Practical Reasons*, Cambridge, MA: Harvard University Press.

—— (1999) *Faces of Intention: Selected Essays on Intention and Agency*, Cambridge: Cambridge University Press.

—— (2006a) *Structures of Agency: Essays*, Oxford: Oxford University Press.

—— (2006b) 'Intention, belief, practical, theoretical', unpublished manuscript, Stanford University.

Coleman, J. L. and Morris, C. W. (eds) (1998) *Rational Commitment and Social Justice: Essays for Gregory Kavka*, Cambridge: Cambridge University Press.

Gauthier, D. (1997) 'Resolute choice and rational deliberation: a critique and a defense', *Nous*, 31: 1–25.

Gigerenzer, G. and Selten, R. (2002) *Bounded Rationality: The Adaptive Toolbox*, Cambridge, MA: MIT Press.

Hammond, P. J. (1976) 'Changing tastes and coherent dynamic choice', *Review of Economic Studies*, 43: 159–173.

Harman, G. (1986) *Change in View*, Cambridge, MA: MIT Press.

Kavka, G. S. (1983) 'The toxin puzzle,' *Analysis*, 43: 33–36.

McClennen, E. F. (1990) *Rationality and Dynamic Choice: Foundational Explorations*, Cambridge: Cambridge University Press.

Mele, A. (1992) 'Intentions, reasons, and beliefs: morals of the toxin puzzle', *Philosophical Studies*, 68: 171–94.

—— (1995) 'Effective deliberation about what to intend: or striking it rich in a toxin-free environment', *Philosophical Studies*, 79: 85–93.

Myerson, R. B. (1991) *Game Theory: Analysis of Conflict*, Cambridge, MA: Harvard University Press.

Neumann, J. von and Morgenstern, O. (1944) *A Theory of Games and Economic Behavior*, Princeton NJ: Princeton University Press.

Osborne, M. J. and Rubinstein, A. (1994) *A Course in Game Theory*, Cambridge, MA: MIT Press.

O'Shaughnessy, B. (1973) 'Trying (as the mental "pineal gland")', *Journal of Philosophy*, 70: 365–386.

Rosenthal, R. (1982) 'Games of perfect information, predatory pricing, and the chain store paradox', *Journal of Economic Theory*, 25: 92–100.

Rubinstein, A. (1998) *Modeling Bounded Rationality*, Cambridge, MA: MIT Press.

Savage, L. J. (1954) *The Foundations of Statistics*, New York: Wiley.

Searle, J. (1983) *Intentionality*, Cambridge: Cambridge University Press.

Selten, R. (1975) 'Reexamination of the perfectness concept for equilibrium points in extensive games', *International Journal of Game Theory*, 4: 25–55.

Sen, A. (1977) 'Rational fools: a critique of the behavioral foundations of economic theory,' *Philosophy & Public Affairs*, 6: 317–344.

Simon, H.A. (1982) *Models of Bounded Rationality*, Vols 1–2. Cambridge, MA: MIT Press.

van Hees, M. and Roy, O. (2007) 'Intentions and plans in game and decision theory', in B. Verbeek (ed.) *Reasons and Intentions*, London: Ashgate.

Velleman, D. (2003) 'What good is a will?', in A. Leist and H. Baumann (eds) *Action in Context*, Berlin: de Gruyter/Mouton.

Verbeek, B. (2002). *Moral Philosophy and Instrumental Rationality: An Essay on the Virtues of Cooperation*, Dordrecht: Kluwer Academic Publishers.

3 Waiving and exercising rights in the theory of social situations

Ruvin Gekker[1]

Introduction

In his seminal paper Sen (1970) has introduced a subject of individual rights into social choice theory. Sen's paradox of a Paretian liberal has provoked some controversies among economists, political scientists and philosophers (for a comprehensive survey, see Sen 1976, 1983; Suzumura 1983; Wriglesworth 1985). Immediately some authors, such as Nozick (1974) and Bernholz (1974), challenged Sen's original formulation of rights within the social choice-theoretic framework. As a result of this criticism, Gardenfors (1981) and Sugden (1985) have suggested an alternative formulation of rights within the game-theoretic framework. Both have claimed that their formulations could better capture our intuition about rights. Indeed, since the publication of a joint paper by Gaertner, Pattanaik and Suzumura (1992) the focus of most researchers has shifted from producing impossibility (possibility) results to discussing an adequacy (or inadequacy) of different formulations of individual rights (see among others Deb 1994; Dowding and van Hees 2003; Hammond 1996; Pattanaik 1996; Pattanaik and Suzumura 1996; Riley 1992; Sen 1992; van Hees 2000).

In this chapter we propose to formulate individual rights within the framework of the theory of social situations developed by Greenberg (1990). Our proposal is motivated by Gardenfors's (1981) suggestion that an individual right can be described as a possibility for an individual i to restrict the set of social states X to a subset Y of X. However, instead of representing individual rights as effectivity functions (for such representation see Deb 1994; Peleg 1998; van Hees 1999), we formalize them using rights-exercising protocols within the theory of social situations. Such representation allows us to avoid some technical problems associated with the formulation of individual rights within cooperative or non-cooperative game-theoretic frameworks. Moreover, it forces us to specify precisely the nature of different rights-exercising protocols that reflect the differences in social environment or institutions. The theory of social situations also provides us with a rather attractive stability or consistency criterion that can be applied uniformly to all rights-exercising protocols.

The structure of this chapter is as follows. First I introduce Sen's and a game form formulation of individual rights and highlight some tensions between them. The following section presents an analysis of individual rights within the framework of the theory of social situations. I conclude with some brief remarks.

Sen's and game form formulations of rights

Sen (1983) explicitly adopts the following formulation of individual rights:

> (3.1) If two social states, x and y, differ only with respect to some aspect which belongs to individual i's recognized personal sphere (RPS), and if i strictly prefers x to y, then in any choice situation where x is available, the society should not choose y.

It should be pointed out that (3.1) is only a necessary condition for individual *i* to have a right. It restricts social choice, based on individual *i*'s preferences over two social states that differ only with respect to *i*'s RPS. Gaertner *et al.* (1992) and Pattanaik (1996) highlight, using Gibbard's (1974) example, some intuitive problems with Sen's formulation of individual rights. They claim that each individual should be able to determine a certain feature or aspect of any social state provided that this aspect is within that individual's RPS. For example, each person has a right to choose the colour of his or her own shirt. Then it seems that the game form formulation of individual rights adequately captures this intuition. Recall that a game form specifies: (i) a finite set N of players; (ii) a finite set S_i of strategies for each player *i* in N; (iii) a finite set X of all feasible outcomes; (iv) an outcome function that specifies precisely one outcome for each *n*-tuple of strategies (for more on game form, see Moulin 1983 or Peleg 1984). If, in addition, we specify preferences of the players, then we have a game in normal (strategic) form.

Continuing with the example of the right to choose the colour of one's own shirt, suppose that players 1 and 2 each have two permissible strategies: wear white shirt (*w*) or wear blue shirt (*b*). Then we have four possible social states: $x=(w,w)$, $y=(b,w)$, $z=(w,b)$ and $w=(b,b)$. Notice that, by choosing *w*, player 1 can ensure that only social states *x* and *z* will prevail in which he or she wears a white shirt. Similarly, by choosing *b*, the player can ensure that social states *y* and *w* prevail in which he or she wears a blue shirt. Of course, what strategies players 1 and 2 will choose will depend on their preferences. Following Gibbard, assume that 1 wants to conform whereas 2 insists on being different. Then the following preference orderings may result:

1	2
x	y
w	z
y	x
z	w

Suppose also that each person is completely ignorant about the other person's preferences. Given this uncertainty, it is reasonable to assume that both 1 and 2 may follow the maxi-min rule. In this case 1 will choose *b*, while 2 will choose *w*. Then the social state *y* will emerge as an outcome of their choices. Notice, however, that the pair of social states (*x,y*) belongs to 1's RPS and the player strictly prefers *x* over *y*. Hence according to (3.1), *y* should not be chosen. The emergence of *y*, therefore, could be construed as a violation of 1's right to choose the colour of his or her shirt.

Sen (1992), however, does not believe that this example brings out the tension between the game form formulation and his own formulation of individual rights. In fact, he believes that the game form formulation entails his own formulation of rights under some proviso (such as absence of uncertainty, or if, in the presence of uncertainty, the desired rankings were such that each individual would have a dominant strategy). According to Sen, 'the violations of liberty with which political philosophy has been traditionally concerned have not been particularly geared to decision problems under uncertainty, or to the gap between the individual's own choices and desires' (Sen 1992: 149). Hence the contribution of Gaertner *et al.* (1992) is in enriching the classical account of liberty by bringing uncertainty into the story.

We believe that Gaertner *et al.* are right in insisting that the game form formulation of individual rights is not in general compatible with Sen's formulation of rights. We will try to bring out the tension between these two formulations of individual rights by using another example (Gibbard 1974), which involves no uncertainty. Angelina wants to marry Edwin, but she will settle for the judge, who wants whatever Angelina wants. Edwin wants to remain single, but he would rather wed Angelina than see her wed the judge. Denote 'both Edwin and Angelina remain single' as *x*, 'Edwin weds Angelina' as *y*, and 'the judge weds Angelina and Edwin remains single' as *z*. Then we have the following pattern of their preferences over $X = \{x,y,z\}$:

Angelina	*Edwin*
y	x
z	y
x	z

Notice that the pair (*x,z*) is in Angelina's RPS and she strictly prefers *z* over *x*. Hence according to (3.1), *x* should not be chosen. Next, the pair (*x,y*) is in Edwin's RPS and he strictly prefers *x* over *y*. Hence, according to (3.1), *y* should not be chosen. The outcome that will emerge after Angelina and Edwin exercise their individual rights is *z*. Yet *z* is the outcome that Edwin likes the least. Gibbard (1974) suggests that in this case Edwin might be better off by bargaining his rights away or by waiving them. However, the game form formulation of individual rights provides a natural solution. Both Angelina and Edwin have two permissible strategies: remain single *(s)* or marry *(m)* (notice that the judge is a fictitious player who simply grants Angelina's wishes). Then we have the following 2×2 game in normal form:

Edwin

		s	m
Angelina	s	x	x
	m	z	y

Given the preference orderings above, the strategy m for Angelina strictly dominates her strategy s. Hence, given common knowledge of rationality, Edwin knows that Angelina will not play her strategy s, which can be eliminated. Since Edwin strictly prefers y over z, his strategy m also strictly dominates his strategy s in the reduced game and hence s can be eliminated. Therefore, Angelina and Edwin will choose their strategies m leading to the outcome y. Of course, $y = (m,m)$ is also a unique Nash equilibrium of the game. The emergence of y does not constitute any violation of Edwin's rights under the game form formulation. On the contrary, Edwin rationally chooses his permissible strategy to marry Angelina rather than to remain single and see her marrying the judge.

Suppose we slightly change Gibbard's original story by strengthening Edwin's desire to remain single as follows: Edwin wants to remain single and feels so strongly about it that he would rather see Angelina wed the judge than to marry her. In this case we have the following preference orderings over X:

Angelina	*Edwin*
y	x
z	z
x	y

Given this preference orderings, the strategy m for Angelina still strictly dominates her strategy s, which can be eliminated. However, now Edwin strictly prefers z over y, and hence his strategy s strictly dominates his strategy m in the reduced game. Hence m can be eliminated. Therefore, the outcome $z = (m,s)$ will emerge, which is also a unique Nash equilibrium of the game. In this case the exercise of rights under the game form formulation will coincide with the social choice or Sen's formulation of individual rights.

Individual rights and the theory of social situations

Gardenfors (1981) has tried to formalize Nozick's account of rights that refers to legal and philosophical analysis of the concept of a right.

> The type of individual right that Sen and Nozick seem to have in mind can be presented in the form 'i may see to it that F' where F is not a particular social state, but a condition on (or a property of) a social state (see, for example, Kanger and Kanger (1966) and Lindahl (1977)). Rights do not establish an ordering of social states but divide them into classes; if a right is exercised,

some class of possible social states is excluded from further consideration and the remaining class of social states may be subject of further restrictions by the exercising of other rights.

(Gardenfors 1981: 343)

The game form formulation of individual rights might be considered as one possible formalization of such an intuition. For example, Edwin by exercising his right to remain single may force the choice of social states in which he remains single, that is $\{x,z\}$. Notice, however, that the normal game form formulation of individual rights abstracts from the dynamic or sequential aspects of rights-exercising. We shall see below that Gardenfors also abstracts from the sequential aspects of rights-exercising by imposing a rather artificial condition on the rights combination.

Gardenfors's formalization takes a right as a possibility for an individual i to restrict the set of social states X to a subset Y of X. A rights system is defined then as a set of pairs (i, Y). First, Gardenfors requires that rights of different individuals be mutually consistent, that is, different individuals should not have conflicting rights. However, in many cases we are interested in the analysis of individual rights in the situations where these rights are conflicting. For example, the right to smoke for one individual may conflict with the right to clean air of another individual. In order to simplify his formalization of rights, Gardenfors also requires that the consistent rights of an individual could be combined without restrictions. This requirement is too strong and fails in many situations. As Gardenfors himself notices 'I may at a certain point of time have the right to drink a bottle of whisky and also have the right to drive my car, but I may not exercise both of these rights at the given point of time' (Gardenfors 1981: 345).

According to Gardenfors, what rights an individual would choose to exercise will depend on his or her preferences over social states. However, since the rights-exercising may induce the sets of social states, Gardenfors extends preferences over single states to preferences over the sets of social states. He views the exercising (or waiving) of a right assigned to an individual as a move in a game. The condition on combinations of rights allows Gardenfors to ignore the sequential aspects of a set of moves and to identify the set of strategies available to an individual with the set of rights assigned to him.

In this chapter, following the lead of Gardenfors, we propose to formulate and analyse individual rights within the framework of the theory of social situations. Similarly to Gardenfors's and the game form formulations of individual rights we distinguish between having a right and exercising that right. However, unlike Gardenfors (1981), we do not impose any restrictions on individual rights. In particular, we will allow different individuals to possess conflicting rights, and we also allow individuals to exercise their rights sequentially. Specifically, we assume that a society with rights consists of an ordered quadruple $\Omega \equiv (N,X,\{R_i\}_{i \in N}, \rho)$, where N is a finite set of individuals, X is a finite set of social states, R_i is a weak preference relation of individual i over X (P_i is the asymmetric part of R_i), and ρ is a rights assignment in a society. As in Gardenfors (1981; see also Deb

1994; Peleg 1998; van Hees 1999), we assume that, if individual i exercises his or her rights, then the original set of alternatives X is restricted to a subset Y of X. Hence for every Y we define a subsociety $\Omega^Y \equiv (N,Y,\{R_i'\},\rho')$, where R_i' and ρ' are the restrictions of R_i and ρ to Y. With each subsociety Ω^Y we will associate a position $G^Y \equiv (N,Y,\{R_i'\}_{i \in N})$. The set of all possible positions is denoted by Γ, that is, $\Gamma \equiv \{G^Y : Y \subseteq X\}$.

The most important concept of the framework is a definition of the rights-exercising protocol. By *the rights-exercising protocol* we understand a mapping δ that for every coalition S, $S \subseteq N$, and every sub-society G^Y, and each alternative $x \in Y$ specifies the set $\delta(S \mid G^Y, x) \subseteq \Gamma$. Next, we define a *standard of behaviour* as a mapping σ that specifies the subset of Y for every subsociety G^Y. The only requirement that we impose on the standard of behaviour is *stability* (or consistency). Formally, given $(N, X, \{R_i\}_{i \in N}, \rho)$ and δ, the standard of behaviour σ is *conservatively stable* (CSSB for short) if for every $G^Y \in \Gamma$ the following condition holds:

$x \in \sigma(G^Y)$ if and only if there exist no coalition $S \subseteq N$ and $G^Z \in \delta(S \mid G^Y, x)$ such that $\sigma(G^Z) \neq \varnothing$ and moreover for all $i \in S$, $y P_i' x$ for all $y \in \sigma(G^Z)$.

Alternatively, we can define a CSSB σ as follows. First, we define the *dominion* of G^Y (CDOM for short) as:

CDOM$(\sigma, G^Y) = \{x \in Y$: there exist $S \subseteq N$ and $G^Z \in \delta(S \mid G^Y, x)$ such that $\sigma(G^Z) \neq \varnothing$, and for all $i \in S$, $y P_i' x$ for all $y \in \sigma(G^Z)\}$.

Then the standard of behaviour σ is a CSSB if and only if for $G^Y \in \Gamma$, $\sigma(G^Y) = Y \setminus$ CDOM(σ, G^Y).

The theory of social situations framework allows different formulations of the rights-exercising protocols that we might want to employ in our analysis of individual rights. For example, individuals might want to know whether sequential rights-exercising is permissible or not, or if they can form coalitions and exercise their rights collectively by signing some binding agreements (in this case the existence of institutions enforcing such agreements is naturally presupposed). It is this flexibility that underscores certain advantages of this framework over the traditional social choice-theoretic framework.

In this chapter we will limit ourselves to only three rights-exercising protocols (many more could be easily defined). Specifically, the first rights-exercising protocol prohibits both sequential rights-exercising and the formation of coalitions, that is, an individual i can exercise his or her right to restrict the set X to $Y \subseteq X \setminus \rho(i)$ only if some element from $\rho(i)$ is currently under consideration, and no prior rights-exercising was performed. Formally, this protocol is described by the correspondence δ^1 as follows:

For every $G^Y \in \Gamma$ for every coalition $S \subseteq N$ and each alternative $x \in Y$,

$\delta^1(\{i\} \mid G^Y, x) \equiv \varnothing$ if $Y \neq X$,

$\delta^1(\{i\} \mid G^X,x) \equiv \{G^Z \in \Gamma : Z = X \backslash \rho(i) \text{ and } x \notin Z\}$,

$\delta^1(S \mid G^Y,x) \equiv \varnothing$ otherwise.

The next rights-exercising protocol allows individuals to exercise their rights even if other members of society did so before. However, it still prohibits the formation of coalitions. Formally, this protocol can be defined as follows:

For every $G^Y \in \Gamma$, for every coalition $S \subseteq N$ and each alternative $x \in Y$,

$\delta^2(\{i\} \mid G^Y,x) \equiv \{G^Z \in \Gamma : Z = Y \backslash \rho(i) \text{ and } x \notin Z\}$,

$\delta^2(S \mid G^Y,x) \equiv \varnothing$ otherwise.

The third rights-exercising protocol allows both the formation of coalitions and sequential rights-exercising. Formally, this protocol might be described as follows:

For every $G^Y \in \Gamma$, for every coalition $S \subseteq N$ and each alternative $x \in Y$,

$\delta^3(S \mid G^Y,x) \equiv \{G^Z \in \Gamma : Z = Y \backslash [\cup \{\rho(i) : i \in S\}] \text{ and } x \notin Z\}$.

Using Theorem 5.4.1 from Greenberg (1990), the following result can be easily established:

Proposition 3.1 Every situation (δ^k,Γ), $k = 1,2,3$ admits a unique CSSB.

As an illustration of the flexibility of the theory of social situations framework, we apply it to the Gibbard's example. We have the following society with rights: $N = \{A(\text{Angelina}), E(\text{Edwin})\}$; $X = \{x,y,z\}$. The preferences are exactly like in Gibbard's example. We will first examine the situation in which Angelina and Edwin both have the right to marry, that is $\rho(A) = \text{marry}$, $\rho(E) = \text{marry}$. In this case, by exercising her right, Angelina may restrict the original set X to $Y = \{y,z\}$ and similarly Edwin by exercising his right may restrict the set X to $Y = \{x,y\}$. We want to investigate how different rights-exercising protocols may affect Angelina's and Edwin's exercising of their rights. The following proposition provides an answer.

Proposition 3.2. The unique CSSB, σ^k, for the associated situation (δ^k,Γ), $k = 1,2,3$ satisfies:

(i) $\sigma^1(G^X) = \{y\}$; (ii) $\sigma^2(G^X) = \{y\}$; (iii) $\sigma^3(G^X) = \{y\}$.

Proof. We shall prove only that (i), ((ii) and (iii) can be handled similarly. After Angelina exercises her rights, $x \in$ CDOM(σ^1, G^X). Similarly, after Edwin exercises his rights, $z \in$ CDOM(σ^1, G^X). Therefore, $\sigma^1(G^X) = X \setminus$ CDOM$(\sigma^1, G^X) = \{y\}$. ∎

Notice that, regardless of the differences in the rights-exercising protocols, the outcome of the rights-exercising through the theory of social situations coincides with the outcome of the rights-exercising through the normal game form. It is not compatible with the outcome emerging through the exercise of rights within the social choice-theoretic framework. What will happen, however, if we endow Edwin with the right to remain single along with his right to marry? Now Edwin by exercising his right to remain single can restrict the original set X to $Y = \{x, z\}$. He can also restrict the set X to $Y = \{x, y\}$ by exercising his right to marry. How does the difference in the rights-exercising protocols affect Angelina's and Edwin's exercising of their rights in this case? The following proposition answers this question.

Proposition 3.3. The unique CSSB, σ^k, for the associated situation (δ^k, Γ), $k = 1, 2, 3$ satisfies:

(i) $\sigma^1(G^X) = \{y\}$; (ii) $\sigma^2(G^X) = \{y, z\}$; (iii) $\sigma^3(G^X) = \{\varnothing\}$.

Proof. We will prove (i) and (ii), leaving (iii) to the reader. In case of (i), Angelina will exercise her right to marry, hence we have $x \in$ CDOM(σ^1, G^X). Similarly, Edwin will exercise his right to marry, therefore $z \in$ CDOM(σ^1, G^X). However, Edwin will not exercise his right to remain single under the rights-exercising protocol δ^1. The reason is simple. If he chooses to exercise this right he will induce the subsociety containing the outcome z, which might make him worse off. Hence $y \notin$ CDOM(σ^1, G^X). Therefore we can conclude that $\sigma^1(G^X) = X \setminus$ CDOM$(\sigma^1, G^X) = \{y\}$.

In case of (ii), we have to explain why Edwin will refrain from exercising his right to marry as well as his right to remain single. Indeed, Edwin has the right to remain single. However, if he chooses to exercise this right he will induce a new agenda $Y = \{x, z\}$. Notice that Edwin and Angelina have opposing preferences over $\{x, z\}$, and each will exercise their rights to eliminate both x and z. Hence $\sigma^2(G^Y) = \varnothing$ and, by exercising his right to remain single, Edwin will create 'chaos'. Therefore, $y \notin$ CDOM(σ^2, G^X). Similarly, Edwin will refrain from exercising his right to marry. Indeed, he must realize that, if he chooses to exercise his right to marry, he will induce a new agenda $Y = \{x, y\}$. However, Edwin and Angelina again have opposing preferences over Y, and each will exercise their rights to eliminate both x and y. As a result, $\sigma^2(G^Y) = \varnothing$. Hence, by exercising his right to marry, Edwin creates the 'chaotic situation'. Therefore, $z \notin$ CDOM(σ^2, G^X). Since Angelina will exercise her right to marry we have $x \in$ CDOM(σ^2, G^X). Hence $\sigma^2(G^X) = X \setminus$ CDOM$(\sigma^2, G^X) = \{y, z\}$. ∎

Notice that the endowment of Edwin with an additional right to remain single does not matter in the case of the rights-exercising protocol δ^1. Remember that under this protocol he can exercise his rights only once (sequential or successive rights-exercising is prohibited). Naturally then Edwin will continue to exercise his right to marry, waiving his right to remain single. Hence the result is the same as when he had only one right to marry. However, the situation is entirely different in the case when sequential rights-exercising is allowed. In this case, not only Edwin will waive his right to remain single but, perhaps paradoxically, he will also waive his right to marry. It is indeed puzzling that giving more rights as well as providing more power to exercise them might lead to rights alienation.

Suppose now that Edwin's desire to remain single is so strong that he would rather see Angelina wed the judge than marry her himself. We will first examine the situation where Edwin will be endowed only with the right to remain single while Angelina will be endowed with her right to marry, that is, $\rho(A)$ = marry, $\rho(E)$ = remain single. How does this change in the rights endowment and in Edwin's preference ordering affect Angelina's and Edwin's exercising of their rights?

Proposition 3.4. The unique CSSB, σ^k, for the associated situation (δ^k, Γ), $k = 1,2,3$ satisfies:

(i) $\sigma^1(G^X) = \{z\}$; (ii) $\sigma^2(G^X) = \{z\}$; (iii) $\sigma^3(G^X) = \{z\}$.

Proof. It is similar to the proof of Proposition 4.2 and is therefore omitted. ∎

Again notice that, regardless of the differences in the right-exercising protocols, the outcome of the rights-exercising through the theory of social situations coincides with the outcome of the rights-exercising through the normal game form. However, this time it also coincides with the outcome that has emerged within the social choice-theoretic framework. We want again to investigate what will happen if we endow Edwin with an additional right to marry. How does the difference in the rights-exercising protocols affect Edwin's and Angelina's exercising of their rights in this case?

Proposition 3.5. The unique CSSB, σ^k, for the associated situation (δ^k, Γ), $k = 1,2,3$ satisfies:

(i) $\sigma^1(G^X) = \{z\}$; (ii) $\sigma^2(G^X) = \{y,z\}$; (iii) $\sigma^3(G^X) = \{\varnothing\}$.

Proof. It is similar to that of Proposition 3 and is therefore omitted. ∎

Again granting more rights as well as providing more power to exercise them leads to an alienation of Edwin's individual rights. This time, despite his strong desire to remain single, he would refrain from exercising his right to do so.

Notice that so far all our rights assignments were in the form of a certain feature of the state that was in the private sphere of an individual i. For example, Edwin by exercising his rights to remain single could exclude y from the set of all social states. Similarly, by exercising his right to marry, he could exclude z from the set of all social states. However, Edwin did not have the power to exclude x from the set of all social states. On the other hand, Angelina did not have a power to exclude z from the set of all social states. And yet it is precisely this power that both Edwin and Angelina may enjoy under the social choice formulation of individual rights. Remember that the pair $\{x,y\}$ is in Edwin's RPS and depending on his preferences he can eliminate either x or y. Similarly, the pair $\{x,z\}$ is in Angelina's RPS and depending on her preferences she can knock out either x or z. What will happen if we mimic the social choice-theoretic rights assignments within the framework of the theory of social situations but exercise those rights using different rights-exercising protocols? Suppose first that Angelina, by exercising her right, can eliminate x from the set of all social states and Edwin, by exercising his right, can knock out y from the set X. In effect, we assume one-sided decisiveness and, since Angelina strictly prefers z over x, we will allow her to eliminate x only. Similarly, since Edwin strictly prefers x over y, we will allow him to knock out y only. Given the modification of Gibbard's example in which Edwin strongly desires to remain single, we have already established that $\sigma^k(G^X)=\{z\}$, $k=1,2,3$ in the case of this rights-assignment (see Proposition 3.4). However, what will happen if in addition to our previous assignment of rights we allow Angelina to eliminate z and Edwin to eliminate x from the set X by exercising their rights? The following proposition provides an answer.

Proposition 3.6. The unique CSSB, σ^k, for the associated situation (δ^k,Γ), $k=1,2,3$ satisfies:

(i) $\sigma^1(G^X)=\{z\}$; (ii) $\sigma^2(G^X)=\{x,z\}$; (iii) $\sigma^3(G^X)=\{\varnothing\}$.

Proof. We will prove (ii) and (iii), leaving (i) to the reader. In case of (ii), we will show that both Angelina and Edwin will refrain from exercising their rights to eliminate x. First, we will show that Angelina will not choose to eliminate x. Because if she will, then she will induce a new agenda $Y=\{y,z\}$, and Edwin and Angelina have opposing preferences over Y. By exercising their rights, they can eliminate both y and z leading to $\sigma^2(G^Y)=\varnothing$. Hence by exercising her right to eliminate x, Angelina will create 'chaos'. For similar reason, Edwin will not choose to eliminate x. Therefore, $x \notin \mathrm{CDOM}(\sigma^2,G^X)$. Angelina also will not choose to eliminate z because, if she does, then she will induce a new agenda $Y=\{x,y\}$, and Edwin and Angelina have opposing preferences over $\{x,y\}$. Hence by exercising their rights, they can eliminate both

x and y leading to $\sigma^2(G^Y)=\varnothing$. Therefore, $z\notin$ CDOM(σ^2,G^Y). Finally, Edwin will exercise his right to eliminate y. By eliminating y, he will induce a new agenda $Y=\{x,z\}$. Angelina strictly prefers z to x and she has a right to eliminate x that she will exercise. Edwin, on the other hand, will not use his right to eliminate x since he strictly prefers x to z. As a result, z would emerge as the final outcome of their rights exercising. Because Edwin strictly prefers z to y he will choose to exercise his right to eliminate y. Hence $y\in$ CDOM(σ^2,G^X) and $\sigma^2(G^X)=X\backslash$CDOM($\sigma^2,G^X$)$=\{x,z\}$.

In case of (iii), Angelina can combine her rights to exclude both x and z, since she prefers y to both of them. Hence both x and z belong to CDOM(σ^3,G^X). Edwin will choose to exercise his right to eliminate y because by eliminating y he will induce a new agenda $Y=\{x,z\}$. Angelina strictly prefers z to x and she has a right to knock out x, which she will use. Edwin, on the other hand, strictly prefers x to z and therefore will waive his right to eliminate x. Therefore, z will emerge as an outcome of rights-exercising. Since Edwin strictly prefers z to y, he will use his right to exclude y from X. Hence $y\in$ CDOM(σ^3,G^X) and $\sigma^3(G^X)=X\backslash$CDOM($\sigma^3,G^X$)$=\varnothing$. ∎

Notice that the endowment of both Angelina and Edwin with the additional rights would not make any difference in the case of the rights-exercising protocol δ^1. However, the situation is somewhat different in the case of δ^2. In this case, perhaps paradoxically, Angelina will waive all her rights. Again a familiar pattern has emerged, namely, granting more rights as well as providing more power to exercise them leads to an alienation of Angelina's individual rights.

After our examination of the Gibbard's example and its modification within the framework of the theory of social situations, the reader might think that a somewhat paradoxical phenomenon of rights alienation could be even established formally, that is, it should be possible to prove, for example, that $\sigma^1\subseteq\sigma^2$. This result would indeed be paradoxical because intuitively we believe that giving more rights to an individual as well as providing more power to exercise them should lead in general to people exercising more of their individual rights rather than fewer, that is, intuitively it should be true that $\sigma^2\subseteq\sigma^1$. However, the following example establishes that neither inclusion holds.

Suppose that Angelina and Edwin are the only people in the train compartment. We also assume that smoking on the train is not prohibited unless someone would object to it. Angelina is addicted to smoking and will smoke provided no one would object. On the other hand, Edwin is a non-smoker who values clean air. At stake here is the right to smoke (or the right to continue smoking) for Angelina and the right to clean air (or the right to object to smoking) for Edwin. Angelina, being addicted to smoking, will definitely start smoking. Edwin then faces two choices: either to object to smoking (o) or to refrain from an objection and let her continue to enjoy her habit (o'). In case of objection, either Angelina will comply and stop smoking (s') or she will ignore it and will continue to smoke *(s)*. Denote 'Edwin objects and Angelina ignores it' as x, 'Edwin objects and Angelina complies' as y, and 'Edwin refrains from an objection and Angelina enjoys her habit' as z. The reader should easily come up with a story justifying the following preferences:

Edwin	Angelina
y	z
z	y
x	x

Notice that the pair (x,z) is in Edwin's RPS, and he strictly prefers z to x. Therefore, according to (3.1), x should not be chosen. The pair (x,y) is in Angelina's RPS, and she strictly prefers y to x. Hence, again according to (3.1), x should not be chosen. The outcomes that will emerge after Edwin and Angelina will exercise their rights are $\{y,z\}$. If we want to formulate their rights using a game form formulation, it is perhaps more natural for this example to utilize an extensive game form. However, we will continue to use a normal game form. Edwin has two permissible strategies: object to smoking (o) or refrain from an objection (o'). Angelina also has two permissible strategies: continue smoking *(s)* (more precisely start smoking and continue) and stop smoking (s') (again more precisely start smoking and then stop). Hence we have the following 2×2 game in normal form:

Angelina

		s	s'
Edwin	o	x	y
	o'	z	z

Given the preference orderings above, we have two Nash equilibria in this game, $y=(o,s')$ and $z=(o',s)$. However, only y is a subgame perfect Nash equilibrium.

Within the theory of social situations we first examine the case in which Angelina will have her right to continue smoking while Edwin will have his right to object to it, that is $\rho(E)=$ object to smoking, $\rho(A)=$ continue smoking. Hence by exercising her right Angelina may restrict the original set $X=\{x,y,z\}$ to $Y=\{x,z\}$, and similarly Edwin by exercising his right might restrict the set X to $Y=\{x,y\}$. What would be the result of their rights-exercising in this case? The following proposition provides an answer.

Proposition 3.7. The unique CSSB, σ^k, for the associated situation (δ^k,Γ), $k=1,2,3$ satisfies:

$$(i) \ \sigma^1(G^X)=\{x,y,z\}; (ii) \ \sigma^2(G^X)=\{x,y\}; (iii) \ \sigma^3(G^X)=\{x,y\}.$$

Proof. We will prove (i) and (ii); (iii) can be handled similarly. In case of (i), Edwin will refrain from exercising his right to object to smoking because if he exercises his right he will induce a subsociety containing social state x, and Edwin strictly prefers z to x. Hence $z \notin \text{CDOM}(\sigma^1, G^X)$. Similarly, and for the same reason, Angelina will refrain from exercising her right to continue smoking. Therefore, $y \notin \text{CDOM}(\sigma^1, G^X)$ and $\sigma^1(G^X) = X \backslash \text{CDOM}(\sigma^1, G^X) = \{x, y, z\}$.

In case of (ii), Edwin will choose to exercise his right to object to smoking. By exercising his right, he will induce a new agenda $Y = \{x, y\}$. Angelina strictly prefers y to x and by exercising her right will eliminate x. Since Edwin strictly prefers y to z, he will exercise his right, that is, $z \in \text{CDOM}(\sigma^2, G^X)$. On the other hand, Angelina will not exercise her right to continue smoking because, by exercising her right, she will induce a new agenda $Y = \{x, z\}$. Edwin strictly prefers z to x, and will not exercise his right to eliminate z. Hence, by exercising her right, Angelina will induce a subsociety containing social state x, and she strictly prefers y to x. Therefore, $y \notin \text{CDOM}(\sigma^2, G^X)$ and $\sigma^2(G^X) = X \backslash \text{CDOM}(\sigma^2, G^X) = \{x, y\}$. ∎

At last we have a situation in which providing more power to exercise individual rights will actually lead people to exercising more of them. Also notice that, in this case, $\sigma^2(G^X) \subset \sigma^1(G^X)$, which corresponds to our intuition about rights-exercising. However, will this inclusion hold if we grant some additional rights to the participants? Specifically, suppose that not only will Angelina have her right to continue smoking, but she will also have the right to stop smoking, that is $\rho(A) = $ continue smoking, $\rho(A') = $ stop smoking, $\rho(E) = $ object to smoking. The preference orderings are exactly as before. The following proposition provides a negative answer.

Proposition 3.8. The unique CSSB, σ^k, for the associated situation (δ^k, Γ), $k = 1, 2, 3$ satisfies:

(i) $\sigma^1(G^X) = \{y, z\}$; (ii) $\sigma^2(G^X) = \{x\}$; (iii) $\sigma^3(G^X) = \varnothing$.

Proof. We will prove (i) and (ii), leaving (iii) to the reader. In case of (i), Angelina will exercise her right to stop smoking and will eliminate x. Hence $x \in \text{CDOM}(\sigma^1, G^X)$. However, she will refrain from exercising her right to continue smoking because, if she does, she will induce a subsociety containing social state x, and she strictly prefers y to x. Therefore, $y \notin \text{CDOM}(\sigma^1, G^X)$. Similarly, and for the same reason, Edwin will refrain from exercising his right to object to smoking. Hence $z \notin \text{CDOM}(\sigma^1, G^X)$ and $\sigma^1(G^X) = X \backslash \text{CDOM}(\sigma^1, G^X) = \{y, z\}$.

In case of (ii), we will show first that Edwin will choose to exercise his right to object to smoking. Indeed, if he does, he will induce a new agenda $Y = \{x, y\}$. Angelina strictly prefers y to x and by exercising her right not to smoke she will eliminate x. Since Edwin strictly prefers y to z, he will choose to eliminate z by exercising his right. Therefore, $z \in \text{CDOM}(\sigma^2, G^X)$. Similarly, Angelina will choose to exercise her right to continue smoking. By exercising her right, she will induce a new agenda $Y = \{x,z\}$. Edwin and Angelina have similar preferences over $\{x,z\}$ and, since Edwin strictly prefers z to x, he will not exercise his right to eliminate z. On the other hand, by exercising her right to stop smoking, Angelina will eliminate x because she also strictly prefers z to x. Hence z will emerge as an outcome and Angelina strictly prefers z to y. Therefore, she will exercise her right to continue smoking and eliminate y, that is, $y \in \text{CDOM}(\sigma^2, G^X)$.

However, Angelina will refrain from exercising her right to stop smoking because if she exercises this right she will induce a new agenda $Y = \{y,z\}$, and Edwin and Angelina have opposing preferences over Y. By exercising their individual rights, they will eliminate both y and z leading to $\sigma^2(G^Y) = \varnothing$. Hence by exercising her right to stop smoking Angelina will create 'chaos'. Therefore $x \notin \text{CDOM}(\sigma^2, G^X)$, and $\sigma^2(G^X) = X \backslash \text{CDOM}(\sigma^2, G^X) = \{x\}$. ∎

Notice that the original rights assignment in this example does not allow Angelina and Edwin to knock out x by exercising their individual rights. However, granting Angelina an additional right to stop smoking does provide her with an opportunity to eliminate x from the set X. It turns out that whether she will use this opportunity or not will depend on the nature of the rights-exercising protocols. For example, Angelina will exercise her right to stop smoking under the rights-exercising protocol δ^1, and she will waive this right under the rights-exercising protocol δ^2. As a result, we have established that $\sigma^1 \cap \sigma^2 = \varnothing$, that is, neither $\sigma^1 \subseteq \sigma^2$ nor $\sigma^2 \subseteq \sigma^1$ holds. Also notice that the outcome x that has emerged under the rights-exercising protocol δ^2 clashes with the outcomes that have emerged under the game form formulation of individual rights. Perhaps even more fundamentally, the emergence of x could be construed as a violation of Edwin's and Angelina's rights under the social choice-theoretic formulation of individual rights. However, the close examination of the proof of Proposition 3.8 shows that both Angelina and Edwin will exercise their individual rights (to smoke and to object to smoking respectively). The emergence of x, therefore, reflects the fact that when individual rights are in conflict someone's rights must give in (for more on the co-possibility as well as compossibility of individual rights, see Dowding and van Hees 2003).

Concluding remarks

In this chapter we have suggested an alternative formulation of rights within the framework of the theory of social situations. We have focused primarily on the analysis of individual rights within this framework, leaving the detailed examination of group rights and their relationship to individual rights until another time. However, Pattanaik (1988) has already shown that the clash may arise between individual and group rights, and that perhaps group rights deserve more scrutiny than they have received so far.

In his paper, Riley (1989) has suggested that any cooperation in the rights-exercising games should be based on the reasonable non-cooperative foundation. Furthermore, he insists that 'if the possibility of coalition formation is taken seriously in a non-cooperative setting, then any solution is appropriately required to be a strong Nash equilibrium' (p. 145). However, Deb, Pattanaik and Razzolini (1997) argue that a strong Nash equilibrium is perhaps too 'strong' in many rights-exercising situations. Instead they suggest a k-strong equilibrium or a coalition-proof Nash equilibrium to model rights-exercising games (Greenberg's (1990) notion of an equilibrium with coalitional commitments or an equilibrium with coalitional contingent threat might also be relevant). Perhaps an additional advantage of the theory of social situations is that it allows a rather uniform treatment of both individual and group rights within the same framework using the same stability or consistency criterion.

Note

1 For helpful discussions and comments on earlier versions of this chapter I would like to thank David Austen-Smith, Rajjat Deb, Wulf Gaertner, Joseph Greenberg, David Kelsey, Martin van Hees, Stefano Vanucci and Shlomo Weber. The usual disclaimer applies.

References

Bernholz, P. (1974) 'Is a Paretian liberal really impossible?', *Public Choice*, 20: 90–107.
Deb, R. (1994) 'Waiver, effectivity and rights as game forms', *Economica*, 61: 167–178.
Deb, R., Pattanaik, P. K. and Razzolini, L. (1997) 'Game forms, rights and the efficiency of social outcomes', *Journal of Economic Theory*, 72: 74–95.
Dowding, K. and van Hees, M. (2003) 'The construction of rights', *American Political Science Review*, 97: 281–293.
Gaertner, W., Pattanaik, P. K. and Suzumura, K. (1992) 'Individual rights revisited', *Economica*, 59: 161–177.
Gardenfors, P. (1981) 'Rights, games and social choice', *Nous*, 15: 341–56.
Gibbard, A. (1974) 'Pareto-consistent libertarian claim', *Journal of Economic Theory*, 7: 388–410.
Greenberg, J. (1990) *The Theory of Social Situations: An Alternative Game-Theoretic Approach*, Cambridge: Cambridge University Press.
Hammond, P. (1996) 'Game forms versus social choice rules as models of rights', in K. J. Arrow, A. K. Sen and K. Suzumura (eds), *Social Choice Re-examined*, London: Macmillan.
Kanger, S. and Kanger, H. (1966) 'Rights and parlamentarism', *Theoria*, 32: 85–115.
Lindahl, L. (1977) *Position and Change: A Study in Law and Logic*, Dordrecht: Reidel.
Moulin, H. (1983) *The Strategy of Social Choice*, Amsterdam: North-Holland.
Nozick, R. (1974) *Anarchy, State and Utopia*, Oxford: Basil Blackwell.
Pattanaik, P. K. (1988) 'On the consistency of libertarian values', *Economica*, 55: 517–524.
—— (1996) 'On modelling individual rights: some conceptual issues', in K. J. Arrow, A. K. Sen and K. Suzumura (eds), *Social Choice Re-examined*, London: Macmillan.
Pattanaik, P. K. and Suzumura, K. (1996) 'Individual rights and social evaluation: a conceptual framework', *Oxford Economic Papers*, 48: 194–212.
Peleg, B. (1984) *Game Theoretic Analysis of Voting in Committees*, Cambridge: Cambridge University Press.

—— (1998) 'Effectivity functions, game forms, games and rights', *Social Choice and Welfare*, 15: 67–80.

Riley, J. (1989) 'Rights to liberty in purely private matters', *Economics and Philosophy*, 5: 121–166.

—— (1992) 'Towards adequate formulations of rights and liberty,' mimeo, Tulane University.

Sen, A. K. (1970) 'The impossibility of a Paretian liberal', *Journal of Political Economy*, 78: 152–157.

—— (1976) 'Liberty, unanimity and rights', *Economica*, 43: 217–245.

—— (1983) 'Liberty and social choice', *Journal of Philosophy*, 80: 5–28.

—— (1992) 'Minimal liberty', *Economica*, 59: 139–159.

Sugden, R. (1985) 'Preference and choice', *Economics and Philosophy*, 1: 213–229.

Suzumura, K. (1983) *Rational Choice, Collective Decisions, and Social Welfare*, Cambridge: Cambridge University Press.

Van Hees, M. (1999) 'Liberalism, efficiency and stability: some possibility results', *Journal of Economic Theory*, 88: 294–309.

—— (2000) *Legal Reductionism and Freedom*, Dordrecht: Kluwer.

Wriglesworth, J. L. (1985) *Libertarian Conflicts in Social Choice*, Cambridge: Cambridge University Press.

4 Consequentialist choice and behavior

A comparison[1]

Nicholas Baigent

Introduction

The purpose of this chapter is to distinguish between two classes of consequentialism based roughly on what an agent is and what an agent does. What an agent is refers to those things, such as preferences, norms, and intentions that may determine choice behavior. What an agent does refers here to the agent's choices.

Two examples will be given. In both, non-consequentialist agents behave in a consequentialist way. Furthermore, the relevant concepts of consequentialism invoked here are not contrived for the purpose, but are prominent in the literature.

The examples suggest that the behavior space, or choice space, may not be the most appropriate space in which to define consequentialism. Rather, it may be more appropriate to define consequentialism in the space of agent characteristics that specify what an agent is rather than what an agent does.

The next section introduces consequentialist behavior as a property of choice functions. After that come examples of consequentialism defined in terms of what may determine choice and contrasts such non-choice consequentialism with choice consequentialism. The final section discusses the examples and draws a conclusion.

Choice consequentialism

Consequentialism as introduced in Hammond (1977) is a property of choices, though Hammond called the property "metastatic consistency." The terminology of consequentialism was introduced later in Hammond (1986). Apart from minor differences,[2] the concept formulated in this section is closest to that in Hammond (1977).

Let X denote a finite set of alternatives and let $K=2^X\backslash\varnothing$ denote the set of all non-empty subsets of X and for all $S \in K$, let $K_s=2^S\backslash\varnothing$ denote the set of all non-empty subsets of S. The binary relation $R \subseteq X \times X$ is a weak order on X if and only if it is complete, reflexive, and transitive. For all weak orders on X and all $S \in K$ the set of R-greatest alternatives in S is given by $G(S,R)=\{x \in (\forall y \in S)xRy\}$. A choice function C on X is Consistent with Optimizing a Weak Order (COWO) if and only if, for all $S \in K$, $C(S) = G(S,R)$.

For all $T \in K$, a choice function C_T on T is a function $C_T : K_T \to K_T$ that, for all $S \in K_T$, $C_T(S) \in K_s$. For simplicity, C_x will be written as C. c will denote the set of all choice functions on X. For all $S \in K$, $\{S,T\}$ is a dichotomous partition of X if and only if $S \neq X$ and $T = X/S$.

In Hammond (1977), partitions on X are induced by "two stage trees," motivated as follows. An agent is seen as facing a choice from X in two stages. In the first stage the agent can narrow down the set of available alternatives from X to subsets partitioning X. Then, at the second stage, a choice is made from the element of the partition chosen at the first stage. However, only dichotomous partitions are used to obtain the agent's results and the only role of the tree structure is to induce a partition. Thus, in this chapter only dichotomous partitions are required.

Roughly expressed, Hammond's choice consequentialism requires that intentions at the first stage of choice be respected at the second stage. Thus, consider an agent with choice function on $X = \{x,y,z\}$ given by: $C(\{x,y,z\}) = C(\{x,y\}) = \{x,y\}$, $C(\{y,z\}) = \{y,z\}$ and $C(\{x,z\}) = \{x\}$.[3] Given the dichotomous partition $\{\{y,z\},\{x\}\}$ of X, this agent may well choose $\{y,z\}$ at the first stage with the intention of choosing $\{y\}$ at the second stage. At the second stage however, it is the choice function $C_{\{y,z\}}$ that is relevant rather than C. Given the original intention at the first stage when all alternatives in X were available, y should then be chosen from $\{y,z\}$ using $C_{\{y,z\}}$. Since the only thing that has changed is the set of available alternatives, if $y \notin C_{\{y,z\}}(\{y,z\})$ then the original intentions must have been affected by what is available and choice cannot be said to depend solely on consequences. Choosing z at the second stage would fail to carry out the intention held at the fist stage to reject z. Thus, if choices depend only on their consequences, then second stage choices should be exclusively all those that would have been chosen at the first stage and are still available.

More formally, a choice function C on X is consequentialist if and only if, for all dichotomous partitions $\{S,T\}$ of X and all $A \in K$, there exists a choice function C_S on S such that: $(\forall S \in K)[(C(A) \cap S \neq \varnothing) \Rightarrow (C(A) \cup S = C_S(S \cap A))]$. Consequentialism and COWO are equivalent properties of choice functions as established by the following result.

> **Theorem** (Hammond 1977): A choice function C on X is consequentialist if and only if it is COWO.

Examples

Example 4.1: Composition of choice functions

For the first example, consider an agent who has two choice functions, C_i and C_j, on X at a pre-choice deliberative stage in the choice process. Furthermore, assume that the agent gives priority to the considerations inducing choice function C_j over those inducing choice function C_i. For example, it may be that, for all $S \in K$, $C_j(S)$ is the set of alternatives in S the choice of which would not violate some moral principle and that C_i is induced by some social norm. If moral principles are given priority then the final choice is given by the composition $C=C_i \circ C_j$ of C_i and C_j. Thus, for all $S \in K$, $C(S)=C_i(C_j(S))$.

Let C_i be given by $C_i(\{x,y,z\})=\{x\}$, $C_i\{x,y\}=\{x\}$, $C_i\{y,z\}=\{y\}$ and $C_i\{x,z\}=\{z\}$, and let C_j be given by $C_j(\{x,y,z\})=\{x,y,z\}$, $C_j(\{x,y\})=\{x,y\}$, $C_j(\{y,z\})=\{y,z\}$ and $C_j(\{x,z\})=\{x\}$. Neither C_i nor C_j are COWO. $C_i(\{x,y,z\})=\{x\}$ would require a preference of x strictly preferred to z, whereas $C_i\{x,z\}=\{z\}$ would require the opposite strict preference between x and z. $C_j(\{x,y,z\})=\{x,y,z\}$ would require a preference for which there is indifference between all alternatives whereas $C_j(\{x,z\})=\{x\}$ requires a strict preference over x and z. However, their composition is a COWO choice function on X and therefore, by Hammond's theorem, it is consequentialist.

In this example, the behavior of the non-consequentialist agent is consequentialist.

Example 4.2: Preference consequentialism

Consequentialism as a property of preferences over extended alternatives was introduced in Suzumura and Xu (2001) and used in Suzumura and Xu (2003). An extended alternative allows non-consequentialist preferences to be formulated.

An extended alternative is a pair (x,S) in which $S \in K$ and $x \in S$. Ω denotes the set of all extended alternatives. Note that $\Omega \neq X \times K$. A binary relation $\geq \subseteq \Omega \times \Omega$ is a weak order on Ω if and only if it is complete, reflexive and transitive. The interpretation of $(x,S) \geq (y,T)$ is that choosing x from S is at least as 'good' as choosing y from T. A weak order on Ω is consequentialist if and only if, for all (x,S), $(x,T) \in \Omega$: $(x,S) \sim (x,T)$. Thus, consequentialist weak orders on Ω draw no distinction between choosing an alternative from different subsets.

For a weak order $\geq$ on Ω, let $C_\geq$ denote the choice function on X such that, for all $S \in K$, $C_\geq (S)=\{x \in S : (\forall y \in S)(x,S) \geq (y,S)\}$. This induces a choice function from a preference on extended alternatives in a natural way as follows. An alternative x in S is chosen from S if and only if choosing it from S is at least as good as choosing anything else from S. However, it does not follow that a consequentialist weak order $\geq$ on Ω induces a consequentialist choice function $C_\geq$ on X. To see this, consider the following example.

Let $X=\{x,y,z\}$ and let $\geq$ be given by the following list in strict descending order: $(x,\{x,y\})$, $(x,\{x,z\})$, $(x,\{x,y,z\})$, $(z,\{x,y,z\})$, $(z,\{x,z\})$, $(y,\{y,z\})$, $(z,\{y,z\})$, $(y,\{x,y\})$, and $(y,\{x,y,z\})$. This weak order on extended alternatives is thoroughly non-consequentialist. In particular, since there is a strict preference over all distinct pairs of extended alternatives the indifference required by consequentialism does not hold over any relevant pair. However, this weak order on extended alternatives induces the following consequentialist choice function $C_\geq$ on X: $C(\{x,y,z\})=C(\{x,y\})=C(\{x,z\})=\{x\}$ and $C(\{y,z\})=\{y\}$. $C_\geq$ is COWO since it chooses the R-greatest alternatives from any subset according to the weak order R on X for which x is strictly preferred to both y and z, and y is strictly preferred to z.

In this example also, the behavior of a non-consequentialist agent is consequentialist.

Conclusion

The examples in the preceding section show that the choices of non-consequentialist agents may in fact be consequentialist. Since choice is invariably considered as depending on the various cares and concerns of agents, this suggests that it may be more appropriate to define consequentialism in terms of whatever is taken to determine choices rather than in terms of choices. Indeed, this is an application of the general concept of external reference in Sen (1993). Then, choices would be defined as consequentialist if they are induced by consequentialist agents and this would avoid the incongruity of the examples in which non-consequentialist agents behave in a way that is consequentialist.

Notes

1   I am very grateful to Ruvin Gekker for his encouragement and patience.
2   In Hammond (1977), metastatic consistency (consequentialism) is a property of a family of choice functions and his main theorem assumes that a single alternative is chosen from every subset. Neither is essential and both are dropped in the later literature as they are here.
3   This choice function is in fact induced by choosing greatest elements from each subset according to the quasitransitive, but not transitive, binary relation on X for which x is indifferent to y, y is indifferent to z, and x is strictly preferred to z.

References

Hammond, P.J. (1977) 'Dynamic restrictions on metastatic choice', *Economica*, 44: 337–350.
—— (1986) 'Consequentialist social norms for public decisions', in W.P. Heller, R.M. Starr, and D.A. Starrett (eds), *Social Choice and Public Decision Making: Essays in Honor of Kenneth J. Arrow*, Vol. 1, Cambridge: Cambridge University Press.
Sen, A.K. (1993) 'Internal consistency of choice', *Econometrica*, 61: 495–521.
Suzumura, K. and Xu, Y. (2001) 'Characterizations of consequentialism and non-consequentialism', *Journal of Economic Theory*, 101: 423–436.
—— (2003) 'Consequences, opportunities, and generalized consequentialism and non-consequentialism', *Journal of Economic Theory*, 111: 293–304.

Part II

Social choice, judgment aggregation and rationality of legal order

5   Social choice, fuzzy preferences and manipulations

Juan Perote-Peña and Ashley Piggins

Introduction

According to philosophers, natural language is infected with vague predicates. For example, predicates such as 'thin', 'red' and 'tall' are commonly taken to be vague. These predicates are 'vague' because they admit borderline cases. Some people are borderline thin, for example. Some reddish-orange patches of colour are borderline red, and so on. The existence of vagueness implies that many of the predicates we commonly use lack sharply defined boundaries. For example, on a scale of height, there is no sharp boundary between people who are tall and people who are not tall. The boundaries of vague predicates are blurred, not sharp.[1]

According to the standard view in philosophy, vagueness creates problems for classical logic.[2] For example, if Jim is borderline thin then the sentence 'Jim is thin' is neither true nor false, violating the principle of bivalence. The law of excluded middle, that 'Jim is thin or Jim is not thin' is true, seems suspect too.

Several theories of vagueness have been proposed. The one most commonly used in the social choice literature is fuzzy set theory.[3] But why are social choice theorists interested in vagueness? One argument put forward in the literature is that preference relations are vague.[4] Here are two examples.

Imagine that you are comparing two possible jobs, and what you care about is how they fare with respect to salary and excitement. Imagine too that one job offers a higher salary than the other, but is less exciting. Which job would you prefer? Often it is hard to say, but not always. For example, one job could offer a much higher salary than the other, and yet be only marginally less exciting. In such cases, it seems plausible that you would prefer the better paid job to the more exciting one. The reason for this is that you are probably willing to trade off slightly less excitement in order to obtain a much higher income. Unfortunately things are not always as straightforward as this. For example, one job could offer a much higher salary than the other, and yet be much less exciting too.

In cases like this, it might be extremely difficult to put the jobs in a clear order. This may be because of the existence of unresolved conflict in the mind of the decision maker. How does this conflict manifest itself? One way is through feeling that your preferences are 'divided' in some sense. For instance, in this example you might feel that to some extent the better paid job is at least as good as the more exciting job. However, at the same time, you might also feel that to some extent the more exciting job is at least as good as the better paid job. These conflicting feelings may be difficult to integrate into a clear expression of preference or indifference.

Here is another example, inspired by an argument made by Sen (1970). Imagine that a social planner is attempting to rank two social states, A and B, in which only two people live. Suppose that person i is better off in A than in B, but that person j is better off in B than in A. In other words, A and B cannot be ranked by the traditional Pareto principle. Does this mean that the planner cannot put the states in order? Quite rightly, Sen argues no. For example, it might be the case that state A is much better for person i than state B, and yet only slightly worse for person j. If so, it would be reasonable for the planner to place A above B in the social ranking. In other words, the planner could judge that the gains to person i in state A outweigh the losses to person j.

However, as Sen points out, this does not mean that it is always possible to rank Pareto incomparable states. For example, if the gains to person i in A are 'similar' to the losses to person j, then the planner may conclude that it is extremely difficult to put the states in a clear order. In cases like this, the planner may feel that his or her preferences are 'divided' in some sense. In other words, the planner might feel that to some extent state A is at least as good as state B. However, at the same time, the planner might also feel that to some extent state B is at least as good as state A. Once again, these conflicting feelings may be difficult to integrate into a clear expression of preference or indifference.

These examples appeal to the fact that preferences are often 'conflicting' or 'ambiguous'. Put more simply, we might just say that in these examples preferences are vague. Fuzzy set theory has been used in the social choice literature to represent preferences like these.[5]

Fuzzy set theory

A fuzzy set is the extension of a vague predicate. So if 'red' is vague then the set of red objects is a fuzzy set. To be precise, let X denote the universal set and let W denote a subset of X in the classical sense, $W \subseteq X$. The set W is characterized by a function $f_W: X \rightarrow \{0,1\}$ where $f_W(x) = 1$ for $x \in W$, and $f_W(x) = 0$ for $x \notin W$. Given $x \in X$, $f_W(x)$ is the degree to which x belongs to W. The generalization to a fuzzy set occurs by permitting this degree to take more than two values, typically by allowing any value in $[0,1]$.[6] So a fuzzy subset G of X is characterized by a function $f_G: X \rightarrow [0,1]$. If $f_G(x) = 1$ then x 'clearly' belongs to G, and if $f_G(x) = 0$ then x 'clearly does not' belong to G. In between there are varying degrees of belonging. If G is a vague property and if x is borderline G, then x's degree of Gness is some number between 0 and 1.

A fuzzy (binary) relation F defined on X is characterized by a function $f_F: X \times X \rightarrow [0,1]$. If the semantic concept this fuzzy relation is meant to represent is (weak) preference, then $f_F(x, y)$ can be interpreted as the degree of confidence that 'x is at least as good as y'. This is not the only possible interpretation of $f_F(x, y)$. It can be interpreted as the degree of truth of the sentence 'x is at least as good as *y'*. Fuzzy relations can be used to represent vague preferences, since the degree to which you are confident that one alternative is at least as good as another is represented by a number in $[0,1]$.[7]

The literature

It is interesting to know whether economic theory can be reconstructed on the basis of fuzzy preferences. The literature on this topic is now quite extensive. For instance, if individuals have fuzzy preferences then how do they make choices?[8] Can we demonstrate that a competitive equilibrium exists and prove counterparts to the first and second welfare theorems?[9] Does Arrow's impossibility theorem hold in the context of fuzzy preferences?[10]

This chapter makes a contribution to this growing body of work. Like much of the literature, our focus is on social choice theory. This literature has been motivated by the idea that fuzziness can have a 'smoothing' effect on preference aggregation and so perhaps the famous impossibility results of Arrow (1951) and others can be avoided. Unfortunately, this is not always the case. In fact, in this chapter a very strong concept of dictatorship emerges.

We investigate the nature of social choice when it is based on fuzzy individual preferences. It is worth emphasising that, even when judgments about social welfare are vague, the final social choice or action must necessarily be non-fuzzy or exact. In this chapter we investigate the structure of exact social choice functions. These exact social choice functions combine non-empty subsets of the set of alternatives with a fuzzy preference profile in order to produce a social choice. These social choices are assumed to be related in a very mild way to the fuzzy social preference that emerges at this profile. We prove that any exact social choice function that has 'minimal links' to a fuzzy social welfare function is dictatorial provided that the latter is strategy-proof and not constant.[11] These fuzzy social welfare functions are referred to as fuzzy aggregation rules. Of course, this result is a version of the celebrated Gibbard–Satterthwaite theorem but in the context of fuzzy preferences and exact social choice functions.[12]

Preliminaries

Let A be a set of social alternatives with the cardinality of $A \geq 3$. Let $N = \{1, \ldots, n\}$, $n \geq 2$, be a finite set of individuals. $A^* = \{(a, b) \in A^2 \mid a \neq b\}$ is the set of ordered pairs of distinct social alternatives.

> **Definition 5.1.** A fuzzy binary relation (FBR) over A^* is a function f: $A^* \rightarrow [0,1]$. An exact binary relation over A^* is an FBR g such that $g(A^*) \subseteq \{0,1\}$.

Let T denote the set of all FBRs over A^*.

> **Definition 5.2.** Let H be the set of all $r \in T$ that satisfy the following conditions.

(i)   For all $(a, b) \in A^*$, $r(a, b) + r(b, a) \geq 1$.
(ii) For all distinct $a, b, c \in A$, $r(a, c) \geq \min \{r(a, b), r(b, c)\}$.

The FBRs in H will be interpreted as fuzzy weak preference relations. Thus, if $r_i \in H$ is interpreted as the fuzzy weak preference relation of individual i, then $r_i(a, b)$ is to be interpreted as the degree to which individual i is confident that 'a is at least as good as b'.

Property (i) is the fuzzy counterpart of the traditional completeness condition, whereas property (ii) is the familiar max–min transitivity condition. Notice that within H are all (exact) complete and transitive weak preference relations. This is one reason why the fuzzy approach to preferences is interesting. It generalizes the traditional theory.

Definition 5.3. A fuzzy aggregation rule (FAR) is a function $\Psi: H^n \to H$.

Intuitively, an FAR specifies a fuzzy social weak preference relation given an n-tuple of fuzzy individual weak preference relations (one for each individual). The elements of H^n are indicated by $(r_1, \ldots, r_n)$, $(r_1', \ldots, r_n')$, etc. We write $r = \Psi(r_1, \ldots, r_n)$, $r' = \Psi(r_1', \ldots, r_n')$ and so on (where Ψ is the FAR). We write $r(a, b)$ to denote the restriction of r to (a, b), and $r'(a, b)$ to denote the restriction of r' to (a, b) and so on.

Let $G(A)$ denote the set of non-empty subsets of A.

Definition 5.4. An exact social choice function (ESCF) is a function d: $G(A) \times H^n \to G(A)$ such that for all $W \in G(A)$ and all $(r_1, \ldots, r_n) \in H^n$, $d(W; r_1, \ldots, r_n) \subseteq W$.

Definition 5.5. Let Ψ be an FAR and d be an ESCF. d has at least minimal links with Ψ if and only if the following property is satisfied.

For all $W \in G(A)$ and all $(r_1, \ldots, r_n) \in H^n$, if there exists $x \in W$ such that $[r(x, y) = 1$ and $r(y, x) = 0]$ for all $y \in W - \{x\}$, then $d(W; r_1, \ldots, r_n) = \{x\}$.

The idea of minimal links between the appropriate d and Ψ is taken from Barrett, Pattanaik and Salles (1986). The intuition behind the idea can be described as follows. If, in a given set W of alternatives, an alternative x is socially strictly preferred to every other alternative in W, then x must be the only socially chosen alternative.

We denote by $(r_1, \ldots, r_i', \ldots, r_n) \in H^n$ the profile obtained from $(r_1, \ldots, r_i, \ldots, r_n)$ when individual i replaces $r_i \in H$ with $r_i' \in H$. We write $r_{-i} \otimes r_i' = \Psi(r_1, \ldots, r_i', \ldots, r_n)$ and $r_{-i} \otimes r_i'\{a, b\}$ denotes the restriction of $r_{-i} \otimes r_i'$ to (a, b). Similarly, $r_{-i} \otimes r_i' \otimes r_j' = \Psi(r_1, \ldots, r_i', \ldots, r_j', \ldots, r_n)$ and $r_{-i} \otimes r_i' \otimes r_j'\{a, b\}$ denotes the restriction of $r_{-i} \otimes r_i' \otimes r_j'$ to (a, b).

Definition 5.6. An FAR Ψ is strategy-proof if and only if it satisfies the following property.

(SP) For all $(a, b) \in A^*$, all $(r_1, \ldots, r_n) \in H^n$, all $i \in N$ and all $r_i' \in H$, both (i) and (ii) hold.

(i) $r(a, b) < r_i(a, b) \rightarrow r_{-i} \otimes r_i' \{a, b\} \leq r(a, b).$
(ii) $r(a, b) > r_i(a, b) \rightarrow r_{-i} \otimes r_i' \{a, b\} \geq r(a, b).$

This condition can be described as follows. Take any pair of alternatives (a, b) and any fuzzy preference profile in which you truthfully report your preferences. At this profile you are confident to some degree that 'a is at least as good as b'. However, imagine that at this profile the fuzzy aggregation rule assigns a larger social degree of confidence to (a, b) than the one you happen to hold. Then, if the fuzzy aggregation rule is strategy-proof, whenever you misrepresent your preferences the social degree assigned to (a, b) will either rise or remain constant. Conversely, if the social degree assigned to (a, b) is smaller than your individual (a, b) value, whenever you misrepresent your preferences the social degree assigned to (a, b) will either fall or remain constant.

Loosely speaking, what this means is as follows. Whenever someone unilaterally switches from telling the truth to lying, the fuzzy social ranking moves 'at least as far away' from their truthful ranking as was initially the case. In other words, whenever someone misrepresents their preferences, the 'distance' between their truthful ranking and the social ranking (weakly) increases. In such circumstances, individuals do not gain by misrepresenting their preferences. We say that a fuzzy aggregation rule is strategy-proof if and only if it satisfies this property.

Obviously there may be other ways of formulating a non-manipulation condition within the framework of fuzzy aggregation, but this one strikes us as a natural place to start. Weaker conditions are possible, but inevitably they would be more controversial as conditions of non-manipulation.

To clarify the nature of this condition, consider Figure 5.1.

In Figure 5.1, we restrict attention to the ordered pair (a, b) and the ordered pair (b, a). Individual js'4 fuzzy preferences are denoted by the vector $(r_j(a, b), r_j(b, a))$. Social preferences are denoted by the vector $(r(a, b), r(b, a))$. If individual j misrepresents his or her preferences, then the new vector of social values $(r^*(a, b), r^*(b, a))$ is constrained to lie in Ω.

Finally, we need a condition to eliminate strategy-proof FARs which are trivial.

Definition 5.7. An FAR Ψ is not constant if and only if it satisfies the following property.

(NC) For all $(a, b) \in A^*$, there exists $(r_1, \ldots, r_n)$, $(r_1', \ldots, r_n') \in H^n$ such that $r(a, b) = 0$ and $r'(a, b) = 1$.

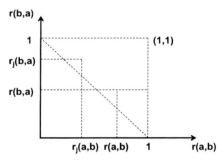

Figure 5.1 An illustration of the strategy proofness condition.

As stated earlier, this condition is mild. It stipulates that, for each pair of social alternatives, two profiles exist in the domain of the fuzzy aggregation rule which produce different social values in $\{0,1\}$ for this pair. This condition rules out fuzzy aggregation rules that assign constant values to pairs of alternatives, irrespective of individual preferences.

Let P denote the set of all subsets of N. A non-empty subset of N is called a coalition. Given a coalition $C = \{i_1, \ldots, i_m\}$, and given $(r_1, \ldots, r_n) \in H^n$, $r_C(a, b)$ denotes $(r_{i1}(a, b), \ldots, r_{im}(a, b)) \in [0,1]^m$.

Note that $r_N(a, b)$ denotes $(r_{i1}(a, b), \ldots, r_{in}(a, b)) \in [0,1]^n$. So given $N = \{1, \ldots, n\}$, $r_{i1}(a, b)$ in the vector $r_N(a, b)$ denotes individual 1's fuzzy preference over (a, b), $r_{in}(a, b)$ in the vector $r_N(a, b)$ denotes individual n's fuzzy preference over (a, b) and so on.

We write $r_C(a, b) \geq r_C'(a, b)$ if $r_i(a, b) \geq r_i'(a, b)$ for all $i \in C$.

We now introduce some other properties that FARs might satisfy.

Definition 5.8. An FAR Ψ is Arrow-like if and only if it satisfies the following two properties.

(IIA) For all $(r_1, \ldots, r_n)$, $(r_1', \ldots, r_n') \in H^n$ and all $(a, b) \in A^*$

$r_N(a, b) = r_N'(a, b)$ implies $r(a, b) = r'(a, b)$

(PC) For all $(r_1, \ldots, r_n) \in H^n$ and all $(a, b) \in A^*$

$\max \{r_N(a, b)\} \geq r(a, b) \geq \min \{r_N(a, b)\}$

Of course, IIA is our version of Arrow's (1951) independence of irrelevant alternatives condition but in the framework of fuzzy aggregation. Similarly, PC is our version of the Pareto condition.

Definition 5.9. An FAR Ψ is neutral if and only if it satisfies the following property. (N) For all $(r_1, \ldots, r_n)$, $(r'_1, \ldots, r'_n) \in H^n$ and all (a, b), $(c, d) \in A^*$,

$$r_N(a, b) = r_N'(c, d) \text{ implies } r(a, b) = r'(c, d)$$

In order to explain this condition, let Ψ be a neutral FAR. Take any $(r_1, \ldots, r_n) \in H^n$ and any $(a, b) \in A^*$. At this profile we have $r_N(a, b) \in [0,1]^n$. In addition, assume that at this profile we also have $r_N(a, b) = r_N(c, d)$ for some $(c, d) \in A^*$. In other words, each individual's (a, b) value is identical to his or her (c, d) value. Then, since Ψ is neutral, we have $r(a, b) = r(c, d)$. This means that the social value assigned by Ψ to (c, d) is identical to the value assigned to (a, b). Furthermore, if $r_N(a, b) = r'_N(c, d)$ at some other profile $(r'_1, \ldots, r'_n) \in H^n$ then we have $r(a, b) = r'(c, d)$ as well. In other words, neutrality is both an intra-profile condition and an inter-profile condition. Loosely speaking, neutrality means that the names of the alternatives do not matter.

The theorem

We now state and prove our dictatorship theorem.

Theorem. Let Ψ be a strategy-proof FAR that is not constant. Let d be an ESCF which has at least minimal links with Ψ. Then there exists an individual $i \in N$ such that for all $W \in G(A)$ and for every $(r_1, \ldots, r_n) \in H^n$, if there exists $x \in W$ such that $[r_i(x, y) = 1$ and $r_i(y, x) = 0]$ for all $y \in W - \{x\}$, then $d(W; r_1, \ldots, r_n) = \{x\}$.

This theorem says the following. If social choices are determined by a choice function which has at least minimal links to an FAR, then the former is dictatorial whenever the latter is strategy-proof and not constant. 'Dictatorship' here means that an individual exists with the following power. In every non-empty subset of A if there exists an element in this subset which this individual prefers to all others, then this element is the only socially chosen alternative.

The proof of this theorem involves a number of steps. In what follows $\mathbf{w}^n$ denotes the vector with $w \in [0,1]$ in all n places.

Lemma 5.1. Let Ψ be a strategy-proof FAR that is not constant. Then Ψ is Arrow-like.

Proof. Let Ψ be a strategy-proof FAR that is NC. We start by proving that Ψ must satisfy IIA. Assume, by way of contradiction, that Ψ does not satisfy IIA. Therefore, $\exists (a, b) \in A^*$ and $\exists (r_1, \ldots, r_n)$, $(r'_1, \ldots, r'_n) \in H^n$ with $r_j(a, b) = r'_j(a, b)$ $\forall j \in N$ such that $r(a, b) \neq r'(a, b)$. Consider the following sequence of fuzzy preference profiles:

$$R^{(0)} = (r_1, \ldots, r_n),$$

$$R^{(1)} = (r'_1, r_2, \ldots, r_n),$$

$$R^{(2)} = (r'_1, r'_2, r_3, \ldots, r_n),$$

$$\vdots$$

$$R^{(n)} = (r'_1, \ldots, r'_n).$$

Assume, without loss of generality, that $r(a, b) = k$ and $r'(a, b) = k'$ with $k' > k$. First of all, compare $r_{-1} \otimes r'_1 \{a, b\}$ with $r(a, b)$. There are two possibilities.

Case 1. $r_{-1} \otimes r'_1 \{a, b\} \neq k$. If $k < r_{-1} \otimes r'_1 \{a, b\} \leq r_1(a, b)$ or $k > r_{-1} \otimes r'_1 \{a, b\} \geq r_1(a, b)$ then SP is violated in the move from $R^{(0)}$ to $R^{(1)}$. Similarly, if $k \leq r_1(a, b) < r_{-1} \otimes r'_1 \{a, b\}$ then SP is violated either in the move from $R^{(0)}$ to $R^{(1)}$ or in the move from $R^{(1)}$ to $R^{(0)}$. If $k \geq r_1(a, b) > r_{-1} \otimes r'_1 \{a, b\}$ then SP is violated either in the move from $R^{(0)}$ to $R^{(1)}$ or in the move from $R^{(1)}$ to $R^{(0)}$. Finally, if $r_1(a, b) > k > r_{-1} \otimes r'_1 \{a, b\}$ or $r_1(a, b) < k < r_{-1} \otimes r'_1 \{a, b\}$ then SP is violated in the move from $R^{(1)}$ to $R^{(0)}$. The only case remaining is Case 2.

Case 2. $k = r_{-1} \otimes r'_1 = \{a, b\}$. We now proceed to move from $R^{(1)}$ to $R^{(2)}$ by changing the fuzzy preferences of individual 2. However, we can treat this case in exactly the same manner as the move from $R^{(0)}$ to $R^{(1)}$ and so $r_{-1-2} \otimes r'_1 \otimes r'_2 \{a, b\} = k$. Repeating this argument for each individual ensures that when we reach $R^{(n)}$ we have $r'(a, b) = k$ which contradicts the assumption that $r'(a, b) = k' > k$.

Therefore, Ψ satisfies IIA.

We now prove that Ψ satisfies PC. First of all, we prove that Ψ satisfies the following property.

(*) For all $(r_1, \ldots, r_n), (r'_1, \ldots, r'_n) \in H^n$ and every $(a, b) \in A^*$, (i) if $r_N(a, b) = 0^n$ then $r(a, b) = 0$ and (ii) if $r'_N(a, b) = 1^n$ then $r'(a, b) = 1$.

To see that (*) holds note that NC implies that there exists $(r_1, \ldots, r_n) \in H^n$ such that $r(a, b) = 0$. Let $(r_1^*, \ldots, r_n^*) \in H^n$ denote a profile such that $r_N^*(a, b) = 0^n$. If $r_N(a, b) = 0^n$ then (i) of (*) holds immediately by IIA. Assume that $r_N^*(a, b) \neq r_N(a, b)$. Therefore, $\exists Q \subseteq N$ such that $r_j(a, b) \neq 0$ for all $j \in Q$. Let $q \in Q$ and note that $r_{-q} \otimes r_q^* \{a, b\} = 0$. If not, then SP is violated in the move from $(r_1, \ldots, r_q, \ldots, r_n) \in H^n$ to $(r_1, \ldots, r_q^*, \ldots, r_n) \in H^n$. If $Q \backslash \{q\}$ is non-empty then let $z \in Q \backslash \{q\}$ and note that $r_{-q-z} \otimes r_q^* \otimes r_z^* \{a, b\} = 0$. If not, then SP is violated in the move from $(r_1, \ldots, r_q^*, r_z, \ldots, r_n) \in H^n$ to $(r_1, \ldots, r_q^*, r_z^*, \ldots, r_n) \in H^n$. Simply repeating this argument for the remaining members of Q ensures that $r^*(a, b) = 0$. Since $(r_1^*, \ldots, r_n^*) \in H^n$ is arbitrary, part (i) of (*) is proved.

The proof of part (ii) of (*) is similar and is, therefore, omitted. We now prove that Ψ satisfies PC.

We prove by contradiction. Assume that $\exists (a, b) \in A^*$, $\exists (r_1, \ldots, r_n) \in H^n$ such that $r(a, b) < \min \{r_N(a, b)\}$. Note that if $r_N(a, b) = 1^n$ then (*) implies that $r(a, b) = 1$ which contradicts the assumption that $r(a, b) < \min \{r_N(a, b)\}$. So $r_N(a, b) \neq 1^n$.

Consider any preference profile $(r_1^*, \ldots, r_n^*) \in H^n$ such that $r_i^*(a, b) = 1$ for all $i \in N$. Consider the following sequence of fuzzy preference profiles:

$$G^{(0)} = (r_1, \ldots, r_n),$$

$$G^{(1)} = (r_1^*, r_2, \ldots, r_n),$$

$$G^{(2)} = (r_1^*, r_2^*, r_3, \ldots, r_n),$$

$$\vdots$$

$$G^{(n)} = (r_1^*, \ldots, r_n^*).$$

Consider $G^{(1)}$. If $r_{-1} \otimes r_1^* \{a, b\} > r(a, b)$ then SP is violated in the move from $G^{(0)}$ to $G^{(1)}$. If $r_{-1} \otimes r_1^* \{a, b\} < r(a, b)$ then SP is violated in the move from $G^{(1)}$ to $G^{(0)}$. Therefore, $r_{-1} \otimes r_1^* \{a, b\} = r(a, b)$.

We can repeat this argument as we move from $G^{(1)}$ to $G^{(2)}$ and so $r_{-1-2} \otimes r_1^* \otimes r_2^* \{a, b\} = r(a, b)$. Again, repeating this argument for each individual ensures that when we reach $G^{(n)}$ we have $r^*(a, b) = r(a, b)$. However, this contradicts (*) and so $r(a, b) \geq \min \{r_N(a, b)\}$.

In order to complete the proof that Ψ satisfies PC, assume that $\exists (a, b) \in A^*$, $\exists (r_1, \ldots, r_n) \in H^n$ such that $r(a, b) > \max \{r_N(a, b)\}$. Note that if $r_N(a, b) = 0^n$ then (*) implies that $r(a, b) = 0$ which contradicts the assumption that $r(a, b) > \max \{r_N(a, b)\}$. So $r_N(a, b) \neq 0^n$.

Consider any preference profile $(r_1^{**}, \ldots, r_n^{**}) \in H^n$ such that $r_i^{**}(a, b) = 0$ for all $i \in N$. Consider the following sequence of fuzzy preference profiles:

$$H^{(0)} = (r_1, \ldots, r_n),$$

$$H^{(1)} = (r_1^{**}, r_2, \ldots, r_n),$$

$$H^{(2)} = (r_1^{**}, r_2^{**}, r_3, \ldots, r_n),$$

$$\vdots$$

$$H^{(n)} = (r_1^{**}, \ldots, r_n^{**}).$$

Consider $H^{(1)}$. If $r_{-1} \otimes r_1 **\{a, b\} < r(a, b)$ then SP is violated in the move from $H^{(0)}$ to $H^{(1)}$. If $r_{-1} \otimes r_1 **\{a, b\} > r(a, b)$ then SP is violated in the move from $H^{(1)}$ to $H^{(0)}$. Therefore, $r_{-1} \otimes r_1 **\{a, b\} = r(a, b)$.

We can repeat this argument as we move from $H^{(1)}$ to $H^{(2)}$ and so $r_{-1-2} \otimes r_1 ** \otimes r_2 **\{a, b\} = r(a, b)$. Again, repeating this argument for each individual ensures that when we reach $H^{(n)}$ we have $r**(a, b) = r(a, b)$. However, this contradicts (*) and so $r(a, b) \leq \max \{r_N(a, b)\}$.

Therefore, Ψ satisfies PC. We have proved that Ψ is Arrow-like. ∎

Lemma 5.2. An Arrow-like FAR Ψ is neutral.

Proof. Case 1: If $(a, b) = (c, d)$ then the result follows immediately from the fact that Ψ is Arrow-like.

Case 2: $(a, b), (a, d) \in A*$. Take $(r_1, \ldots, r_n) \in H^n$ such that $r_N(b, d) = 1^n$. Then PC implies that $r(b, d) = 1$. Since r is max–min transitive, we have $r(a, d) \geq \min \{r(a, b), r(b, d)\}$. Therefore, $r(a, d) \geq \min \{r(a, b), 1\}$ and so $r(a, d) \geq r(a, b)$. In addition, since $r_N(b, d) = 1^n$ and individual preferences are max–min transitive, it follows that $r_N(a, d) \geq r_N(a, b)$.

Select a profile $(r_1*, \ldots, r_n*) \in H^n$ such that $r_N*(b, d) = 1^n$ and $r_N*(d, b) = 1^n$. From the argument above we know that $r*(a, d) \geq r*(a, b)$ and $r_N*(a, d) \geq r_N*(a, b)$. However, an identical argument shows that $r*(a, b) \geq r*(a, d)$ and $r_N*(a, b) \geq r_N*(a, d)$. Therefore, it must be the case that $r*(a, b) = r*(a, d)$ and $r_N*(a, b) = r_N*(a, d)$.

Since $(r_1*, \ldots, r_n*) \in H^n$ is arbitrary, this condition holds for all profiles $(r_1, \ldots, r_n) \in H^n$ such that $r_N(b, d) = 1^n$ and $r_N(d, b) = 1^n$. Let F^n denote the set of such profiles. Take any profile $(r_1', \ldots, r_n') \in H^n$ such that $r_N'(a, b) = r_N'(a, d)$. Then there exists a profile $(r_1'', \ldots, r_n'') \in F^n$ such that $r_N'(a, b) = r_N'(a, d) = r_N''(a, b) = r_N''(a, d)$. IIA implies that $r'(a, b) = r'(a, d) = r''(a, b) = r''(a, d)$.

Take any pair of distinct profiles $(r_1*, \ldots, r_n*), (r_1**, \ldots, r_n**) \in H^n$ such that $r_N*(a, b) = r_N**(a, d)$. Then there exists a profile $(r_1***, \ldots, r_n***) \in F^n$ such that $r_N*(a, b) = r_N**(a, d) = r_N***(a, b) = r_N***(a, d)$. IIA implies that $r*(a, b) = r**(a, d) = r***(a, b) = r***(a, d)$.

Case 3: $(a, b), (c, b) \in A*$. Take $(r_1, \ldots, r_n) \in H^n$ such that $r_N(a, c) = 1^n$. Then PC implies that $r(a, c) = 1$. Since r is max–min transitive, we have $r(a, b) \geq \min \{r(a, c), r(c, b)\}$. Therefore, $r(a, b) \geq \min \{1, r(c, b)\}$ and so $r(a, b) \geq r(c, b)$. In addition, since $r_N(a, c) = 1^n$ and individual preferences are max–min transitive, it follows that $r_N(a, b) \geq r_N(c, b)$.

Select a profile $(r_1*, \ldots, r_n*) \in H^n$ such that $r_N*(a, c) = 1^n$ and $r_N*(c, a) = 1^n$. From the argument above we know that $r*(a, b) \geq r*(c, b)$ and $r_N*(a, c) \geq r_N*(c, b)$. However, an identical argument shows that $r*(c, b) \geq r*(a, b)$ and $r_N*(c, b) \geq r_N*(a, b)$. Therefore, it must be the case that $r*(a, b) = r*(c, b)$ and $r_N*(a, b) = r_N*(c, b)$.

Since $(r_1*, \ldots, r_n*) \in H^n$ is arbitrary, this condition holds for all profiles $(r_1, \ldots, r_n) \in H^n$ such that $r_N(a, c) = 1^n$ and $r_N(c, a) = 1^n$. Let G^n denote the set of such profiles. Take any profile $(r_1', \ldots, r_n') \in H^n$ such that $r_N'(a, b) = r_N'(c, b)$. Then there exists a profile $(r_1'', \ldots, r_n'') \in G^n$ such that $r_N'(a, b) = r_N'(c, b) = r_N''(a, b) = r_N''(c, b)$. IIA implies that $r'(a, b) = r'(c, b) = r''(a, b) = r''(c, b)$.

Take any pair of distinct profiles $(r_1*, \ldots, r_n*)$, $(r_1**, \ldots, r_n**) \in H^n$ such that $r_N*(a, b) = r_N**(c, b)$. Then there exists a profile $(r_1***, \ldots, r_n***) \in G^n$ such that $r_N*(a, b) = r_N**(c, b) = r_N***(a, b) = r_N***(c, b)$. IIA implies that $r*(a, b) = r**(c, b) = r***(a, b) = r***(c, b)$.

Case 4: (a, b), $(c, d) \in A*$ with a, b, c, d distinct. Take $(r_1, \ldots, r_n) \in H^n$ such that $r_N(b, d) = r_N(d, b) = r_N(a, c) = r_N(c, a) = \mathbf{1}^n$. Then PC implies that $r(d, b) = 1$. Since r is max–min transitive, we have $r(a, b) \geq \min \{r(a, d), r(d, b)\}$. Therefore, $r(a, b) \geq \min \{r(a, d), 1\}$ and so $r(a, b) \geq r(a, d)$. However, an identical argument shows that $r(a, d) \geq r(a, b)$ and so $r(a, b) = r(a, d)$. In addition, since $r_N(d, b) = r_N(b, d) = \mathbf{1}^n$ and individual preferences are max–min transitive, it follows that $r_N(a, b) = r_N(a, d)$.

We can repeat this argument to show that $r(a, d) = r(c, d)$ and $r_N(a, d) = r_N(c, d)$. Since $(r_1, \ldots, r_n) \in H^n$ is arbitrary, this condition holds for all profiles $(r_1, \ldots, r_n) \in H^n$ such that $r_N(b, d) = r_N(d, b) = r_N(a, c) = r_N(c, a) = \mathbf{1}^n$. Let J^n denote the set of such profiles.

Take any profile $(r_1', \ldots, r_n') \in H^n$ such that $r_N'(a, b) = r_N'(c, d)$. Then there exists a profile $(r_1'', \ldots, r_n'') \in J^n$ such that $r_N'(a, b) = r_N'(c, d) = r_N''(a, b) = r_N''(c, d)$. IIA implies that $r'(a, b) = r'(c, d) = r''(a, b) = r''(c, d)$.

Take any pair of distinct profiles $(r_1*, \ldots, r_n*)$, $(r_1**, \ldots, r_n**) \in H^n$ such that $r_N*(a, b) = r_N**(c, d)$. Then there exists a profile $(r_1***, \ldots, r_n***) \in J^n$ such that $r_N*(a, b) = r_N**(c, d) = r_N***(a, b) = r_N***(c, d)$. IIA implies that $r*(a, b) = r**(c, d) = r***(a, b) = r***(c, d)$.

Case 5: (a, b), $(b, a) \in A*$. Take any profile $(r_1, \ldots, r_n) \in H^n$ such that $r_N(a, b) = r_N(a, c) = r_N(b, c) = r_N(b, a)$. Cases (2) and (3) imply that $r(a, b) = r(a, c) = r(b, c) = r(b, a)$. Let W^n denote the set of such profiles. Take any profile $(r_1', \ldots, r_n') \in H^n$ such that $r_N'(a, b) = r_N'(b, a)$. Then there exists a profile $(r_1'', \ldots, r_n'') \in W^n$ such that $r_N'(a, b) = r_N'(b, a) = r_N''(a, b) = r_N''(b, a)$. IIA implies that $r'(a, b) = r'(b, a) = r''(a, b) = r''(b, a)$.

Take any pair of distinct profiles $(r_1*, \ldots, r_n*)$, $(r_1**, \ldots, r_n**) \in H^n$ such that $r_N*(a, b) = r_N**(b, a)$. Then there exists a profile $(r_1***, \ldots, r_n***) \in W^n$ such that $r_N*(a, b) = r_N**(b, a) = r_N***(a, b) = r_N***(b, a)$. IIA implies that $r*(a, b) = r**(b, a) = r***(a, b) = r***(b, a)$.

Therefore Ψ is neutral. ∎

Given that Ψ is neutral we can complete the proof in the following way. Take any $(a, b) \in A*$. Take a profile $(r_1, \ldots, r_n) \in H^n$ such that $r_N(a, b) = \mathbf{0}^n$. By PC it must be the case that $r(a, b) = 0$. Take some other profile $(r_1*, \ldots, r_n*) \in H^n$ such that $r_N*(a, b) = 1$. By PC it must be the case that $r*(a, b) = 1$.

Consider the following sequence of fuzzy preference profiles:

$$W^{(0)} = (r_1, \ldots, r_n),$$

$$W^{(1)} = (r_1{}^*, r_2, \ldots, r_n),$$

$$W^{(2)} = (r_1{}^*, r_2{}^*, r_3, \ldots, r_n),$$

$$\vdots$$

$$W^{(n)} = (r_1{}^*, \ldots, r_n{}^*).$$

At some profile in this sequence, say $W^{(2)}$, the social value assigned to (a, b) must rise from zero to a value strictly greater than zero. By PC, the latest this can happen is when we reach $W^{(n)}$. We shall assume, without loss of generality, that this happens at $W^{(2)}$ when individual 2 raises his or her (a, b) value from 0 to 1.

Now consider the profile $W^{(\alpha)} = (r_1{}^*, r_2, r_3{}^*, \ldots, r_n{}^*)$. We claim that the value of (a, b) at this profile is 0. To see this, note that, by assumption, the value of (a, b) at $W^{(1)}$ is zero. We can construct a profile $(r_1{}^{**}, \ldots, r_n{}^{**}) \in H^n$ in which individuals have the following preferences over three alternatives a, b and c. Individual preferences over (a, b) at this profile are the same as they are over (a, b) at $W^{(\alpha)}$. Individual preferences over (a, c) at this profile are the same as they are over (a, b) at $W^{(1)}$. Finally, individual preferences over (b, c) at this profile are the same as they are over (a, b) at $W^{(2)}$. We write $aRb \leftrightarrow r^{**}(a, b) = 1$ and $aPb \leftrightarrow aRb \wedge r^{**}(b, a) = 0$. Therefore at $(r_1{}^{**}, \ldots, r_n{}^{**}) \in H^n$ individuals hold the following preferences:

Individual 1: $aRbRc$

Individual 2: $bRcPa$

Everyone else: $cPaRb$.

Neutrality implies that $r^{**}(a, b)$ is identical to the value (a, b) takes at $W^{(\alpha)}$. Similarly, it implies that $r^{**}(b, c) = s > 0$ and that $r^{**}(a, c) = 0$. Note that by max–min transitivity $r^{**}(a, c) \geq \min \{r^{**}(a, b), s\}$ and so $r^{**}(a, b) = 0$. Therefore, the value (a, b) takes at $W^{(\alpha)}$ is zero. At $W^{(\alpha)}$ individual 2 assigns the value 0 to (a, b) but everyone else assigns the value 1. Despite this, the social value of (a, b) is 0. Neutrality implies that this will remain the case whenever these preferences are replicated over any other pair of distinct social alternatives at any profile.

Now consider any profile $W^{(\alpha\alpha)} = (r_1{}', \ldots, r_n{}') \in H^n$ in which individual 2 assigns the value 0 to some pair of distinct social alternatives. Furthermore, at this profile, individual 1 assigns the value t_1 to this pair, individual 3 assigns the value t_3 to this pair, and so on with $t_1, t_3, \ldots, t_n \in [0,1]$. The SP condition implies that the social value assigned to this pair must remain at 0 for all $t_1, t_3, \ldots, t_n \in [0,1]$.

Let us now return to $W^{(\alpha)}$. To recall, individual 2 assigns the value 0 to (a, b) at this profile but everyone else assigns the value 1. Despite this, the social value of (a, b) is 0. Completeness implies that, at this profile, individual 2 must assign the value 1 to (b, a) and so must society. This is true irrespective of everyone else's (b, a) value. Neutrality implies that any profile $W^{(\beta\beta)} = (r_1, \ldots, r_n) \in H^n$ in which individual 2 assigns the value 1 to some pair of distinct social alternatives, and in which individual 1 assigns the value t_1^* to this pair, individual 3 assigns the value t_3^* to this pair, and so on with $t_1^*, t_3^*, \ldots, t_n^* \in [0,1]$, must be consistent with the social welfare function assigning a value of 1 to this pair.

Fix some ordered pair (a, b). By the above argument, whenever individual 2 assigns a value of 1 to this pair then so must society, irrespective of everyone else's (a, b) value. Imagine now that individual 2 lowers his or her (a, b) value to some value in $[0,1]$. If this value is 0 then the social value of (a, b) must be 0 given the argument above about $W^{(\alpha\alpha)}$. Imagine that individual 2 selects a value v whereby $1 > v > 0$. If the social value of (a, b) exceeds v then individual 2 can profitably misrepresent by lowering his or her value to 0. If the social value of (a, b) is below v then individual 2 can profitably misrepresent by raising his or her value to 1. Neither of these things can happen and so the social value must be equal to v.

We have proved that individual 2 can impose his or her (a, b) preferences on society at every profile in the domain of the fuzzy aggregation rule Ψ. Since Ψ is neutral individual 2 can impose his or her preferences on society at every profile in the domain of Ψ.

Since d is an ESCF that has at least minimal links with Ψ, we have demonstrated the following. There exists an individual $i \in N$ such that for all $W \in G(A)$ and for every $(r_1, \ldots, r_n) \in H^n$, if there exists $x \in W$ such that $[r_i(x, y) = 1$ and $r_i(y, x) = 0]$ for all $y \in W - \{x\}$, then $d(W; r_1, \ldots, r_n) = \{x\}$. ∎

Conclusion

This chapter is a contribution to the literature on social choice with fuzzy preferences.

What is responsible for the impossibility theorem in this chapter? The requirement that the fuzzy aggregation rule should not be constant is mild. It requires that, for each pair of social alternatives, two profiles exist in the domain of the fuzzy aggregation rule that produce different social values in $\{0, 1\}$ for this pair. This is reminiscent of the standard non-imposition axiom in social choice theory. This condition rules out fuzzy aggregation rules that assign constant values to pairs of alternatives, irrespective of individual preferences.

Given this, one can suspect that the theorem derives from (1) our requirement that the fuzzy aggregation rule be strategy-proof and (2) the assumption we make about the transitivity of fuzzy preferences. Let us deal with our strategy-proofness condition first. As we mentioned in the chapter, weaker conditions are possible, but inevitably they would be more controversial as conditions of non-manipulation.

Consider now transitivity. As with all papers that deal with fuzzy preferences, the way the transitivity condition is formulated is crucial. In this chapter, our fuzzy preferences (both individual and social) are assumed to satisfy 'max-min' transitivity. This is probably the most widely used transitivity assumption in the literature on fuzzy relations, although it is somewhat controversial.[13]

It is certainly the case that weaker transitivity conditions exist. However, we are aware of no experimental evidence that shows that people with fuzzy preferences do not satisfy max–min transitivity. In the absence of such evidence, we feel that this condition cannot simply be dismissed out of hand. This fact, combined with its status as the most widely used condition in the literature, means that max–min transitivity is a natural place to start.

With these arguments in mind, it is worth emphasizing that our objective in this chapter is to establish a baseline impossibility theorem that can serve as a useful benchmark for future work.

Notes

1 Keefe and Smith (1997: 1–57) is an excellent introduction to the philosophical literature on vagueness. They describe several competing theories of vagueness.
2 The standard view has been challenged by Williamson (1994).
3 Fuzzy set theory was invented by Lotfi Zadeh in 1965 and has grown enormously since then. Excellent accounts of the theory are contained in Zimmerman (1991) and Dubois and Prade (1980).
4 See, for example, Barrett and Pattanaik (1989: 229–31) and Salles (1998). A comprehensive survey of the growing literature in social choice is Salles (1998). See also the interesting book by Billot (1995).
5 Alternative representations of preferences are possible that could capture what we are attempting to model here. These are discussed in Piggins and Salles (2007).
6 In so-called 'ordinal' versions of fuzzy set theory [0,1] can be replaced by an abstract set on which a particular mathematical structure is defined. See Goguen (1967), Barrett, Pattanaik and Salles (1992) and Basu, Deb and Pattanaik (1992).
7 There is a large literature on the foundations of fuzzy preference. A sample includes Orlovsky (1978), Ovchinnikov (1981), Basu (1984), Billot (1987, 1995), Dutta, Panda and Pattanaik (1986), Dutta (1987), Jain (1990), Ponsard (1990), Dasgupta and Deb (1991, 1996, 2001), Ovchinnikov and Roubens (1991, 1992) and Banerjee (1993, 1994).
8 Orlovsky (1978), Ovchinnikov (1991), Basu (1984), Dutta, Panda and Pattanaik (1986), Barrett, Pattanaik and Salles (1990), Dasgupta and Deb (1991), Banerjee (1993) and Pattanaik and Sengupta (2000).
9 Panda and Pattanaik (2002).
10 Barrett, Pattanaik and Salles (1986), Dutta (1987), Banerjee (1994), Richardson (1998) and Dasgupta and Deb (1999). Results using lattice theory have been obtained by Leclerc (1984, 1991) and Leclerc and Monjardet (1995).
11 To the best of our knowledge, the only other papers that consider the manipulability problem in a fuzzy framework are Tang (1994), Abdelaziz, Figueira and Meddeb (2007), Côrte-Real (2007) and Perote-Peña and Piggins (2007).
12 Gibbard (1973) and Satterthwaite (1975). An important precursor to the present study in the case of exact preferences is Pattanaik (1973, 1978).
13 Barrett and Pattanaik (1989) and Dasgupta and Deb (1996, 2001).

References

Abdelaziz, F. B., Figueira, J. R. and Meddeb, O. (2007) 'On the manipulability of the fuzzy social choice functions', *Fuzzy Sets and Systems*, 159: 117–184.

Arrow, K. J. (1951) *Social Choice and Individual Values*, New York: Wiley.

Banerjee, A. (1993) 'Rational choice under fuzzy preferences: the Orlovsky choice function', *Fuzzy Sets and Systems*, 53: 295–299.

—— (1994) 'Fuzzy preferences and Arrow-type problems in social choice', *Social Choice and Welfare*, 11: 121–130.

Barrett, C. R. and Pattanaik, P. K. (1989) 'Fuzzy sets, preference and choice: some conceptual issues', *Bulletin of Economic Research*, 41: 229–253.

Barrett, C. R., Pattanaik, P. K. and Salles, M. (1986) 'On the structure of fuzzy social welfare functions', *Fuzzy Sets and Systems*, 19: 1–10.

—— (1990) 'On choosing rationally when preferences are fuzzy', *Fuzzy Sets and Systems*, 34: 197–212.

—— (1992) 'Rationality and the aggregation of preferences in an ordinally fuzzy framework', *Fuzzy Sets and Systems*, 49, 9–13.

Basu, K., Deb, R. and Pattanaik, P. K. (1992) 'Soft sets: an ordinal reformulation of vagueness with some applications to the theory of choice', *Fuzzy Sets and Systems*, 45: 45–58.

Basu, K. (1984) 'Fuzzy revealed preference', *Journal of Economic Theory*, 32: 212–227.

Billot, A. (1987) *Préférence et utilité floues: applications à la théorie de l'équilibre partiel du consommateur*, Paris: Presses Universitaires de France.

—— (1995) *Economic Theory of Fuzzy Equilibria*, Berlin: Springer.

Côrte-Real, P. (2007) 'Fuzzy voters, crisp votes', *International Game Theory Review*, 9: 67–86.

Dasgupta, M. and Deb, R. (1991) 'Fuzzy choice functions', *Social Choice and Welfare*, 8: 171–182.

—— (1996) 'Transitivity and fuzzy preferences', *Social Choice and Welfare*, 13: 305–318.

—— (1999) 'An impossibility theorem with fuzzy preferences', in H. de Swart (ed.), *Logic, Game Theory and Social Choice: Proceedings of the International Conference, LGS '99, May 13–16, 1999*, Tilburg: Tilburg University Press.

—— (2001) 'Factoring fuzzy transitivity', *Fuzzy Sets and Systems*, 118: 489–502.

Dubois, D. and Prade, H. (1980) *Fuzzy Sets and Systems: Theory and Applications*, New York: Academic Press.

Dutta, B. (1987) 'Fuzzy preferences and social choice', *Mathematical Social Sciences*, 13: 215–229.

Dutta, B., Panda, S. C. and Pattanaik, P. K. (1986) 'Exact choice and fuzzy preferences', *Mathematical Social Sciences*, 11: 53–68.

Gibbard, A. F. (1973) 'Manipulation of voting schemes: a general result', *Econometrica*, 41: 587–601.

Goguen, J. A. (1967) 'L-fuzzy sets', *Journal of Mathematical Analysis and Applications*, 18: 145–174.

Jain, N. (1990) 'Transitivity of fuzzy relations and rational choice', *Annals of Operations Research*, 23: 265–278.

Keefe, R. and Smith, P. (1997) *Vagueness: A Reader*, Cambridge: MIT Press.

Leclerc, B. (1984) 'Efficient and binary consensus functions on transitively valued relations', *Mathematical Social Sciences*, 8: 45–61.

—— (1991) 'Aggregation of fuzzy preferences: a theoretic Arrow-like approach', *Fuzzy Sets and Systems*, 43: 291–309.

Leclerc, B. and Monjardet, B. (1995) 'Lattical theory of consensus', in W. Barnett, H. Moulin, M. Salles and N. Schofield (eds), *Social Choice, Welfare and Ethics*, Cambridge: Cambridge University Press.

Orlovsky, S. A. (1978) 'Decision-making with a fuzzy preference relation', *Fuzzy Sets and Systems*, 1: 155–167.

Ovchinnikov, S. V. (1981) 'Structure of fuzzy binary relations', *Fuzzy Sets and Systems*, 6: 169–195.

—— (1991) 'Social choice and Lukasiewicz logic', *Fuzzy Sets and Systems*, 43: 275–289.

Ovchinnikov, S. V. and Roubens, M. (1991) 'On strict preference relations', *Fuzzy Sets and Systems*, 43: 319–326.

—— (1992) 'On fuzzy strict preference, indifference and incomparability relations', *Fuzzy Sets and Systems*, 49: 15–20.

Panda, S. and Pattanaik, P. K. (2002) 'On optimality and competitive equilibria in the presence of fuzzy preferences', *Arthaniti*, 1: 22–31.

Pattanaik, P. K. (1973) 'On the stability of sincere voting situations', *Journal of Economic Theory*, 6: 558–574.

—— (1978) *Strategy and Group Choice*, Amsterdam: North-Holland.

Pattanaik, P. K. and Sengupta, K. (2000) 'On the structure of simple preference-based choice functions', *Social Choice and Welfare*, 17: 33–43.

Perote-Peña, J. and Piggins, A. (2007) 'Strategy-proof fuzzy aggregation rules', *Journal of Mathematical Economics*, 43: 564–580.

Piggins, A. and Salles, M. (2007) 'Instances of indeterminacy', *Analyse und Kritik*, 29: 311–328.

Ponsard, C. (1990) 'Some dissenting views on the transitivity of individual preference', *Annals of Operations Research*, 23: 279–288.

Richardson, G. (1998) 'The structure of fuzzy preferences: social choice implications', *Social Choice and Welfare*, 15: 359–369.

Salles, M. (1998) 'Fuzzy utility', in S. Barbera, P. J. Hammond and C. Seidl (eds), *Handbook of Utility Theory*, Vol. 1: *Principles*, Dordrecht: Kluwer.

Satterthwaite, M. (1975) 'Strategy-proofness and Arrow's conditions: existence and correspondence theorems for voting procedures and social welfare functions', *Journal of Economic Theory*, 10: 187–217.

Sen, A. (1970) 'Interpersonal aggregation and partial comparability', *Econometrica*, 38: 393–409.

Tang, F.-F. (1994) 'Fuzzy preferences and social choice', *Bulletin of Economic Research*, 46: 263–269.

Williamson, T. (1994) *Vagueness*, London: Routledge.

Zimmerman, H.-J. (1991) *Fuzzy Set Theory and its Applications*, Boston: Kluwer.

6 Judgment aggregation under constraints

Franz Dietrich and Christian List

Introduction

There has been much recent work on the problem of 'judgment aggregation': how can the judgments of several individuals on logically connected propositions be aggregated into corresponding collective judgments (for example, List and Pettit 2002; Pauly and van Hees 2006; Dietrich 2006; Nehring and Puppe forthcoming)? To illustrate, consider the much-cited example of the 'doctrinal paradox' (Kornhausser and Sager 1986). Suppose a three-member court has to make collective judgments (acceptance/rejection) on three connected propositions:

a   The defendant did action X.
b   The defendant had a contractual obligation not to do action X.
c   The defendant is liable for breach of contract.

Suppose further that legal doctrine imposes the constraint that action and obligation (the two *premises*) are necessary and sufficient for liability (the *conclusion*), in short $c \leftrightarrow (a \wedge b)$. It can then happen that the majority judgments on the two premises (a and b) conflict with the majority judgment on the conclusion (c), relative to that constraint. Suppose, for example, the first judge holds both a and b to be true; the second holds a but not b to be true; and the third holds b but not a to be true. If each judge individually respects the constraint that $c \leftrightarrow (a \wedge b)$, then the majority judgments – in support of a and b and against c – violate the given constraint, as shown in Table 6.1.

The conflict may disappear if we modify the constraint. For example, the majority judgments $\{a, b, \neg c\}$ pose no problem if a and b are considered necessary but not sufficient for liability (so that the constraint is $c \rightarrow (a \wedge b)$ instead of $c \leftrightarrow (a \wedge b)$, or if we introduce a third premise d (so that the constraint is $c \leftrightarrow (a \wedge b \wedge d)$, or if we drop the constraint altogether.

Our aim in this chapter is to investigate judgment aggregation on general agendas of propositions with general sets of constraints. This framework is suitable for modelling not only the court example but also many other judgment aggregation problems. Judgments on budget items, for example, are required to respect budgetary constraints. If propositions a, b and c state, respectively, that spending

Table 6.1 The doctrinal paradox

	a	b	c
Individual 1	True	True	True
Individual 2	True	False	False
Individual 3	False	True	False
Majority	True	True	False

on education, healthcare and defence should be increased, then a budgetary constraint could stipulate that not all three can be accepted together, formally $\neg(a \wedge b \wedge c)$. Judgments on binary ranking proposition such as 'x is preferable to y', 'y is preferable to z' and 'x is preferable to z' are connected by constraints such as transitivity or acyclicity. Judgments of biologists on whether two organisms fall into the same species are constrained by the assumption that belonging to the same species is an equivalence relation.

We explain how constraints between propositions can be naturally incorporated into the judgment aggregation model. Constraints have of course played a role in earlier work, particularly in the computer science literature under the label 'integrity constraints' (Konieczny and Pino-Perez 2002). See also the notion of 'context' in Nehring and Puppe (forthcoming) and that of the 'axioms' in Dietrich (2007).

We present two general impossibility theorems that depend on the nature of those constraints. The results are corollaries of results in Dietrich and List (2007a), but have a somewhat different interpretational flavour. They are also closely related to results by Dokow and Holzman (2005) and prior results by Nehring and Puppe (2002).

To illustrate our approach, we apply our two theorems to the aggregation of judgments on binary relations (which can represent various forms of comparisons), distinguishing between different constraint sets on such binary relations. In particular, we consider strict orderings, acyclic binary relations and equivalence relations. This application generalizes earlier results by List and Pettit (2004), Dietrich (2007), Dietrich and List (2007a) and Nehring and Puppe (forthcoming) on the representation of preference aggregation in the judgment aggregation model (a related result drawing on the 'property space' framework is Nehring 2003). A comprehensive bibliography on judgment aggregation can be found online (List 2004–7).

The model

We consider a group of individuals $N = \{1, 2, \ldots, n\}$ ($n \geq 2$). The propositions on which judgments are made are represented in logic, following List and Pettit (2002, 2004). We use Dietrich's (2007) generalized model.

Logic

A *logic* is an ordered pair $(\mathbf{L}, \vdash)$, where (i) $\mathbf{L}$ is a non-empty set of sentences, called *propositions*, closed under negation (i.e. if $p \in \mathbf{L}$ then $\neg p \in \mathbf{L}$, where $\neg$ denotes 'not') and (ii) $\vdash$ is an *entailment relation*, where, for each set $S \subseteq \mathbf{L}$ and each proposition $p \in \mathbf{L}$, $S \vdash p$ is read as 'S entails p' (we write $p \vdash q$ to abbreviate $\{p\} \vdash q$).[1] A set $S \subseteq \mathbf{L}$ is *inconsistent* is $S \vdash p$ and $S \vdash \neg p$ for some $p \in \mathbf{L}$, and *consistent* otherwise. We require the logic to satisfy the following minimal conditions.[2]

L1   For all $p \in \mathbf{L}$, $p \vdash p$ (self-entailment).
L2   For all $p \in \mathbf{L}$ and $S \subseteq T \subseteq \mathbf{L}$, if $S \vdash p$ then $T \vdash p$ (monotonicity).
L3 $\varnothing$ is consistent, and each consistent set $S \subseteq \mathbf{L}$ has a consistent superset $T \subseteq \mathbf{L}$ containing a member of each pair $p, \neg p \in \mathbf{L}$ (completability).

In standard propositional logic, $\mathbf{L}$ contains propositions such as a, b, $a \wedge b$, $a \vee b$, $\neg(a \rightarrow b)$ (where $\wedge$, $\vee$, $\rightarrow$ denote 'and', 'or', 'if–then', respectively). The set $\{a, a \rightarrow b\}$ entails proposition b, for example, whereas the set $\{a \vee b\}$ does not entail a. Examples of consistent sets are $\{a, a \rightarrow b, b\}$ and $\{a \wedge b\}$, examples of inconsistent ones $\{a, \neg a\}$ and $\{a, a \rightarrow b, \neg b\}$.

Agenda

The *agenda* is the set of propositions on which judgments are made, defined as a non-empty subset $X \subseteq \mathbf{L}$ expressible as $X = \{p, \neg p : p \in X_+\}$ for a set $X_+ \subseteq \mathbf{L}$ of unnegated propositions. Notationally, we assume that double negations cancel each other out (i.e. $\neg\neg p$ stands for p).[3] In the three-member court example, $X = \{a, \neg a, b, \neg b, c, \neg c\}$.

Constraints

A *constraint set* is a consistent subset $C \subseteq \mathbf{L}$. It is meant to represent logical inter-connections that are stipulated to hold between propositions. In the three-member court example, $C = \{c \leftrightarrow (a \wedge b)\}$. We say that a set $S \subseteq \mathbf{L}$ *entails* a proposition $p \in \mathbf{L}$ *relative to C*, formally $S \vdash_C p$, if $S \cup C \vdash p$. We say that a set $S \subseteq \mathbf{L}$ is *consistent relative to C* if $S \cup C$ is consistent, and *inconsistent relative to C* otherwise. Hereafter we refer to *C-entailment* and *C-(in)consistency*. The relationship between *C-*(in)consistency and *C*-entailment is analogous to that between (in)consistency and entailment *simpliciter*, which can be seen as the special cases of *C-*(in)consistency and *C*-entailment for $C = \varnothing$. A set $S \subseteq \mathbf{L}$ is *minimally C-inconsistent* if S is *C*-inconsistent but every proper subset of S is *C*-consistent. A proposition $p \in \mathbf{L}$ is *C-contingent* if $\{p\}$ and $\{\neg p\}$ are *C*-consistent. Informally, a *C*-contingent proposition is one whose truth or falsity is not settled by the constraints in C alone.

Individual judgment sets

Each individual i's judgment is the set $A_i \subseteq X$ of propositions that he or she accepts. On a belief interpretation, A_i is the set of propositions believed by individual i to be true; on a desire interpretation, the set of propositions desired by individual i to be true. A judgment set A_i is:

- *C-consistent* if, as just defined, $A_i \cup C$ is consistent;
- *C-deductively* closed if it contains all propositions $p \in X$ such that $A_i \cup C \vdash p$ (i.e. $A_i \vdash_C p$);
- *complete* if it contains a member of each proposition-negation pair p, $\neg p \in X$.

A *profile* is an n-tuple $(A_1, \ldots A_n)$ of individual judgment sets.

Aggregation functions

An *aggregation function* is a function F that maps each profile $(A_1, \ldots, A_n)$ from some domain of admissible ones to a collective judgment set $F(A_1, \ldots, A_n) = A \subseteq X$, the set of propositions that the group as a whole accepts. The judgment set A can be interpreted as the set of propositions collectively believed to be true or as the set collectively desired to be true. Below we impose minimal conditions on aggregation functions (including on the domain of admissible profiles and the co-domain of admissible collective judgment sets). Standard examples of aggregation functions are:

- *majority voting*, whereby $F(A_1, \ldots, A_n)$ is the set of propositions $p \in X$ for which the number of individuals with $p \in A_i$ exceeds that with $p \notin A_i$;
- *dictatorship*, where $F(A_1, \ldots, A_n) = A_i$ for some antecedently fixed individual $i \in N$; and
- *inverse dictatorships*, where $F(A_1, \ldots A_n) = \{\neg p : p \in A_i\}$ for some antecedently fixed individual $i \in N$.

Why explicit constraints?

We could avoid explicit reference to constraints by building them into the logic. Indeed, whenever the logic $(\mathbf{L}, \vdash)$ satisfies L1, L2 and L3, then so does the logic $(\mathbf{L}, \vdash_C)$ induced by the constraint set C. C-consistency in $(\mathbf{L}, \vdash)$ translates into standard consistency in $(\mathbf{L}, \vdash_C)$, and C-deductive closure in $(\mathbf{L}, \vdash)$ translates into standard deductive closure in $(\mathbf{L}, \vdash_C)$. This is in fact the only insight needed to translate existing theorems into theorems with explicit constraints.

Why, then, should we use explicit constraints at all? First of all, constraints introduce a different perspective on the notion of consistency. For a judgment set to be logically inconsistent is somewhat different and perhaps more dramatically 'irrational' than to be more C-inconsistent, i.e. incompatible with the given constraints. If constraints are built into the logic, the distinction between these two kinds of inconsistency disappears: all inconsistencies are by definition logical ones.

Second, the nature of the appropriate set of constraints is often unclear or controversial. For example, what are the correct budgetary constraints or legal constraints when a government cabinet makes decisions? It may thus be interesting to vary the constraint set C, so that we can express the fact that a judgment set is C-consistent yet C'-inconsistent (for distinct C, $C' \subseteq \mathbf{L}$). If reaching C-consistent collective judgments turns out to be unrealistic, the group might look for C'-consistent collective judgments for a 'less ambitious' constraint set C', say a proper subset $C' \subseteq C$. There is a long tradition in social choice theory of considering differently strong rationality constraints on preferences: one may or may not require completeness, one may or may not require full transitivity, etc. As discussed later, each set of rationality conditions on preferences corresponds to a particular constraint set.

Third, if it is unclear for some proposition $p \in \mathbf{L}$ whether or not it should constrain the group decision, a natural move is to put it into the agenda X (rather than into the constraint set C), i.e. to let the group decide whether or not p should constrain the judgments on the (other) propositions in the agenda. For instance, the 'legal doctrine' in the introductory court example or the condition of a balanced budget might be made part of the agenda X rather than of the constraint set C.

When a constraint becomes a proposition upon decision, its correct logical representation becomes crucial. Let us illustrate this point using the two examples just mentioned. First, consider the court example, and suppose the 'legal doctrine' (that action and obligation are necessary and sufficient for liability) is not imposed on the judges but put up for decision. One might be tempted to represent the legal doctrine as a material biconditional $c \leftrightarrow (a \wedge b)$. This, however, is a problematic representation. Consider the resulting agenda $X = \{a, \neg a, b, \neg b, c, \neg c, c \leftrightarrow (a \wedge b), \neg(c \leftrightarrow (a \wedge b))\}$. When a judge rejects the legal doctrine, what he or she rejects is in fact not the material biimplication $c \leftrightarrow (a \wedge b)$; indeed, he or she may well believe that a, b and c are all true or false (so that $c \leftrightarrow (a \wedge b)$ holds). Rather the judge rejects the binding nature of a and b for c. One might say that the judge rejects a *subjunctive* biconditional between c and $a \wedge b$, or perhaps he or she rejects the proposition $\blacksquare (c \leftrightarrow (a \wedge b))$, where $\blacksquare$ is a modal necessity operator ('necessarily, i.e. in all possible worlds, it is the case that …'). If the legal doctrine is represented using a subjunctive biconditional or modal necessity operator, negating the resulting proposition becomes logically consistent with assigning arbitrary truth values to a, b and c, so that the previous problem is avoided.

Similarly, suppose a government faces a decision problem, and suppose a balanced budget is not imposed as a constraint but represented by a proposition p in the government's agenda X. One might be tempted to specify p as the disjunction $\vee_{q \in S} q$, where each proposition $q \in S$ describes a way in which the budget can be balanced (such as 'low spending on education and average spending on social security and …'). The problem here is similar to that just identified in the court example. An individual who rejects the requirement that the budget *must* be balanced may still hold other beliefs that entail a balanced budget (i.e. that entail $\vee_{q \in S} q$): he or she may see no *necessity* of a balanced budget yet favour low total spending for other reasons. A more appropriate representation of the balanced budget requirement might be to let p be the proposition $O(\vee_{q \in S} q)$, where O is a deontic 'ought' operator ('it is required that …'). Since $O(\vee_{q \in S} q)$ states that the budget *ought* to be balanced, it becomes consistent (in standard deontic logic) to negate $O(\vee_{q \in S} q)$ while asserting $\vee_{q \in S} q$, which removes the problem that arises when p is defined as $\vee_{q \in S} q$.

However, if a constraint is not part of the agenda but part of the constraint set C, its misrepresentation is less problematic. The reason is that propositions in C cannot be negated, and often the logical interconnections induced by the (non-negated) constraints in the form of C-consistency and C-deductive closure do not change if these constraints are misspecified in the sense just illustrated. In the court example, for instance, the material biimplication $c \leftrightarrow (a \wedge b)$ imposes exactly the same constraints on a, b and c as a subjunctive one, and also as the proposition $(c \leftrightarrow (a \wedge b))$, namely that a, b, c can have only truth values (T, T, T) or (F, F, F) or (F, F, T) or (F, T, F). For this reason, when giving concrete examples of constraint sets in this chapter we usually omit modal or deontic necessity operators and do not address the nature of (bi)conditionals. For instance, when we later consider the transitivity constraint on preferences, we model it as the statement that 'preferences *are* transitive', not the statement that 'references *are necessarily* transitive' (and similarly for other constraints on preferences).[4]

Impossibility results

Can we find attractive aggregation functions? The answer to this question depends on two things. First, it depends on what conditions we impose on the aggregation function. If, for example, we do not seek to achieve C-consistency at the collective level (for an appropriate C), majority voting may be a perfectly fine solution. Likewise, in the absence of any democratic requirements, a dictatorship of one individual arises as a possibility, which generates C-consistent and complete judgment sets. If the only democratic requirement is non-dictatorship and we allow collective judgments to be incomplete but retain their C-consistency and C-deductive closure, then oligarchies arise as a solution; here, any proposition is accepted if and only if all members of a fixed set $M \subseteq N$ of 'oligarchs' accept it.[5]

Second, the question of whether we can find attractive aggregation functions depends on how the propositions in the agenda are logically connected, which in turn depends on the constraint set C. More constraints can often make aggregation problems harder to solve. If the court in the original example did not have to respect the constraint that action and obligation are necessary and sufficient for liability ($c \leftrightarrow (a \wedge b)$), then the majority judgments resulting from the individual judgments in Table 6.1 would not be considered inconsistent.

Let us address these questions in general terms. Consider some given agenda X and constraint C. The theorems to be presented here are C-relativized versions of existing theorems from Dietrich and List (2007a). We choose to focus on theorems that require complete and C-consistent (hence also C-deductively closed) collective judgment sets. But one could equally obtain theorems that require merely C-consistent and C-deductively closed (possibly incomplete) collective judgment sets, by adapting results by Dietrich and List (forthcoming) and Dokow and Holzman (2006), or theorems that require just C-consistent collective judgment sets, by adapting recent results by Dietrich and List (2007b).

More precisely, we here require the aggregation function to satisfy the following conditions:

Universal C-domain. The domain of F is the set of all possible profiles of C-consistent and complete individual judgment sets on the agenda X.

Collective C-rationality. F generates C-consistent and complete collective judgment sets on the agenda X.

Systematicity. For any propositions $p,q \in X$ and profiles $(A_1, \ldots, A_n)$, $(A^*_1, \ldots, A^*_n) \in Domain(F)$, if [for all individuals i, $p \in A_i$ if and only if $q \in A^*_i$] then [$p \in F(A_1, \ldots, A_n)$ if and only if $q \in F(A^*_1, \ldots, A^*_n)$).

Universal C-domain requires that the aggregation function accept as admissible any possible profile of fully rational individual judgment sets respecting the constraints in the set C. Collective C-rationality requires that the aggregation function produce as output a fully rational collective judgment set respecting the same constraints. Systematicity requires, first, that the collective judgment on each proposition depend only on individual judgments on that proposition and, second, that the pattern of dependence be the same for all propositions. The first part of the condition is the *independence* part, the second the *neutrality* part.

Call agenda X *minimally C-connected* if it satisfies the following conditions:

(i) X has minimal C-inconsistent subset Y with $|Y| \geq 3$, and
(ii) X has a minimal C-inconsistent subset Y such that $(Y \backslash Z) \cup \{\neg z : z \in Z\}$ is C-consistent for some subset $Z \subseteq Y$ of even size.[6]

It is easy to see that the agenda $X = \{a, \neg a, b, \neg b, c, \neg c\}$ in the three-member court example with constraint set $C = \{c \leftrightarrow (a \wedge b)\}$ satisfies minimal C-connectedness. On the other hand, if C were the empty set, the agenda $X = \{a, \neg a, b, \neg b, c, \neg c\}$ would not be minimally C-connected: it would violate both (i) and (ii). Thus the question of whether or not an agenda is minimally C-connected depends crucially on the strength of the constraint set C.

The following is a corollary of Dietrich and List's (2007) Theorem 1, which in turn generalizes earlier results on systematicity by List and Pettit (2002) and Pauly and van Hees (2006).

Theorem 6.1. For a minimally C-connected agenda X, every aggregation function F satisfying universal C-domain, collective C-rationality and systematicity is a (possibly inverse) dictatorship.

The agenda condition of Theorem 6.1 (minimal C-connectedness) is tight if the agenda is finite or the logic is compact (and $n \geq 3$ and X contain at least one C-contingent proposition), i.e. minimal C-connectedness is also necessary, and not merely sufficient, for characterizing (possibly inverse) dictatorships by the conditions of Theorem 6.1.[7] The same holds for the agenda conditions of the other theorems stated below.

There are two ways in which Theorem 6.1 can be turned into a characterization of dictatorships as opposed to possibly inverse ones. One way is to impose an additional unanimity condition on the aggregation function:

Unanimity

For any unanimous profile $(A, \ldots, A) \in Domain(F)$, $F(A, \ldots, A) = A$.

Theorem 6.1a. For a minimally C-connected agenda X, every aggregation function F satisfying universal C-domain, collective C-rationality, systematicity and unanimity is a dictatorship.

The other way to obtain a characterization of dictatorships from Theorem 6.1 is to impose an additional asymmetry condition on the agenda. Call agenda X *C-asymmetric* if there exists a C-inconsistent subset $Y \subseteq X$ such that $\{\neg y : y \in Y\}$ is C-consistent.

Theorem 6.1b. For a minimally C-connected and C-asymmetric agenda X, every aggregation function F satisfying universal C-domain, collective C-rationality and systematicity is a dictatorship.

Systematicity, however, is a strong condition on an aggregation function, and it is interesting to ask whether we can obtain a characterization of dictatorships using the weaker condition of independence, which retains the independence part of systematicity but drops the neutrality part.

Independence

For any proposition $p \in X$ and profiles $(A_1, \ldots, A_n)$, $(A^*_1, \ldots, A_n) \in Domain(F)$, if [for all individuals i, $p \in A_i$ if and only if $p \in (A^*_i]$ then $[p \in F(A_1, \ldots, A_n)$ if and only if $p \in F(A^*_1, \ldots, A_n)$.

Let us define the agenda condition of *C-path-connectedness*, building upon Nehring and Puppe's (2002) condition of *total blockedness*.[8] For any $p, q \in X$, we write $p \vdash_c^* q$ if $\{p, \neg q\} \cup Y$ is C-inconsistent for some $Y \subseteq X$ that is C-consistent with p and with $\neg q$.[9] Now an agenda X is *C-path-connected* if:

(iii) for every C-contingent p, $q \in X$, there exist $p_1, p_2, \ldots, p_k \in X$ (with $p = p_1$ and $q = p_k$) such that $p_1 \vdash^*_C p_2$, $p_2 \vdash^*_C p_3$, $\ldots$, $p_{k-1} \vdash^*_C p_k$.

The agenda in the three-member court example above is minimally C-connected but not C-path-connected, but, as shown below, preference aggregation problems can be represented by agendas that are both minimally C-connected and C-path-connected. Call an agenda *strongly C-connected* if it is C-path-connected and satisfies (ii). It then follows (for finite X or a compact logic) that X also satisfies (i) and hence that it is minimally C-connected as well.

> **Theorem 6.2.** For a strongly C-connected agenda X, every aggregation function F satisfying universal C-domain, collective C-rationality, independence and unanimity is a dictatorship.

This result is the C-relativized version of a result proved independently by Dietrich and List (2007b) and Dokow and Holzman (2005).[10] Both of these results extend a prior result by Nehring and Puppe (2002) with an additional monotonicity condition on F.

Finally, all results in this section continue to hold under generalized definitions of minimal and strong C-connectedness.[11]

An application: binary relations

To illustrate the results above, we apply them to the aggregation of binary comparisons, such as betterness judgments or judgments of (a given type of) equivalence. Such judgments are given by a binary relation over a set of objects to be compared, e.g. policy alternatives, job candidates or organisms to be classified into species. We use the following construction, drawing on List and Pettit (2004), Dietrich (2007) and Dietrich and List (2007a).

A simple predicate logic

We consider a predicate logic with constraints $x, y, z, \ldots \in K$ (representing objects), variables $v, w, v_1, v_2, \ldots$ (ranging over objects), identity symbol $=$, a binary relation symbol P (representing the comparative relation in question), logical connectives $\neg$ (not), $\wedge$ (and), $\vee$ (or), $\rightarrow$ (if–then), and universal quantifier $\forall$. Formally, **L** is the smallest set such that:

- **L** contains all propositions of the forms $\alpha P \beta$ and $\alpha = \beta$, where α and β are constants or variables, and
- whenever **L** contains two propositions p and q, then **L** also contains $\neg p$, $(p \wedge q)$, $(p \vee q)$, $(p \rightarrow q)$ and $(\forall v)p$, where v is any variable.

We drop brackets when there is no ambiguity.

Constraint sets

We consider some alternative constraint sets. We begin with the constraint set on fully rational strict preferences, the paradigmatic binary relation in social choice theory:

$$C_{\text{fully rational}} = \begin{cases} (\forall v_1)(\forall v_2)(v_1 P v_2 \rightarrow \neg v_2 P v_1) \\ (\forall v_1)(\forall v_2)(\forall v_3)(v_1 P v_2 \wedge v_2 P v_3) \rightarrow v_1 P v_3) \\ (\forall v_1)(\forall v_2)(\neg v_1 = v_2 \rightarrow (v_1 P v_2 \vee v_2 P v_1)) \end{cases} 12$$

The three displayed propositions in $C_{\text{fully rational}}$ are the constraints of asymmetry, transitivity and connectedness. To represent weak preferences rather than strict ones, $C_{\text{fully rational}}$ needs to be redefined as the set of rationality conditions on weak preferences (i.e. reflexivity, transitivity and connectedness); see also Dietrich (2007).[13]

Contrast this with the constraint set on merely acyclic (but not necessarily fully rational) strict preferences, representing a weaker notion of rationality:

$$C_{\text{acyclic}} = \begin{cases} \neg(\alpha_1 P \alpha_2 \wedge \ldots \wedge \alpha_{m-1} P \alpha_m \wedge \alpha_m P \alpha_1 \\ : \alpha_1 \ldots \alpha_m \in K \ldots \text{pairwise distinct}, m \geq 1 \end{cases} 14$$

The propositions in C_{acyclic} rule out any cycle of any length $m \geq 1$. In particular, irreflexivity is enforced (take $m = 1$). Transitivity, however, is not required. Thus the set $\{xPy, yPz, \neg xPz\}$, while inconsistent relative to $C_{\text{fully rational}}$, is consistent relative to C_{acyclic}.

Next we consider the constraint set on equivalence relations, suitable for classifying objects:

$$C_{\text{equivalence}} = \begin{cases} (\forall v)(v P v) \\ (\forall v_1)(\forall v_2)(\forall v_3)(v_1 P v_2 \wedge v_2 P v_3 \rightarrow v_1 P v_3) \\ (\forall v_1)(\forall v_2)(v_1 P v_2 \rightarrow P v_1) \end{cases} 15$$

The three displayed propositions in $C_{\text{equivalence}}$ are the constraints of reflexivity, transitivity and symmetry. Although this constraint set would obviously not be imposed when P represents a *preference* relation (since 'better than' is neither reflexive nor symmetric), it may be imposed on a relation of *equal suitability* between job candidates (since 'is as suitable as' is plausibly an equivalence relation) or on the relation of *belonging to the same species* among organisms.

Each of these constraint sets C induces its own notions of C-consistency and C-deductive closure.

The agenda

The *binary-relation agenda* is the set X of all propositions of the form xPy, $\neg xPy \in \mathbf{L}$, where x and y are constants. The question of which agenda condition is met by the binary-relation agenda depends crucially on the given constraint set. The following lemma holds:

Lemma 6.1. The binary-relation agenda X (with $|K| \geq 3$) is

a   strongly C-connected when $C = C_{\text{fully rational}}$;
b   minimally, not not strongly, C-connected when $C = C_{\text{acyclic}}$;
c   minimally, but not strongly, C-connected when $C = C_{\text{equivalence}}$.

In part (a), the C-path-connectedness part is a variant of a lemma by Nehring (2003); for instance $xPy \vdash_C^* xPz$ because $\{xPy, yPz\} \vdash_C xPz$ (where x, y, $z \in K$ are pairwise distinct). In parts (a) and (b), minimal C-connectedness holds since any cycle $Y = \{xPy, yPz, zPx\} \subseteq X$ defines a minimal C-inconsistent set, which becomes C-consistent by negating two elements. In part (c), minimal C-connectedness holds because any set of type $Y = \{xPy, yPz, \neg xPz\} \subseteq X$ (with x, y, z pairwise distinct) is minimally C-inconsistent and becomes C-consistent by negating any two members.

By this lemma, Theorems 6.1, 6.1a and 6.1b apply to the binary relation agenda for any of the three constraint sets C. This allows the conclusion that it is impossible to aggregate preference relations – whether fully rational or just acyclic – or equivalence relations in a systematic and non-degenerate way, unless we restrict the domain of individual inputs or allow some kind of collective irrationality (such as incomplete collective judgment sets).

By part (a), the stronger impossibility of Theorem 6.2 applies when the constraint set is $C_{\text{fully rational}}$. It is impossible to aggregate fully rational preference relations in an independent, unanimity preserving and non-dictatorial manner, again unless we restrict the domain of individual inputs or allow collective irrationality. The latter is precisely Arrow's famous theorem on the aggregation of preferences (in the case where indifference between distinct options is excluded).

In conclusion, the present approach allows us to derive a large number of general results on aggregation problems with various constraints in a simple unified framework. An interesting question for future research is how the results are affected when different constraints are imposed at individual and collective levels, for example, when the constraints on collective judgments are weaker than those on individual ones or vice versa.

Notes

1   Formally, $\vdash \subseteq P(\mathbf{L}) \times \mathbf{L}$, where $P(\mathbf{L})$ is the power set of $\mathbf{L}$.
2   Alternatively we may assume three conditions on the consistency notion (jointly equivalent to L1–L3): (C1) All sets $\{p, \neg p\} \subseteq \mathbf{L}$ are inconsistent; (C2) subsets of consistent sets $S \subseteq \mathbf{L}$ are consistent; (C3) L3 holds. In many (non-paraconsistent)

logics, the notion of entailment is uniquely determined by that of consistency (via $A \vdash p \Leftrightarrow [A \cup \{\neg p\}$ is inconsistent]), so that the two notions are interdefinable. If we restrict attention to logics with interdefinabiity, or if we are ultimately interested only in whether judgments are consistent (not in whether they are deductively closed), we can use the system of consistent sets rather than the relation $\vdash$ as the primitive logical notion (and assume C1–C3). For details see Dietrich (2007).

3   Strictly speaking, when we use the symbol $\neg$ hereafter, we mean a modified negation symbol $\sim$, where $\sim p := \neg p$ if p is unnegated and $\sim p := q$ if $p = \neg q$ for some q. This convention is to ensure that $p \in X$ implies $\neg p \in X$.

4   On subjunctive implications in judgment aggregation, see Dietrich (forthcoming); on modal operators for representing legal prescriptions, see List (2006) and Dietrich (2007).

5   More precisely, an oligarchy F is defined by $F(A_1, \ldots, A_n) = \cap_{i \in M} A_i$ for all profiles $(A_1, \ldots, A_n)$ in the universal C-domain (as defined below), where $M \subseteq N$ is a fixed non-empty set of 'oligarchs'. Oligarchies generate C-consistent and C-deductively closed (but usually incomplete) collective judgment sets, as the intersection of C-consistent and C-deductively closed sets is C-consistent and C-deductively closed. To avoid dictatorship, there must be at least two oligarchs; if all individuals are oligarchs, F is unanimity rule, an anonymous rule with considerable collective incompleteness.

6   This clause is for finite X equivalent to a C-relativized version of Dokow and Holzman's (2005) *non-affineness* condition: the set of admissible yes/no views on the propositions in X (corresponding to C-consistent and complete judgment sets on X) is a non-affine subset of $\{0,1\}^X$.

7   If X is not minimally C-connected, there exists an aggregation function that satisfies universal C-domain, collective C-rationality and systematicity and is not a (possibly inverse) dictatorship. Let M be a subset of $\{1, \ldots, n\}$ of odd size at least 3. If part (i) of minimal C-connectedness is violated, then majority voting among the individuals in M satisfies all requirements. If part (ii) is violated, the aggregation rule F with universal C-domain defined by $F(A_1, \ldots, A_n) := \{p \in X$: the number of individuals $i \in M$ with $p \in A_i$ is odd$\}$ satisfies all requirements. The second example is based on Dokow and Holzman (2005).

8   The relationship between C-path-connectedness and total blockedness arises when $C = \varnothing$. For a compact logic, $\varnothing$-path-connectedness is equivalent to total blockedness; generally $\varnothing$-path-connectedness is weaker than total blockedness.

9   For non-paraconsistent logics, in the sense of L4 in Dietrich (2007), $\{p, \neg p\} \cup Y$ is C-inconsistent if and only if $\{p\} \cup Y \vdash_C q$.

10   Dokow and Holzman restrict the agenda to be finite (with only contingent propositions) and for this case show the tightness of the agenda assumptions (if $n \geq 3$).

11   In the definitions of minimal and strong C-connectedness, (i) and (ii) can be weakened, namely to the C-relativized versions of the conditions (i*) and (ii*) given in Dietrich (2007). All theorems presented survive the weakening, and the agenda assumptions of Theorems 6.1, 6.1a and 6.1b become right even for infinite X in a non-compact logic (again provided that X contains a contingent proposition and $n \geq 3$). The weakened conditions become equivalent to the original ones for finite X or a compact logic.

12   For technical reasons, the constraint set also contains, for each pair of distinct constants x, y, the condition $\neg x = y$.

13   Transitivity and connectedness are as defined above. Reflexivity can be stated by the proposition $(\forall v)(vPv)$. For aesthetic reasons, one might also replace the predicate symbol P by R in the logic.

14   Again, the constraint set also contains, for each pair of distinct constants x, y, the condition $\neg x = y$.

15   Again, the constraint set also contains, for each pair of distinct constants x, y, the condition $\neg x = y$.

References

Dietrich, F. (2006) 'Judgment aggregation: (im)possibility theorems', *Journal of Economic Theory*, 126: 286–98.

Dietrich, F. (2007) 'A generalised model of judgment aggregation', *Social Choice and Welfare*, 28(4): 529–565.

—— (forthcoming) 'The possibility of judgment aggregation on agendas with subjunctive implications', *Journal of Economic Theory*.

Dietrich, F. and List, C. (2007a) 'Arrow's theorem in judgment aggregation', *Social Choice and Welfare*, 29: 19–33.

—— (2007b) 'Judgment aggregation with consistency alone', working paper, London School of Economics.

—— (forthcoming) 'Judgment aggregation without full rationality,' *Social Choice and Welfare*.

Dokow, E. and Holzman, R. (2005) 'Aggregation of binary evaluations', working paper, Technion Israel Institute of Technology.

—— (2006) 'Aggregation of binary evaluations with abstentions', working paper, Technion Israel Institute of Technology.

Konieczny, S. and Pino-Perez, R. (2002) 'Merging information under constraints: a logical framework', *Journal of Logic and Computation*, 12: 773–808.

Kornhausser, L.A. and Sager L.G. (1986) 'Unpacking the court', *Yale Law Review*, 96: 82–117.

List, C. (2004–7) 'Judgment aggregation: a bibliography on the discursive dilemma, doctrinal paradox and decisions on multiple propositions'. Available at http://personal.lse.ac.uk/list/.

—— (2006) 'Republican freedom and the rule of law', *Politics, Philosophy and Economics*, 5(2): 201–220.

List, C. and Pettit, P. (2002) 'Aggregating sets of judgments: an impossibility result', *Economics and Philosophy*, 18: 89–110.

—— (2004) 'Aggregating sets of judgments: two impossibility results compared', *Synthese*, 140: 207–235.

Nehring, K. (2003) 'Arrow's theorem as a corollary', *Economics Letters*, 80: 379–82.

Nehring, K. and Puppe, C. (2002) 'Strategy proof social choice on single-peaked domains: possibility, impossibility and the space between', working paper, University of California at Davis.

—— (forthcoming) 'Consistent judgment aggregation: the truth-functional case', *Social Choice and Welfare*.

Pauly, M. and van Hees, M. (2006) 'Logical constraints on judgment aggregation', *Journal of Philosophical Logic*, 35: 569–85.

7 Rationality and the legal order

Gerald Pech

Introduction

Legal order and rational choice

In this chapter I am concerned with the rational design of a legal system. This problem has been analyzed on a number of analytical levels: social choice theory asks how an assignment of rights can be achieved that is consistent with axioms such as liberty and Pareto-optimality (Sen 1970).[1] Whereas Sen provided an impossibility result, it has since been shown that under a more extensive definition of rights his result can be substantially weakened (van Hees 1999). But more obvious problems remain: sufficiently extensive assignments of rights lack co-possibility and, therefore, it is not obvious how one would choose between different assignment of rights, given that each assignment is Pareto-optimal.

Normative constitutional economics seeks to answer the latter question. In an appropriately constructed hypothetical decision-making situation and given certain restrictions on preferences a society, may be able to unanimously agree on a range of otherwise contentious issues (Harsanyi 1955; Rawls 1971; Buchanan 1975). By making specific assumptions one may arrive at specific constitutional rules. For example, if citizens are concerned about suffering exploitation at the hands of their rulers they may be able to agree on constitutional constraints on the power to tax (Brennan and Buchanan 1980). Positive constitutional economics, on the other hand, is concerned with the way constitutional rules affect choices and which choices over constitutional rules are actually made.[2]

This chapter develops a positive analysis of the legal system founded in the constitution. I am interested in the incentives for the rulers that the legal system provides. In his constructive approach, Gersbach (2005) develops constitutional mechanisms to overcome asymmetric information problems found in the democratic process. What I am looking for are mechanisms ensuring the self-enforceability of the legal system. In analogy to Weingast's (1997, 2005) analysis of self-enforceable constitutions, self-enforceability of the legal order is understood as its stability in the view of possible transgressions by the ruler of the state. If citizens are concerned about transgressions by their rulers against the legal order, then in the spirit of the constitutional economics tradition, it can be argued that self-enforceability is in itself normatively desirable.

Self-enforceability of the constitution

Self-enforceability constraints in private contracts have been extensively analyzed. It makes sense to take account of such a constraint when there are limits to the legal enforceability of a contract.[3] But if anything, such issues are more pressing when the social contract is concerned (see, for example, Merville and Osborne 1990). A contract that sets up a government also assigns it the means to force others to comply, and there is no outside enforcer who forces the government to play by the rules. Even unseating it in elections or its compliance with court decisions needs at least some sort of consent on the side of the government. Once a ruler has decided to abandon constitutional rule, such checks and balances often pose very little real obstacle. So the public is ultimately left with revolution as a disciplinary device of last resort. This is a rather costly enforcement mechanism.[4] A constitutional contract might, however, be self-enforcing if the following holds: given the consequences (legal or other) that unfold after a violation of the contract by one party, each party to the contract at any point in time wants to abide by the contract. And, where a consequence is threatened in the contract, it is in the interest of the party in charge of bringing about this consequence to actually do so.

The previous literature has treated self-enforceability problems of the social contract either in terms of broad coordination problems within society (Weingast 1997, 2005) or between different societies, one succeeding the other (Kotlikoff, Persson, and Svennson 1988). In a broader context, the question of what a sustainable – or self-enforcing – constitutional contract is is not unlike asking about the sustainable – or time-consistent – inflation rate (Barro and Gordon 1983). In both cases, the asset under consideration – paper money or the constitutional contract – has no obvious intrinsic value. Its value is determined by the actions of political or economic agents in relation to the asset and expectations over those actions. Such actions may take the form of signing contracts that promise payments of money or challenging the actions of the sovereign. If agents interact repeatedly, many equilibria may be sustainable. Weingast (2005) in his analysis of constitutional history shows the importance of historical events in triggering the emergence of behavioral standards and shaping expectations.

Rules generate outcomes and such rules may be supported in dynamic equilibrium in which no party expects to obtain a better outcome if it defects. Lagunoff (2001) shows that this is the case for tolerant legal standards, Dixit, Grossman, and Gul (2000) for the rights of legislative minorities, and Gersbach (2004) for the one person one vote rule. Interdependent institutional arrangements have been analyzed by Bös and Kolmar (2003) for the combination of property rights and redistributive policies and by Gibbons and Rutten (2004) for contract enforcement and public goods. Taking a slightly different route, Barbera and Jackson (2004) analyze voting rules that satisfy the property self-stability, i.e. if a vote is taken over voting rules when applying the voting rule, the same rule is returned as a voting outcome. I agree with this literature on the importance of rules for generating sustainable outcomes. I ask under what circumstances a ruler will accept the constitutional rule book over no rule at all. To do so I view legal rules as elements that in their entirety establish the order of the state (Maddox 1982), which in turn creates certain incentives for the rulers. I focus on a particular rule, the rule of law, and its interaction with property rights. I show that a constitutional rule book containing the rule of law may be self-enforcing in that any potential ruler wants to accept it and in accepting it she makes sure that any defecting ruler gets punished. As a consequence, the rule of law creates incentives for the government not to overturn the allocation of property rights founded in the constitutional order.

The difference between the analysis of isolated rules and the analysis of mechanisms built into the legal system is that the latter approach considers consequences that are intended by the legal order. Consider the following trivial example: a simple rule may state that 'the president is elected by a simple majority of the votes'. A complete mechanism would specify what this person can do when elected but also what happens if a person declares herself president without being elected. Suppose this specification is that her words shall not be obeyed. This mechanism is self-enforcing if it is in the interest of the addressee not to obey and, therefore, no one will seek to declare herself president without being elected.

Main argument and outline of the chapter

The term 'rule of law' is associated with different meanings. It may be understood as non-arbitrariness of legal practice, a set of formal characteristics that the rules of the legal system have to fulfill, or the subordination of administration and legislature to a law possessing higher authority (Phillips and Jackson 1987). In a constitutional system – with the possible exception of the British constitution – the constitution is a law of superior authority that puts limits to what legislation may be adopted. By what I shall call the legality principle under the rule of law, laws have to be legal, that is, in accordance with the constitution and its principles or, even stronger, a political ideal (Hayek 1960: ch. 14). Unconstitutional laws do not bind a government if this government accepts the constitution. A constitutional government, on the other hand, guarantees the constitutional rights of its citizens. So understood, the rule of law is a negative commitment for a constitutional government not to enforce laws that violate constitutional rights of its citizens.

I discuss the consequences of the legality principle under the rule of law in an application to property rights. There is a chain of successive governments, each with an exogenously fixed lifespan. A government may win political support by redistributing property toward its cronies. Only the first government that engages in this activity can gain support by doing so. Otherwise, the government is only interested in its tax revenue. A constitutional successor government is prevented from honoring illegal redistributive measures, and illegitimate property holders expect a reduction in their rewards from investing in the property if the successor government acts under the constitution. So, whenever the tax base reacts negatively to an expected loss of rewards, tax revenue tends to be smaller for an unconstitutional government. Essentially, I solve the problem of the missing enforcer by delegating the enforcement of rule compliance by the government today to its successor government. The choice of whether the future government will act constitutionally or not is, however, for the future government to make. I therefore have to show that it is optimal for the future government to act constitutionally. Under certainty I find that defection and non-defection are equilibria of this game. However, I provide conditions under which the only trembling-hand perfect equilibrium of the game between successive governments and its citizens is that every government chooses to be legitimate with a probability approaching 1. Under trembling-hand perfection no (unconstitutional) government can rule out the possibility that it might be succeeded by a constitutional government. In fact, if the punishment that a constitutional government exercises under the rule of law is sufficiently great, a defecting government will put the greatest possible weight on the possibility that it is succeeded by a constitutional government. As a consequence, if the prize is sufficiently small and the punishment under the rule of law greater than the greatest possible punishment if the government abides by the constitution, each government will abide by the constitution.

There are some assumptions in this chapter, most of which I make to facilitate the exposition. I assume that the government also dominates the legislature, so I do not distinguish between the legislative branch and the administration. Moreover, I do not model political constraints resulting from a re-election objective. The way I set up the problem, the distribution of property rights is historically given together with the constitution. Indeed, for the constitutional order to be self-enforcing under the rule of law mechanism it is necessary that there is only one legitimate constitutional order and that the legality of laws is derived from this order. My focus on a completely deterministic constitution ignores the possibility of constitutional reform. At certain points in history it might well be that a trade-off between (property) rights is considered. For example, when slaves were given liberal rights, this infringed on the property rights of slave owners (Weingast 2005). Although I believe that allowing for constitutional reform would not pose a major problem to my approach, there are clearly important issues arising from the possibility of having competing concepts of a legitimate order. The theory I am developing in this contribution has applications to credibility problems in foreign direct investment (Pech 2007) and to the sustainability of fiscal rules (Neumärker and Pech 2002).

The next section sets up the model. The section after it derives the main results. The succeeding section extends the model in various directions and discusses the results: first discussing the effect of the rule of law understood as non-arbitrariness; second introducing costs in law enforcement; third taking up the issue of competing concepts of legitimacy; and fourth connecting my findings to the discussion of self-governance. The final section concludes.

The model

Constitutional rules

The constitution has two elements.

R1   The property rights of proper owners are guaranteed.
R2   If a property right has been violated, the proper owner has claim to restitution.

Under the rule of law, a government that violates the constitution by expropriating property cannot establish property rights that bind a lawfully acting government.[5] A lawfully acting government, on the other hand, cannot redistribute property when it deems this to be advantageous. However, the government has a choice whether or not to act according to the constitution: during its fixed tenure it has the power to impose even its unlawful acts. So how does the constitution affect the government's decision to act lawfully?

It is important to emphasize the different role of the two constitutional rules: R1 is a positive commitment to obey property rights. But it is well known that with no other provision such a commitment is typically not credible (see, for example, Persson and Tabellini 1990). Credibility problems are particularly severe if the government is short-lived. R2 on the other hand imposes a negative commitment that prevents a lawfully acting government from honoring an unlawful distribution of property rights. A government might be willing to accept the second commitment whereas accepting the first commitment typically involves sacrificing an opportunity to advance its own interest. If some incoming government is expected to accept the constitution including R2 after a period of unlawfulness, this may well affect the utility of an unlawful predecessor government.

As we have pointed out in the introduction, the rule of law requires not only legality of law but also its non-arbitrariness. Non-arbitrariness is sometimes believed to imply that laws should be generally followed. In this view, if the law establishes a right, such as a property right, the positive implication is that it will never be infringed. But in fact, an absolute guarantee of property rights is difficult to achieve. In practice, the boundaries between conflicting claims to property may be blurred. For example, the exact location of the border between adjacent farms may be disputed. The property right of a farmer may be curtailed by a right of way of the owner of a neighboring farm or the wider public but it may be uncertain whether anybody will actually make use of this right of way. In short, in the case of property rights the arguments of Dowding and van Hees (2003) equally apply, that we have to distinguish between a formal right and the degree by which it is exercised. From this perspective, constitutional rule R1 is probably too strong if it is to be applied not only in the relationship between government and citizens but also in those cases where the government adjudicates in conflicts between citizens. The following, weaker formulation, takes account of these arguments:

R1′   The government must not seize property from its proper owner.

The decisive point here is that the government does not try to intentionally redistribute property to itself or other citizens. Although stopping short of establishing an absolute right, R1′ can still be seen as guaranteeing non-arbitrariness in the exercise of government power.

Governments

We assume that the government in period t is interested in tax revenues R_t and that it may seize a prize Δ_t by violating the constitution and undertaking unlawful redistribution. If the government in t defects to the non-constitutional state, indexed by n, its utility is $w_t^n = R_t^n + \Delta_t$. If it stays constitutional, it receives the payoff $w_t^c = R_c^t$. The prize may be seized only by the first government that violates the constitution. That is, $\Delta_t > 0$ after a history of compliance and $\Delta_t = 0$ for any history in which defection has occurred before t. We are thinking of the prize as political support that is bought by distributing confiscated land to the government's clientele. It is quite plausible that the same trick cannot be played by a successor government, even if it does not care about property rights: once land has been distributed to the poor, there are presumably fewer landless people to be bought off and some of the landless people are likely to be the former legitimate owners. A government that wants to redistribute land towards them might as well do it by way of restitution and, thereby, act lawfully.

In order to seize the prize, the government has to expropriate a share of at least $x \geq x^{min}$ of its citizens. By R1′, the latter measure puts the government in violation of the constitution. After an expropriation, a share $x' \geq x^{min}$ of citizens are new (and illegitimate) landowners. The index N designates decision variables of new landowners. A share $(1 - x')$ of citizens are old (and legitimate) landowners. We indicate those by the index L.

If the successor government of an unlawful government chooses to be unconstitutional – in which case it neither seizes a prize nor makes any restitution – the property rights of legitimate owners are enforced with a probability of α^L and the property rights of a land owner that has benefited from seizures by the predecessor government with probability α^N. We assume that a future unconstitutional government acts independently of its unconstitutional predecessor and sets $\alpha^N = \alpha^L = \alpha$. Furthermore, we assume that the unconstitutional government does not change the share of illegitimate ownership that it inherits from its predecessor.[6] We assume that $\alpha \geq 1 - x^{min}$, that is, the redistribution necessary to seize the prize is at least as great as the implicit expropriation rate in the absence of a prize. All expropriation undertaken by a redistributing government results in a restitution claim. A constitutional government enforces property rights of legitimate owners with rate b. We assume that $\beta \geq \alpha$ and, in view of rule R1′, β may be smaller than 1.

Economic sector

Citizens live for two periods. The population is organized in family units or clans. At any given time, each unit consists of an old and a young household. If the family does not possess land, it receives a subsistence income, which we normalize to be zero. If the family possesses land, it passes the land and any obligation connected with the land down the family line. The same goes for the restitution claim of an expropriated family. There is no operative bequest motive but at the beginning of each period the land is transferred to the young household. In return, the old household receives an income transfer within the family from the young household, which depends on the value of the land transferred. This is a stylized version of an arrangement that is not uncommon in agricultural societies.

The young household in period t may undertake a costly effort e_t to improve the quality of the land. The return on land f depends on efforts in the current and previous period, so for the young household the production function is $f(e_t, \bar{e}_{t-1})$. In the beginning of period $t+1$, when the land is transferred, its value is $\delta f(e_t, \bar{e}_{t-1})$. We assume that $\delta f(0, e^*) \geq f(e^*, e^*)$ at the highest stationary value e^* that can be supported in this economy. The government imposes a tax on all output. We define θ as the revenue-maximizing tax rate.[7] θ may be obtained from an underlying tax evasion or production decision.[8] For simplicity, we assume that θ does not vary with the tax base.

Let C_t^1 be the consumption of a household that is young in t, and C_t^2 be the consumption of a household that is old in t. The utility function of a household i that is young in t is $U_t^i = C_t^1 + P^i u(C_{t+1}^2) - v(e_t)$. It discounts its old age utility with the probability P^i that the family still possesses the land in $t+1$. This probability depends on the legal status of the landowner.

We assume that land seizures do not affect the technical conditions of production or the age of owners. As we show in the appendix, an increase in certainty of claims to property P increases effort, i.e. de/dP. In the following we treat an individual's tax base $f(e_i, \bar{e})$ as a choice variable ξ^i. Because ξ^i increases in e^i it corresponds to P^i: if $P^i > P^{i\prime}$ then $\xi^i > \xi^{i\prime}$. By our assumption on the utility function, $\xi^i = \xi(P^i)$. Given θ, government's tax revenue is:

$$ R_t = \theta \left[x' \xi_t^N + (1 - x') \xi_t^L \right] $$

Note that the shift of ownership from a young household that owes inter-generational transfers, to a young household that does not, does not change incentives to exercise effort. Regarding the timing, we suppose that in the beginning of each period the government decides on its constitutional status. Accordingly, it may redistribute land or return land to households holding a restitution claim. Afterwards, any legitimate landowner that possesses land transfers it to the young household of its family. Subsequently, decisions on effort are made.

Results

Let $\pi^c | c_t$ be the probability that a constitutional government follows a constitutional government and $\pi^c | n_t$ the probability that a constitutional government follows an unlawful one. A new landowner's property right is enforced by an unconstitutional government with probability a and by a constitutional government with probability 0. For him or her, the expected return in the second period on the investment[9] is:

$$P^N|n_t = \alpha(1 - \pi^c|n_t) \tag{7.1}$$

An owner who holds on to a legitimate property right under the unlawful regime has a prospect of having the property right honored by a future unconstitutional government with probability α and of a future constitutional government with probability β, so her prospects are:

$$P^L|n_t = \beta\pi^c|n_t + \alpha(1 - \pi^c|n_t) \tag{7.2}$$

Suppose that the prize is positive, i.e. $\Delta_t > 0$. A legitimate landowner under the constitutional regime in t anticipates $(1 - x')$ from an unconstitutional successor government that wants to seize the prize in the subsequent period and β from the constitutional future regime, which gives:

$$P^L|c_t = \beta\pi^c|c_t + (1 - x')(1 - \pi^c|c_t) \tag{7.3}$$

If the prize in t is zero, a legitimate landowner under a constitutional regime expects α from a future unconstitutional government. Therefore, instead of (7.3) we have:

$$P^{L\prime}|c_t = \beta\pi^c|c_t + \alpha(1 - \pi^c|c_t) \tag{7.4}$$

Tax receipts for the constitutional government – with only legitimate landowners – in the current period is:

$$R^c = \theta\xi(P^L|c_t) \tag{7.5}$$

The tax base of the non-constitutional government with a share x' of illegitimate land ownership is:

$$R^n = x'\theta\zeta(P^N|n_t) + (1 - x')\zeta(P^L|n_t) \tag{7.6}$$

Figure 7.1 summarizes the possible game paths that a government in t after a constitutional history can follow and the resulting payoffs. In view of the fact that we are dealing with an infinite succession of self-interested governments it is perhaps unsurprising that few sequences of actions can be ruled out as an equilibrium outcome, even if we focus on subgame perfect equilibria: for a range of parameter constellations a government may defect immediately from the constitution, defection may be delayed or it may not defect at all. In fact, the only type of

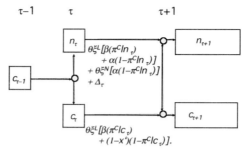

Figure 7.1 Game between subsequent governments and citizens.

equilibrium that we can rule out is one in which a government defects and a subsequent government switches back to the constitutional state. This kind of sequence is ruled out because it is not a Nash equilibrium. If a future government switches back, the previous government would not have wanted to defect. The crucial point why switching back cannot occur along an equilibrium path is that under the rule of law the switching government imposes a punishment on the previous government. For this punishment to be effective, the lowest government income in the constitutional state, $\theta\zeta^{L}(1-x')$, which is obtained if the next government is unconstitutional, has to be lower than income in the non-constitutional state if the switch back occurs. If the switch back occurs, a share of $(1-x')$ landowners expect an enforcement rate of β whereas a share of x' landowners expect an enforcement rate of 0. We focus on such equilibria in which a defecting government selects the lowest expropriation rate, $x'=x^{\min}$. The punishment is effective and the rule of law matters if $\zeta(1-x^{\min})>(1-x^{\min})\zeta(\beta)+x^{\min}\zeta(0)$. If the rule of law matters and the prize is not too high, we can rule out that in equilibrium there is a switch back. For the game, starting in $t=1$ the following proposition holds:

Proposition 7.1. Suppose that a defecting government selects $x'=x^{\min}$. If $\zeta(1-x^{\min})>(1-x^{\min})\zeta(\beta)+x^{\min}\zeta(0)+\theta^{1}\Delta$ only the following paths are compatible with subgame perfect equilibrium in pure strategies: never defect $\{c_s\}^{\infty}_{s=1}$; defect and never switch back $\{n_s\}^{\infty}_{s=1}$ delay and allow a subsequent government to defect $\{c_1, \ldots, c_{\tau-1}, c_{\tau}, n_{\tau+s}\}^{\infty}_{s=1}$.

For the argument made in this chapter it is important to note that, although a switch back cannot occur along an equilibrium path of the overall game, switching back is an equilibrium in the subgame that starts after a previous defection. In fact, the equilibrium strategy configuration supporting the constitutional path involves the t-government not defecting and the $t+1$-government switching back in the event that a defection has taken place in t. The argument I develop in the remainder of the chapter is based on the fact that, if a government cannot rule out that a switch back *may* happen in a case when it actually *does* defect, such an expectation will deter the defection in the first place.[10]

The condition $\xi(1-x^{min}) > (1-x^{min})\xi(\beta) + x^{min}\xi(0)$ under which the rule of law matters may or may not be fulfilled for an economy. For $\beta < 1$, weak concavity of ξ implies the condition. If ξ is convex and $(1-x^{min}) \ll \beta$ it may be violated. On the other hand, concavity is not necessary. In the limiting case $\beta \rightarrow \alpha \rightarrow (1 - x^{min}) < 1$ the rule of law always matters:

Corollary 7.1. Suppose that $\alpha = (1-x^{min}) = \beta$ and that a defecting government selects $x = x^{min}$. If $\Delta < (1-\alpha) [\xi(a) - \xi(0)]$ only the following paths are compatible with subgame perfect equilibrium: never defect $\{c_s\}^{\infty}_{s=1}$; defect and never switch back $\{n_s\}^{\infty}_{s=1}$; delay and allow a subsequent government to defect $\{c_1, \ldots, c_{\tau-1}, c_{\tau}, n_{\tau+s}\}^{\infty}_{s=1}$.

From the corollary it follows that if the constitutional government is free to pick the same enforcement rate α as the unconstitutional government then there is always an expropriation rate x' and a prize which are sufficiently small to satisfy the condition in Proposition 7.1.

The two stationary equilibria of Proposition 7.1 are 'on a knife's edge' in that they rely on an infinite sequence of governments following a policy that accommodates those equilibria. Furthermore, on the constitutional path there are further defections, which themselves can be part of a subgame perfect equilibrium. At the same time, the switch back after some defection is ruled out on the basis of saying that, if this were part of an equilibrium, the government would not have wanted to defect in the first place. If strategies are so sensitive to what future governments are doing, it is sensible to undertake some sensitivity analysis. In the following we construct trembling-hand perfect strategies that are based on the assumption that every strategy in a game is played with at least some small probability e, i.e. we impose the constraint $\pi^c | \bullet \in (\varepsilon, 1-\varepsilon)$.

First, we find that, if the defecting government in t puts positive weight on its successor government playing the constitutional strategy, it decides to defect with the minimal expropriation rate x^{min}.

Lemma 7.1. For all $\varepsilon > 0$, a defecting government wants to select the $x' = x^{min}$.

Proof. Because there is no strategic advantage of selecting a higher x', it suffices to focus on the immediate payoff. Let $\pi^c | n_t = \gamma$. Given γ, a defecting government in τ maximizes its expected payoff $\gamma(1-x')\theta\xi(\beta) + (1-\gamma)\theta\xi(a) + \Delta_\tau$ such that $x' \geq x^{min}$. For all $\gamma > 0$ this expression is maximized when x' is minimized. ∎

In order to construct trembling-hand perfect strategies we can use (7.1)–(7.4) and impose the constraint $\pi^c \in (\varepsilon, 1-\varepsilon)$. Under a condition slightly weaker than $\xi(1-x^{min}) > (1-x^{min})\xi(\beta) + x^{min}\xi(0)$ condition in Proposition 7.1, in the period after a defection the government almost certainly is constitutional. As it cannot rule out that the successor government performs a switch back with positive probability, it is deterred from choosing the non-constitutional state. Going back one stage further, we have to ascertain that a government does not want to defect if it foresees that its successor government almost certainly wants to be constitutional, no matter what happens after it plays constitutional itself. Here, we have to invoke the condition of Proposition 7.1. If this condition holds, there is $\Delta > 0$ such that

$$\Delta_t < \theta[\xi(1-x^{min})-(1-x^{min})\xi(\beta)-x^{min}\xi(0)] \tag{7.7}$$

is fulfilled and it is optimal for the government to act lawfully.

Proposition 7.2. If $\xi(1-x^{min}) > (1-x^{min})\xi(\beta)+x^{min}\xi(0)+\theta^{-1}\Delta_t$ in the unique trembling-hand perfect equilibrium each government almost certainly chooses to be lawful.

Proof. Consider the situation after a defection of the government in τ. For $\pi^c|c_{\tau+1}=n^c|n_{\tau+1}$ it is immediate from using (7.1) and (7.4) in (7.5) and (7.6) that the government in $\tau+1$ wants to be constitutional. The critical case occurs if $\pi^c|n_\tau=1-\epsilon$ and $\pi^c|c_\tau=\epsilon$. For $\epsilon \to 0$ we have $P^{L'}|c_\tau \to \alpha$ and $P^L|n_\tau \to \beta$. Inserting in (7.5) and (7.6) shows that $(1-x^{min})\xi(\beta)<\xi(\alpha)$ is a sufficient condition to have $\tilde{w}_{\tau+1}^c > \tilde{w}_{\tau+1}^n$ in the perturbed game with $\Delta_{\tau+1}=0$ and the government in $\tau+1$ puts the maximum weight on the constitutional strategy.

Now consider the decision to defect in $\tau \geq 1$. Again, the critical case occurs for $\pi^c|c_{\tau\tau}=(1-\epsilon)$. Given that $\pi^c|n_\tau=(1-\epsilon)$ and $\epsilon \to 0$ the condition for the government in τ not to defect is $\xi(1-x^{min}) > (1-x^{min})\xi(\beta)+x^{min}\xi(0)+\theta^{-1}\Delta_\tau$. ∎

Inspection of the conditions in Proposition 7.1 and Proposition 7.2 reveals that all trembling-hand perfect strategies are also subgame perfect as one would expect (Selten 1975). By analogy to Corollary 7.1, we obtain the following corollary of Proposition 7.2:

Corollary 7.2. Suppose that $\alpha=(1-x^{min})=\beta$. If $\Delta_1<(1-\alpha)$ $[\xi(\alpha)-\xi(0)]$ in the only trembling-hand perfect equilibrium all governments are almost certainly constitutional.

From the corollary it follows that, if $\alpha<1$, the constitutional government is free to pick the same enforcement rate as the unconstitutional government, and if the prize and the expropriation rate are sufficiently small, then in the trembling hand perfect equilibrium of the game the rule of law serves as a defense of the constitution. To put this negatively, we may say that, if the prize is great and if the prospect of the government going for the prize creates immense uncertainty, then the rule of law tends to be an insufficient defense of the constitution unless ξ is concave. The rule of law is a good defense, however, if defections by some government involve only minor deviations from the lawful path.

Extensions and discussion

Is generality harmful to stability?

Comparing our results of Propositions 7.1 and 7.2, on the one hand, with Corollaries 7.1 and 7.2, on the other hand, it appears that generality under the rule of law (i.e. a high β) weakens the defense of the constitution. Indeed, the rule of law, and in particular the generality of law, is often seen as a disincentive for the government to act lawfully. In order to make the government deliver general law enforcement, the citizenry needs to have some threat against the government (Weingast 1997). However, one would not expect that, in a model where the driving force is citizens' trust in institutions, the expectation of general law enforcement can impede the emergence of the 'good' institutional state. Closer inspection of the condition reveals that the problem is not the possibility of having a high rate of law enforcement after a switch back (this is the term $(1-x^{min})\theta\xi\,(\beta)$) but the lack of such a high rate of law enforcement after staying constitutional for one period. The latter is expressed in the term $\theta\xi(1-x^{min})$. Unfortunately, we cannot dismiss the possibility that the future government wants to defect even if the present government stays constitutional.

Our conjecture that generality should increase the threshold for defecting from the constitution is probably informed by a focus on stationary solutions. If we focus on the stationary subgame perfect equilibria of the game, the condition for defecting from the constitution is different from the one in Proposition 7.2: a government which believes that a future government will employ the same threshold as itself may not defect if $\Delta < \theta[\xi(\beta)-\xi(\alpha)]$. Of course, it remains an equilibrium that the government defects: a government which considers switching for some $\Delta\_>\Delta'$ and believes that a future government has the same critical level Δ' may rationalize any such defection. All we can say is, given that the 'good' equilibrium prevails, its scope now increases with β for $\beta<1$.

Costly law enforcement

Suppose the enforcement of property rights in state i, $i\in\{c,n\}$ creates a cost $h'(\phi)$, where ϕ is the degree of enforcement.[11] In general, we would expect that a constitutional government finds it less costly to enforce its laws, because professional ethical standards and effects of negative commitment facilitate cooperation of civil servants and the judiciary. For example, bureaucrats or judges might be prepared to resist unconstitutional laws but also have concerns regarding their careers or liberty. Negative commitment mechanisms in the area of disciplinary measures in the public service would be likely to encourage such resistance and impose a cost on government (Pech 2007). In the following we assume, however, that the enforcement cost function is the same for the constitutional and nonconstitutional regimes.

We can define an optimal enforcement level if current revenue R_t depends not only on expected future enforcement but also on current enforcement of property rights, i.e. if we had $R_t(\phi_t,\phi_{t+1})$. So far, we have analyzed only the effect of expectations of future enforcement. Say that a non-constitutional government selects ϕ_t such as to maximize w_t^n and that $\phi_t^n = \alpha$. If the constitution imposes a binding constraint on government behavior, the constitutional government will select $\phi_t^c = \beta > \alpha$. For a constitutional government followed by an infinite sequence of constitutional governments we have $R_t^n = \theta\xi(\alpha,\alpha) - h(\alpha)$ and for a non-constitutional government followed by an infinite sequence of non-constitutional governments we have $R_t^c = \theta\xi(\beta,\beta) - h(\beta)$.[12] In order for our previous results to hold we have to require that $R_t^c \geq R_t^n$ and that the switch back payoff is smaller than the worst outcome under the constitution, i.e. that $\xi(\beta, 1-x^{min}) > (1-x^{min}) \xi(\alpha,\beta) + x^{min}\xi(\alpha,0)$. We should stress here that each unconstitutional government maximizes only its own welfare when employing its instruments. Under positive commitment, constitutional governments may reach higher revenue along the constitutional path.

Singularity of the constitutional contract

We have essentially assumed that the constitution has arbitrarily assigned some property rights and backed them up with the force of constitutional law. Nevertheless, it is crucial for our argument that the constitutional contract is not replaceable by anything else which induces legality of laws. If this were the case, arbitrary paths could be supported in an equilibrium. Therefore, it is necessary for our results that only one type of constitutional arrangement is conceivable. This is the case if the constitution is shaped by generally held ethical beliefs and if there is no obvious alternative order with which those beliefs are compatible. This dependency on ethical beliefs also seems to open the way for constitutional adjustments and a theory of constitutional evolution as the consensus on what is desirable changes. This also includes the development of the constitutional order, which is undertaken by the constitutional courts and, to the extent that this ensures continuing legitimacy of the constitutional order, this seems to be an entirely positive thing.

Our result that the constitution has to be a singular document strengthens a point made by Hayek:

> The rule of law is therefore not a rule of the law, but a but a rule concerning what the law ought to be, a meta-legal doctrine or a political ideal. It will be effective only to the extent that the legislator feels bound by it. In a democracy this means that it will not prevail unless it forms part of the moral traditions of the community, a common ideal shared and unquestionably accepted by the majority.
>
> (Hayek 1960: 121)

Legality of norms derived from the constitution versus legitimacy via self-governance

The findings of this chapter shed some new light on a long-standing debate in constitutional theory (Kahn 1992): if the source of legitimacy is self-governance, then, so one argument runs, there is no reason why a historic document should in any way constrain the choices a society makes to settle issues among its citizens. The new perspective that our theory offers is this: deriving decisions via a historically established process according to pre-defined notions about what is in accordance with the constitution may prevent the party empowered by the social contract from abusing its position. Under the conditions presented in this chapter we can delegate to the future government the task of forcing the present-day government to abide by the constitution. This, however, can only work if each government knows that the decisions of its successor government will be guided by the historically given constitution. Only such a document can specify the legality or illegality of the present-day government's actions and deprive an illegal act of its appearance of legitimacy – which it would otherwise have just because it is carried out by an entity called government.[13] One can easily see that, in the absence of such a document, not only could the present-day society freely redistribute property, which one might argue it should when using some process considered legitimate on other grounds, but what the government as the empowered agent could be tempted to do is to redistribute property without relying on any other process than the exercise of its might.

Conclusion

This chapter presents some first steps on the way to a theory of self-enforcing legal order. We have shown that the negative commitment of a constitutional government not to enforce illegal laws, which follows from the rule of law, is a powerful device in preventing violations of the constitutional order. We have analyzed the illegal redistribution of property rights under a constitution that prevents a constitutional successor government from honoring such illegitimate property rights. The rule of law may deter defections from the constitution if the government and the private sector believe that a switch back to the constitution will eventually take place and the tax base – which in part is provided by illegitimate landowners – reacts negatively to the expectation of a switch back. In that case the government will resist the temptation of defecting from the constitution if the political prize it secures by doing so is not too high. We have shown that the rule of law matters if either the tax base is concave in the probability of enforcement of property rights or for a defecting government the necessary expropriation rate is sufficiently small. Together with the observation that the expectation of compliance with the constitution by future governments strengthens the incentive effect of the rule of law we may conclude that the stabilizing properties of the rule of law unfold in particular in a conservative environment in which a government considers only small deviations from the constitutional order. If the rule of law matters, in the only trembling-hand perfect equilibrium of the game the government following upon a defecting government is constitutional with a probability approaching 1.

Appendix 7A: The household's optimization problem

The young household's problem is:

$$\max U_t = C_t^1 + Pu(C_{t+1}^2) - v(e_t) \quad \text{such that}$$
$$C_t^1 = (1-\theta)f(e_t, \overline{e}_{t-1}) - \overline{C}_{t-1}^2$$
$$C_{t+1}^2 = (1-\theta)\delta f(e_t, \overline{e}_{t-1})$$

The physical constraint $e_t \leq e^{max}$ is assumed to be non-binding. Standard assumptions ($v' > 0$, $v'' > 0$, $f' > 0$, $f'' < 0$, $u' > 0$, $u'' < 0$) apply. The first-order condition for this problem is:

$$\frac{\partial U_t}{\partial e_t} = \overline{f} + P\delta u'f - (1-\theta)^{-1}v' = 0$$

Totally differentiating this expression gives $de/dP = -f'\delta u'A^{-1}$ with $A = f''(1 + P\delta u') + (f')^2 P\delta^2 u'' - (1-\theta)^{-1}v''$. Using standard assumptions, $A < 0$ and $de/dP > 0$ as desired.

Appendix 7B: Proof of Proposition 7.1

Let $\sigma_t | h_{t-1}$ be the strategy of the government in t dependent on the history up to $t-1$ and let $w_t(\sigma_t | h_{t-1})$ be the utility of that government. A history is a vector $h_{t-1} = \{\hat{\sigma}_0, \hat{\sigma}_1, \dots \hat{\sigma}_{t-1}\}$ where $\hat{\sigma}_k \in \{n_k, c_k\}$ are strategy choices of the government in period k. We assume that $h_0 = \{c_0\}$.

$\xi_{t_j} | h_t$ is the strategy for a type j citizen. We assume that the history h_t contains only strategy choices of the government. Such an assumption appears appropriate because we have a chain of single period games in which each government is matched with a cohort of citizens who invest during its reign. We can, therefore, use the concept of subgame perfect Nash equilibrium for solving this game. It is well known that, if strategies depend on a history of the game which includes decisions of the private sector, the appropriate concept is that of sequentially rational Nash equilibrium (Persson and Tabellini 1990).

Show that $\{cs\}_{s=1}^{\infty}$ is compatible with equilibrium. Let $h_{\tau-1} = \{c_0, \dots, c_{\tau-1}\}$. Suppose that $\sigma_{\tau+1}$ specifies $\sigma | \{c_\tau, h_{\tau-1}\} = c_{\tau+1}$, $\sigma | \{n_\tau, h_{\tau-1}\} = c_{\tau+1}$. Then $\sigma | h_{\tau-1} = c_\tau$ is an equilibrium strategy: citizens' equilibrium choices are $\xi^L(c_\tau) = \xi^L(n_\tau) > \xi^N(n_\tau)$. Therefore, for $x' > 0$: $R_\tau^c > R_\tau^n$ and $w_\tau^c > w_\tau^n$. $\sigma_{\tau+1}$ is a best response if the same strategy (always play constitutional) is played in $\tau + 2$ and, therefore, is an equilibrium strategy.

Suppose now instead that $\sigma_{\tau+1}$ specifies $\sigma | \{c_\tau, h_{\tau-1}\} = n_{\tau+1}$, $\sigma | \{n_\tau, h_{\tau-1}\} = n_{\tau+1}$. This gives $\xi^L(n_\tau) = \xi^N(n_\tau) \geq \xi^L(c_\tau)$. Therefore, $R_\tau^n \geq R_\tau^c$ and $w_\tau^n \geq w_\tau^c$ so $\sigma | h_{\tau-1} = n_\tau$ is an equilibrium strategy. $\sigma_{\tau+1}$ is a best response if the same strategy (always play unconstitutional) is played in $\tau + 2$ and, therefore, is an equilibrium strategy. Consequently, $\{n_s\}_{s=1}^{\infty}$ is compatible with equilibrium.

We have to show that, under the condition given in the preposition, it does not occur along an equilibrium path of play that some government plays n_t for $t>0$ given h_0 and a subsequent government, at $t'>t$, plays $c_{t'}'$. Say a strategy $\sigma_{\tau+1}$ specifies $\sigma|\{n_\tau, h_{\tau-1}\}=c_{\tau+1}$. The payoff in n_τ is $(1-x^{min})\theta\xi(\beta)+x^{min}\theta\xi(0)+\Delta_\tau$. On the constitutional path,

$$\min_{\sigma|\{n_\tau,h_{\tau-1}\}} w_\tau^c = \xi(1-x^{min}) > w_\tau^n$$

and the government in τ plays $\sigma|h_{\tau-1}=c_\tau$ if $\sigma|\{n_\tau, h_{\tau-1}\}=c_{\tau+1}$. The argument does not depend on $c_{\tau-1}\in h_{\tau-1}$ so it holds for all histories $h'_{\tau-1}$.

Under the same condition whereby a switch back is not an equilibrium, delaying defection is an equilibrium. Say a strategy $\sigma_{\tau+1}$ specifies $\sigma|\{c_\tau, h_{\tau-1}\}=n_{\tau+1}$ and $\sigma|\{n_\tau, h_{\tau-1}\}=c_{\tau+1}$. The condition that delaying in τ is optimal is $\xi(1-x^{min})>(1-x^{min})$ $\xi(\beta)+x^{min}\xi(0)+\theta^{-1}\Delta_\tau$. Defecting in $\tau+1$ is an equilibrium if the continuation strategies prescribe $\sigma|\{c_{\tau+}, h_\tau\}=n_{\tau+2}$ and $\sigma|\{n_{\tau+1}, h_\tau\}=n_{\tau+2}$, which are equilibrium strategies as shown above. Therefore, $\{c_1, ..., c_{\tau-1}, c_\tau, n_{\tau+s}\}_{s=1}^\infty$ is compatible with equilibrium.

Notes

1 For a treatment of legal norms along these lines see van Hees (2000).
2 See Voigt (1997) for an overview. Aghion, Alesina and Trebi (2004) compare the importance of normative versus positive factors for explaining the formation of constitutional rules.
3 See, for example, Thomas and Worrall (1988) on collective wage agreements and Thomas and Worrall (1994) on foreign direct investment.
4 See Acemoglu and Robinson (2006) and Filipovich and Sempere (2006) on institutional stability supported by the threat of revolution or counterrevolution.
5 One example is the expropriation of property by the government of the German Democratic Republic.
6 For a succession of unconstitutional governments, not differentiating between L and N is an equilibrium policy. If a government anticipates a constitutional successor and wants to increase the share of legitimate owners it chooses to be constitutional itself.
7 As all income is immediately consumed, income and consumption tax are equivalent in this economy. We have to assume that expropriation is not a perfect substitute for tax, which is quite plausible as government would find it difficult to turn a non-negligible amount of seized property into money.
8 For details see below.
9 A constitutional government might grant the new landowner some compensation for his or her expenses if he or she can claim to have acted in good faith. It will not, however, grant the full market value of the return on the investment, which is sufficient for our argument to hold.
10 Neumärker and Pech (2002) construct an incomplete information game in which a switch back may occur and a government anticipating this event is deterred from defecting from the constitution.
11 ϕ may be interpreted as the provision of law and order but may as well be the tax recovery rate $\phi=1-\theta$ with h the revenue loss due to tax avoidance.
12 On conditions for the existence of equilibria for a similar class of games see Leininger (1986).

13 In fact, this argument is far from theoretical. Many states have to carry the burden of external debt accumulated by former governments whose only legitimacy resulted from their position of power.

References

Acemoglu, D. and Robinson, J. A. (2006) *Economic Origins of Dictatorship and Democracy*, Cambridge: Cambridge University Press.
Aghion, P., Alesina, A., and Trebi, F. (2004) 'Endogenous political institutions', *Quarterly Journal of Economics*, 119: 565–611.
Barbera, S. and Jackson, M. O. (2004) 'Choosing how to choose: self-stable majority rules and constitutions', *Quarterly Journal of Economics*, 119: 1011–1048.
Barro, R. J. and Gordon, D. B. (1983) 'Rules, discretion, and reputation in a model of monetary policy', *Journal of Monetary Economics*, 14: 101–121.
Bös, D. and Kolmar, M. (2003) 'Anarchy, efficiency, and redistribution', *Journal of Public Economics*, 87: 2431–2457.
Brennan, G. and Buchanan, J. M. (1980) *The Power to Tax*, Cambridge: Cambridge University Press.
Buchanan, J. M. (1975) *The Limits of Liberty*, Chicago: University of Chicago Press.
Dixit, A., Grossman, G. M., and Gul, F. (2000) 'The dynamics of political compromise', *Journal of Political Economy*, 108: 531–568.
Dowding, K. and van Hees, M. (2003) 'The construction of rights', *American Political Science Review*, 97: 281–293.
Filipovich, D. and Sempere, J. (2006) 'Constitutions as self-enforcing redistributive schemes', mimeo, El Colegio de México.
Gersbach, H. (2004) 'Why one person one vote?', *Social Choice and Welfare*, 23: 449–464.
—— (2005) *Designing Democracy: Ideas for Better Rules*, Berlin: Springer.
Gibbons, R. and Rutten, A. (2004) 'Institutional interactions: an equilibrium approach to the state and civil society', working paper.
Harsanyi, J. (1955) 'Cardinal welfare, individualistic ethics, and interpersonal comparisons of utility', *Journal of Political Economy*, 61: 309–321.
Hayek, F. A. (1960) *The Constitution of Liberty*, Chicago: University of Chicago Press.
Kahn, P. W. (1992) *Legitimacy and History*, New Haven, CT: Yale University Press.
Kotlikoff, L. L., Persson, T. and Svennson, L. E. O. (1988) 'Social contracts as assets: a possible solution to the time-consistency problem', *American Economic Review*, 78: 662–677.
Lagunoff, R. (2001) 'A theory of constitutional standards and civil liberty', *Review of Economic Studies*, 68: 109–132.
Leininger, W. (1986) 'Altruism and perfect equilibria', *Review of Economic Studies*, 53: 349–367.
Maddox, G. (1982) 'A note on the meaning of "constitution"', *American Political Science Review*, 76: 805–809.
Merville, L. J. and Osborne, D. K. (1990) 'Constitutional democracy and the theory of agency', *Constitutional Political Economy*, 1: 21–47.
Neumärker, K. J. B. and Pech, G. (2002) 'The rule of law and the sustainability of the fiscal constitution', CRIEFF working paper, University of St Andrews.
Pech, G. (2007) 'Legal constraints and the credibility of policies towards foreign direct investment', mimeo.

Persson, T. and Tabellini, G. (1990) *Macroeconomic Policy, Credibility and Politics*, Chur, Switzerland: Harwood.

Phillips, O. H. and Jackson, P. (1987) *O. Hood Phillips' Constitutional and Administrative Law*, 7th edn, London: Sweet and Maxwell.

Rawls, J. (1971) *A Theory of Justice*, Oxford: Oxford University Press.

Selten, R. (1975) 'Reexamination of the perfectness concept for equilibrium points in extensive games', *International Journal of Game Theory*, 4: 25–55.

Sen, A. K. (1970) 'The impossibility of a Paretian liberal', *Journal of Political Economy*, 78: 217–245.

Thomas, J. and Worrall, T. (1988) 'Self-enforcing wage contracts', *Review of Economic Studies*, 54: 541–554.

—— (1994) 'Foreign direct investment and the risk of expropriation', *Review of Economic Studies*, 61: 81–108.

Van Hees, M. (1999) 'Liberalism, efficiency, and stability: some possibility results', *Journal of Economic Theory*, 88: 294–309.

—— (2000) *Legal Reductionism and Freedom*, Dordrecht: Kluwer Academic Publishers.

Voigt, S. (1997) 'Positive constitutional economics: a survey', *Public Choice*, 90: 11–53.

Weingast, B. (1997) 'The political foundations of democracy and the rule of law', *American Political Science Review*, 91: 245–263.

—— (2005) 'The constitutional dilemma of economic liberty', *Journal of Economic Perspectives*, 19: 89–108.

Part III

Philosophical aspects of normative social choice

8 Distributing causal responsibility in collectivities[1]

Matthew Braham and Manfred J. Holler

Introduction

For a wide range of moral and legal theories, fixing responsibility on a person for some state of the world consists of an answer to two logically distinct questions:

1 *Causal responsibility.* Is it true that the person's actions contributed to the occurrence of that state of the world?
2 *Volitional responsibility.* Are the person's actions performed in ignorance or under compulsion?

This chapter is concerned *exclusively* with the first question for situations in which states of the world are brought about not by individuals as such but by a collection of individuals. That is, what we are interested in here is merely the basis for factual judgments about the connection of a person to a certain state of affairs that is a consequence of joint decisions and actions of the individual members of a collectivity,[2] and *not* with the epistemological and metaphysical issues of determining whether, for instance, a person knew, or could have known, of the consequences of their action; or if the person acted freely or under compulsion. Nor will we be concerned with the normative issue of determining the grounds for saying that a contribution to a collective action is sufficiently significant to warrant credit or blame for the outcome that the collectivity brought about. We denote this bare judgment of a factual connection between a person's actions and a state of the world as 'causal responsibility'.[3]

That there is an unsolved difficulty in ascribing causal responsibility in collectivities is well known. It is what Thompson (1980), in his analysis of the moral responsibility of public officials has called the 'problem of many hands': 'Because many different officials contribute in many ways to decisions and policies of government, it is difficult even in principle to identify who is morally responsible for political outcomes' (ibid.: 905). Or as Ladd (1970: 513) metaphorically put it: 'The efforts of individuals in organizations are like strands in a rope; together they make up the rope, although any particular strand is dispensable. That is why the activities of the individual are simply lost in the complex social process.'

The same phenomenon has been denoted by Hardin (1988) as the 'responsibility paradox'.

There are many germane examples of the 'many hands problem' in the philosophical and legal literature. Feinberg (1968), for instance, discusses the case of Jesse James's train robbery in which an armed man holds up a car full of passengers. If the passengers had risen up as one and rushed at the robber, one or two of them would have perhaps been shot, but collectively they would have overwhelmed him and saved their own and others' property. Feinberg asks to what extent are any of the passengers responsible for the loss of their property given that none alone could have prevented Jesse James walking off with it? Hardin (1988: 156–157) discusses a similar case in which a driver gets his car stuck in the snow and it requires four people to push it out, but the more than four people standing at the bus stop watching the incident do not help him. Hardin asks in what way each of the people standing around is responsible for the car remaining in the snow.

A more convincing case concerns the group of managers and engineers at McDonnell Douglas who knew of the design faults in early DC-10s that led to these planes dropping out of the sky in the 1970s but nevertheless allowed these planes to, fatally, go into service. As it turned out, no single individual could be declared as having been directly responsible for the harm that occurred. Other examples are the My Lai and Sebrenica massacres, or the collapse of the Bank of Credit and Commerce International (BCCI) that greatly dented international confidence in the British banking system. The list is endless.[4]

The aim of this chapter is as follows. We argue that the conventional way of ascribing causal responsibility is inappropriate when it comes to collective action. That is, insofar as the many hands problem exists in terms of identifying causal contributions to collective actions it does so only on account of a deeply rooted and pervasive conception of social causality. That conception is the one that tries to locate at least one person who can be said to have independently and with his or her 'own hands' created and implemented the collective outcome. It is the conception of 'cause' as 'authorship'. In the technical language that we will introduce, such a conception is that of 'strong necessity' or the application of the canonical counterfactual 'but for test'. In legal terminology it is the concept of cause as *sine qua non* – 'making a difference'. There is, however, an alternative conception of cause, that of 'weak necessity/strong sufficiency' that can be found in the philosophical and legal literature, which goes by the acronym of NESS (*n*ecessary *e*lement of a *s*ufficient *s*et) or INUS (*i*nsufficient but *n*ecessary part of a condition which is itself *u*nnecessary but *s*ufficient for the result). This is a weaker conception that embeds the 'but-for' test in a set theoretic framework. We argue that, given that (i) the 'many hands problem' is really nothing else but a case of causal over-determination, and (ii) the INUS/NESS conception was designed precisely for the case of causal over-determination, it is more appropriate to apply this conception of cause than the more conventional 'but-for' conception when trying to identify causal responsibility in collectivities. Inasmuch as the 'many hands problem' concerns the identification of causal contributions, the NESS/INUS conception of cause defuses the problem.

Although composing an answer to this ascription problem is clearly of fundamental theoretical and practical import – especially for liberals – because it is at the very root of individual accountability in public life, little effort has been devoted to meeting it head on. As far as we can ascertain, with the exception of French's short chapter in his book *Collective and Corporate Responsibility* (1984), the literature on responsibility in collectivities generally assumes the 'many hands problem' as *prima facie* true (which it is, given the conventional concept of causation) and then looks for a way to circumvent the problem via the concept of *collective responsibility*.[5] This is the idea that the collectivity per se should be charged with causal responsibility (and possibly other forms of responsibility), and if any form of responsibility is to descend to its members then it is by dint of association ('mere membership') or some other reason such as being a beneficiary of the outcome that the collectivity brought about.

It does not take much to recognize that that circumventing the 'many hands problem' via the concept of collective responsibility is only to jump out of the logical pan and into the conceptual fire because the concept itself is wrought with taxing metaphysical and ethical problems of its own. The hypostatization of groups is anything but straightforward and the problem of the 'membership' or 'benefits' criteria is that, as Lewis (1948) observed quite some time ago, this form of collective responsibility implicates each of us in one another's actions so that praise and blame will then fall upon us all without discrimination. This makes it very hard to maintain that there are any properly moral distinctions to be drawn between one course of action and another.[6]

Finding a general method for determining the specific and distinctive connections between a member of a collectivity and an outcome that a collectivity brought about obviously greatly simplifies matters, particularly in cases where there are reasons to hand out punishment or demand remedial action. In such cases we may have good reason to avoid calling the innocent to account.

Causal relations

To untangle the factual judgments about whether or not a certain individual's actions (which include decisions) were causally connected to the occurrence of a certain state of the world we need to recap the basics of causation.[7] A 'cause' is a relation between events, processes or entities in the same time series, in which one event, process or entity C has the efficacy to produce or be part of the production, of another, the effect x, i.e. C is a condition for x. Arguments among philosophers and legal theorists about what actually constitutes this efficacy are often concerned with whether or not the efficacy is a *necessity* or *sufficiency* requirement.

There are three senses for each of these. Starting with necessity, in descending order of stringency:

Strict necessity C is necessary for the occurrence of x whenever x occurs.

Strong necessity   C was necessary for *x* on the particular occasion.

Weak necessity   C was a necessary element of some set of existing conditions that was sufficient for the occurrence of *x*.

For sufficiency:

Strict sufficiency   C is sufficient by itself for the occurrence of *x*.

Strong sufficiency   C was a necessary element of some set of existing conditions that was sufficient for the occurrence of *x*.

Weak sufficiency   C was an element of some set of existing conditions that was sufficient for the occurrence of *x*.

There are three remarks to be made here. First, it is obvious that we can instantly dispense with the concept of weak sufficiency for the simple reason that it is trivially satisfied by *any* condition C by simply adding C to an already existing set of conditions that is sufficient for *x*, although C is totally irrelevant as regards *x*. That is, weak sufficiency can fail to satisfy the simple counterfactual test of efficacy known as the 'but-for' test in a very unacceptable way. According to this test, C was a cause of some result *x* only if *but for* the occurrence of C, then *x* would not have occurred. Suppose, for example, a house burns down and evidence is found that there was a short-circuit, there was flammable material nearby, there was no automated and efficient water sprinkler, and all three conditions together are sufficient for the house burning down. Now add the fact that there is also evidence that a Bob Dylan CD was in an unplugged CD player in the house. In absence of some empirically ascertainable laws of nature that govern the spontaneous combustion of unplugged CD players with a Bob Dylan CD loaded in the deck, it is entirely unreasonable that the CD player with the Bob Dylan CD should qualify as having causal status for the fire.

Second, there is no question that if C is strictly necessary for *x* then C should be ascribed causal status for *x*; and if C is strongly necessary for *x* then C should also be ascribed causal status for *x*. In both cases C obviously satisfies the 'but-for' test. Yet strict necessity is inadequate to cover causal relations in general because it will often not be fulfilled. It would mean that evidence of an electrical short-circuit that combined with other conditions and resulted in a house burning down would not qualify for causal status given that it is not true that for all instances of a house burning down there must have been an electrical short-circuit. Strict sufficiency is also inadequate because it too may fail to exist: it is rare that a single condition C is sufficient for *x*. Strict sufficiency also rules out ascribing the electrical short-circuit causal status for the house burning down given that it alone cannot lead to the fire; the presence of flammable material etc. is also called for. Moreover, the fact that C may be strictly sufficient for *x* and was present on the occasion of *x*'s occurrence does not imply that C actually caused *x*; *x* may have been brought about by another strictly sufficient condition that was also present on the occasion.[8]

Third, although strong necessity is ostensibly an attractive candidate for ascribing causality, it too can easily crumble in cases of *causal over-determination*. These are those circumstances in which the causes of an event are cumulatively more than sufficient to generate the effect. That is, there exist situations in which a strongly necessary condition will fail to exist. This is the nub of the 'many hands problem'.

Causal over-determination comes in two broad types, which Wright (1985: 1775) has usefully labelled as *duplicative* and *pre-emptive* causation. A case of duplicative causation is one in which two similar and independent causal processes C_1 and C_2, each of which is sufficient for the same effect x, may culminate in x at the same time. It will be best to turn quickly to some examples.

> **Assassination 1.** Assassin$_1$ and Assassin$_2$ independently and simultaneously aim and shoot at Victim such that each shot is sufficient to kill Victim at exactly the same moment.

Clearly, neither assassin was strongly necessary for Victim's death because, ceteris paribus, if either had not fired Victim would have died anyway from the shot fired by the other assassin. Although one could argue that this example is intuitively resolved by saying that a cause is strictly sufficient, strictly necessary or strongly necessary, this will not work for the following case.

> **Assassination 2.** Victim is held up in his car by Assassin$_1$, Assassin$_2$ and Assassin$_3$ who together tie him up and lock him in his car and then push the car over a cliff killing Victim. It is sufficient for Victim's death that only two assassins hold up Victim and push the car over the cliff.

To simplify matters, we need only focus on the pushing of Victim's car over the cliff. Obviously, the pushing of Victim's car by any assassin alone is neither strictly necessary nor strictly sufficient nor strongly necessary for Victim's death. The absence of strict sufficiency and necessity is obvious: no single pushing by an assassin can kill Victim, and no single act of pushing must be performed with the pushing by the other assassins to push Victim's car over the cliff. To determine strong necessity we again apply the simple counterfactual but-for test by holding the pushing by the other assassins constant and ask whether the car would have gone over the cliff killing Victim had the third assassin not been pushing. The answer is obviously affirmative, because it takes the pushing of at least two assassins for this to happen and, since under the circumstances this is true, then the car would have gone over the cliff and killed Victim. Thus, the pushing by the third assassin cannot be attributed as having causal status for Victim's death. The same holds true for the pushing by the other two assassins.

We can now turn to pre-emptive causation. This is the case in which an effect x is brought about by some actual sufficient condition(s) C_1 such that had C_1 not occurred then x would have been brought about by some alternative sufficient condition(s) C_2. There are two subcases of pre-emptive causation:

(i) The alternative set of conditions C_2 emerged after C_1 brought about x.
(ii) The alternative set of conditions C_2 did not emerge because C_1 emerged and brought about x.

The canonical example of type (i) pre-emptive causation is:

> **Assassination 3.** Assassin$_1$ shoots and kills Victim, who is embarking on a trek across the desert, just as Victim was about to take a swig from his water bottle which was poisoned by Assassin$_2$.

Here strong necessity comes to grief given the failure of the but-for test to allocate causal status to either assassin: Assassin$_1$ cannot be said to have caused Victim's death on the occasion in question because, had he not shot and killed Victim, Assassin$_2$'s poisoning would have, given that Victim was just about to take a swig from the water bottle; and Assassin$_2$ cannot be said to have caused Victim's death because it was in fact Assassin$_1$'s shot that did it and not her poisoning of Victim's water.

A type (ii) case is:

> **Assassination.** Assassin$_1$ shoots and kills Victim and Assassin$_2$ decides not to poison Victim's water bottle (but would have had Assassin$_1$ not shot Victim).

Here strong necessity comes to grief because Assassin$_1$ cannot be considered as having caused Victim's death on the occasion in question because, had he not shot and killed Victim, then Assassin$_2$ would have poisoned Victim's water; yet Assassin$_2$ cannot be attributed as causal for Victim's death because she had not in fact poisoned the water; she only would have done if Assassin$_1$ had not shot Victim.

Defusing the 'many hands problem'

From the six criteria that are available for determining what qualifies as a cause we have still to deal with the equivalent criteria of weak necessity and strong sufficiency. These criteria were actually introduced by Hart and Honoré (1959), Mackie (1965, 1974), and Wright (1985, 1988) in various different forms to deal with causal ascriptions when an outcome is a result of a complex of conditions.

The idea behind the weak necessity/strong sufficiency requirement is that, to be ascribed causal status for an event x, a prior event C need not be *the* cause, as in the sense of its being the single sufficient condition present on the occasion, or *a* cause in the senses of strict or strong necessity; it need merely be shown to be a 'causally relevant condition' of x. That is, weak necessity/strong sufficiency drops what can actually be considered a deeply rooted and too narrow presupposition that, to be ascribed causal status for *x*, *C* must be *directly* related to *x* in that *any* state of affairs is brought about by *some* singularly identifiable prior event. This is the idea of 'cause as authorship'. In its place comes a conception of causality that allows for an *indirect* relation between a prior event *C* and its consequence *x*; but – and this is important – the indirect relation still maintains a necessity requirement. This is obtained by combining a sufficiency and necessity requirement in a set-based framework. That is, weak necessity/strong sufficiency means it need not be the case that a *single* condition is sufficient for *x* but that a *set* of conditions be sufficient (strict sufficiency is then the special case of a singleton set) on this occasion and combines this with a necessity requirement in that the members of this set are necessary for the set to be sufficient.

Mackie (1965) denoted a test of weak necessity/strong sufficiency by the acronym INUS, which we defined earlier as 'an *i*nsufficient but *n*ecessary part of a condition which is itself *u*nnecessary but *s*ufficient for the result'. In Wright's (1985, 1988) simpler mnemonic, 'a *n*ecessary *e*lement of a *s*ufficient *s*et' or NESS – a mnemonic that we will use for the rest of this chapter.[9]

We can formally define the NESS criterion as follows. First define a set of events or states of affairs *S* as *minimally sufficient* for *x* if no proper subset of *S* is itself sufficient for *x*. This implies that *S* is the conjunction of conditions each of which is necessary (non-redundant) for *S* to be sufficient (i.e. each of the conjuncts in *S* satisfies the but-for test for the sufficiency of *S*). If *S* is not minimally sufficient it means that it contains events that are not an integral part of any set of actual conditions that is minimally sufficient for *x* and therefore these events could not properly be classified as a cause of *x* because by being redundant they are devoid of any causal efficacy for *x* coming about.

Next, define the set $M = \{S_1, S_2, \ldots, S_n\}$ as the collection of every *minimally sufficient set* (MSC) of conditions for *x*. An event *C* is, then, a NESS for *x* if, and only if, *C* is an element (conjunct) of some S_i. For instance, if *x* can be written as *x* = (*AB* or *CD*) with (*AB* or *CD*) being the necessary and sufficient condition for *x* (either for all instances of *x* or on this particular occasion), then *C* is a NESS for *x* by dint of it being a member of a disjunct, *CD*, which is minimally sufficient for *x* and therefore *C* is to be ascribed causal status for *x* if under the circumstances *D* were present, i.e.:

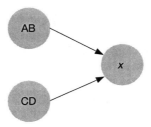

The attractive feature of weak necessity/strong sufficiency is that it is general enough to cover strict and strong necessity and strict sufficiency: (a) if *C* is a member of every S_i for *any* instance of x, then C is strictly necessary for x; (b) if C was a member of every S_i for a given instance of x then C is strongly necessary for x; and (c) if C is sufficient for one S_i, then C is strictly sufficient for x.

To see how NESS works in cases of duplicative causation the idea is to resolve the excess sufficient set into its component MSCs. Consider again Assassination 1. Each assassin's act of shooting is a necessary element of some S_i and S_j and therefore the behaviour of each marksman can be attributed causal status for Victim's death because the behaviour of each marksman was necessary to complete a set of conditions (the marksman possessing a loaded gun in good working order, the absence of protection to the victim, etc.) sufficient for Victim to die and each of these conditions was present on the occasion in question.

In Assassination 2, we see that, given that it is true that the pushing of the car by each of the three assassins belongs to at least one S_i consisting of pushing by two assassins and each of these MSCs was present on the occasion (the excess sufficient set being a superset of each of these MSCs), then the pushing by each assassin qualifies for causal status for Victim's death.[10]

It is similarly easy to disentangle the cases of pre-emptive causation. Here the idea is to check if a particular act is an element of an MSC that forms a pre-empting cause. In Assassination 3, Assassin$_1$'s act of shooting is a necessary element of some S_i and therefore a cause, although Assassin$_2$'s poisoning of the water is not, because, although poisoned water would be sufficient for killing Victim, in the circumstances it cannot be an actual sufficient condition because Victim has already been killed by Assassin$_1$'s shot. In Assassination 4, Assassin$_1$'s act of shooting is a cause of Victim's death, but Assassin$_2$'s intention to poison Victim's water is not. What the NESS condition does in cases of pre-emptive causation is to evaluate the claim that C_1 could not be a causal factor of x because of the existence of an alternative cause C_2 that either emerged or could have emerged subsequent to the occurrence of C_1. This fact does not vitiate the causal status of C_1.[11]

Before concluding this section, there is still a class of problems to deal with that have thus far not been highlighted but are important because they represent so many instances of collective action. Very generally, it is the case when one event C_1 is sufficient for x but there is a second simultaneous event C_2 that is neither sufficient for x nor necessary for a sufficient set. Yet, C_2 still 'contributes' in some manner. Call this *redundant causation.*

> **Assassination 5.** Victim is held up in his car by Assassin$_1$ who ties and locks him up in his car. Together with Assassin$_2$, Assassin$_1$ pushes the car over the cliff, killing Victim. Assassin$_1$ is sufficient for holding up Victim and pushing the car over the cliff. Assassin$_2$ cannot prevent Assassin$_1$ killing Victim.

To make this example more concrete, suppose that it requires at least 2 units of force to push Victim's car over the cliff. Suppose further that Assassin$_1$ has the physical strength to push with 0, 1, 2 or 3 units of force, whereas Assassin$_2$ can only push with 0 or 1 unit of force. Finally, suppose Assassin$_1$ and Assassin$_2$ together push the car over the cliff with 3 units and 1 unit of force respectively.

The question here is, given that Assassin$_1$ is sufficient for the death of Victim, to what extent did Assassin$_2$ contribute to Victim's death? We need to answer this question because otherwise we would have to abandon the very idea that moral responsibility entails causal contribution if we want to say that Assassin$_2$ is blameworthy for her part in Victim's death. It is fair to say that this is a 'weak' version of the 'many hands problem'. Here, too, there is a way out using the NESS test.

What we are after is to find an MSC such that the pushing by both assassins makes up this set. To accomplish this, we have to replace the but-for test with an alternative counterfactual analysis. In the standard but-for test we hold the actions of all others constant and vary the action of the agent i in whom we are interested and check if by doing this the remaining actions are still sufficient for the outcome. For the case of redundant causation, however, we have to hold the action of i constant and vary the action of some other agent j and ask if by doing so i would become a necessary member of a sufficient set. That is, we ask if there is a feasible combination of actions such that i satisfies the NESS test. If the answer is affirmative, then we can say that i's action is a causally relevant factor for the given outcome. In Assassination 5 we hold constant the force that Assassin$_2$ applied to the car (1 unit) and ask if Assassin$_1$ can apply an amount of force such that when combined with Assassin$_2$'s force the combination is just sufficient for Victim's car to roll over the precipice. In other words, if Assassin$_1$ can regulate his strength, by applying 1 unit of force, which he can, then Assassin$_2$ satisfies the NESS test, and not otherwise. We now have the answer we were looking for.

It is worth remarking that this reasoning drives a further wedge between a particular type of counterfactual analysis (the but-for test) and a causal ascription. It is just too restrictive to only consider the *i-variants* in actions; we must also consider the *j-variants* – or the potential causal contributions.

The salient point that emerges so far is that, inasmuch as the 'many hands problem' encompasses a 'whodunnit' question, it is a species of causal over-determination. It is a problem that can easily be defused by the NESS test and expanding the type of counterfactual analysis that we perform. Hence the countless situations in our institutional and social lives in which duplicative and pre-emptive causal over-determination takes place, such as in committees, hierarchies and group action, can all be scrutinized using the concept of weak necessity/strong sufficiency. As long as we assume that every socially engendered event x has a socially engendered cause, then it is always possible to fix causal responsibility on some agent because by definition there is at least one MSC that brought it about.

Consequently, the paradoxical conclusion drawn by some ethical theorists that the causal criterion seems to eliminate moral responsibility in some circumstances where it ought to be maintained does not follow. There is no need to expunge causality from a theory of responsibility; there is only a need to expunge the causal criterion that generates the 'many hands problem'. Despite the belief by some authors that the concept of strong necessity is a weak notion of causality, it is clearly not sufficiently weak.[12]

Social power

Having clarified the nature of the NESS test, we can now turn to the question of social power. This is important because, in one of the few attempts to get around the 'many hands problem' without recourse to the concept of collective responsibility, French (1984) invoked the concept of social power and did so in such a way as to have made use of the NESS test in disguise. Of course it can now be asked what our analysis contributes over and above French's. The answer is threefold. First, French did not undertake a systematic analysis of causal over-determination and show how his solution fits into this literature. Second, and more importantly, although French's use of social power is entirely appropriate for the case that he analyses, in some circumstances it is not. Social power is a special case of social causality and will therefore spread responsibility too narrowly.[13]

The case that French considers is that of the Canby Saloon Crowd, a story adapted from Walter Van Tilburg Clark's *The Ox Bow Incident*. In French's version, a motley and distinct crowd of 15 people are gathered in the Canby Saloon in a small town in Nevada on a winter's night in 1885. A brawl spontaneously breaks out and in typical fashion the saloon is razed. One of the characters in this crowd is a gristly Ma Grier. French asks to what extent is she accountable for the brawl and its attendant consequences *in toto* (including the fact that, at the other end of the bar from where she was, a stranger in town was being bashed by some of the locals) given that she alone could not have started or ended the brawl?

In French's terms, the crowd had 'power' to start and end the brawl in the sense of an 'ability', but it is not clear how that group power is distributed among its constituent members. French's thesis is that an answer to this distribution question is an answer to the question of what a person could have done to alter the state of affairs in a particular situation and this is a person's power. In other words, French's wanted to know whether it is true that Ma Grier (or any other character in the story) could be ascribed the ability to bring about the outbreak or the end of the brawl at any moment.

To answer this question, French drew on Goldman's (1972) theory of social power. Stripped of the trimmings and trappings of his controversial theory of basic actions, and altering the notion somewhat, Goldman's definition of social power is constructed as follows:

Individual power   An individual i has power with respect to some state of affairs x if, and only if, i had an action (or sequence of actions) such that the performance of this action (or sequence of actions) under stated or implied conditions resulted in x but x would not have resulted if i had not performed this action (or sequence of actions).

Collective power   A collection of individuals T has power with respect to x if, and only if, each of the members of that collection have an action (or sequence of actions) such that the performance of these actions (or sequence of actions) under stated or implied conditions resulted in x but x would not have resulted if *any* member of T had not performed these actions (or sequence of actions).

Social power   An individual i has some power with respect to x if, and only if, i is a member of some T with collective power.[14]

Following our discussion of causal relations, it is easy to see that Goldman's definition of individual power is based on 'strong necessity'; his definition of collective power that of a 'minimal sufficient set'; and the definition of social power is based on 'weak necessity/strong sufficiency' – the *NESS* test.[15] That is, to be ascribed as having *some* power with respect to an outcome x that is brought about by a collectivity is to be weakly necessary/strongly sufficient for a collectivity to have power with respect to x.

Using this structure, French argued in precisely the same manner in which we unravelled the causal relations in Assassination 2. *If*, among all the brawling members of the Canby Saloon crowd, Ma Grier had an action that together with the action of others constituted a minimally sufficient set with respect to bringing the brawl to an immediate halt, *then* Ma Grier had social power with respect to the brawl (and all its attendant consequences). The fact that Ma Grier was not strongly necessary (had individual power) with respect to ending the brawl does not imply that she was powerless *tout court*. She had *some* power in the form of *social power* and therefore can be called to account for the brawl *in toto*.

To decipher the difference between power and causality we need to note the following observations. The first is that Goldman's definitions of power are incomplete. They are in fact definitions of mere causal contribution and not social power, although both Goldman and French want to capture the latter and not the former. What is missing is the reference to 'resistance' or 'opposition'. Although this is only of secondary importance in the article by Goldman upon which French draws, it does take a primary role in a later paper (Goldman 1974). In that paper Goldman adopts the Weberian notion of power as the 'ability to realize one's will *despite the* (possible) *resistance or opposition of others*' (Goldman 1974: 231, emphasis in the original) and it is fair to say that French presupposes it as well.[16]

In a game-theoretic framework, a player or a set of players (called a 'coalition') has power with respect to x if that player (coalition) can guarantee x when the other players (complement coalition) act to resist this player's attempt to obtain this outcome. This is not a trivial restriction because it implies a much narrower counterfactual analysis than we use to determine a causal contribution. To determine a player's power for some outcome x we look not at the actual actions that were performed, but at the actions that each player *would* perform *if* they wanted to guarantee x and then counterfactualize opposition such that the joint action space of the opposition consists of actions that would be performed if the players wanted to guarantee not-x (irrespective of the fact that they may fail).

Formally, let X be a set of outcomes and $N=\{1,\ldots, n\}$ of players. Let $G=(a_1, \ldots, a_n, \pi)$ be a game form on X. Each a_i is a set of actions; π is a function from the set of action combinations, or plays, onto X. Given X and N, a coalition $T \subseteq N$ is α-*effective* for $A \subseteq X$ if, and only if, (i) T is non-empty: there is an action profile a_T such that for any action profile a_{N-T} of others, $\pi(a_T, a_{N-T}) \in A$; (ii) T is empty: $A=X$. That is, a coalition T has *power* with respect to some outcome x, where $A=\{x\}$, if it is α-*effective* for $\{x\}$.

Goldman's concept of collective power with respect to x is the α-*effectivity* of T for $\{x\}$ and *individual power* is the case in which $T=\{i\}$ is α-*effective* for

$\{x\}$. Goldman's concept of a social power is given by a player's membership of a *minimum winning coalition* (MWC) which is coalition T that is α-*effective* for $\{x\}$ but no proper subset is as well. That is, i has some power with respect to x if $i \hat{\mathrm{I}} T$ is α-*effective* for $\{x\}$ but $T-\{i\}$ is not, i.e. i can force an outcome $(X-A$ or not-$x)$ against the resistance of the remaining members of T.

The second observation is that an MWC is a special case of an MSC. Without enlarging on the details, which can be found in Braham (2008), a power ascription refers only to particular MSCs. That is, in a game-theoretic framework an MSC is an action profile a_T that is minimally sufficient for $\{x\}$ in the sense that (i) a_T is sufficient for $\{x\}$, and (ii) any unilateral departure from T, holding the actions of all other members of T constant, means that $a_{T-\{i\}}$ is not sufficient for $\{x\}$. In contrast, an MWC refers only to those MSCs in which each player chooses that action which is the most conducive to *guaranteeing* a particular outcome, given the possibility that others will oppose them.

In Assassination 5, for instance, for power we only consider the case in which both assassins exert their full force in pushing the car regardless of the fact that in actual fact both assassins may have exerted equal force. Given that Assassin$_1$'s full force is sufficient for the death of Victim, his action alone constitutes the sole MWC, even though the set of MSCs contains action profiles that include contributions by Assassin$_2$. Hence there is a crucial weakness in using the concept of power to allocate responsibility because it excuses Assassin$_2$ even though she made a causal contribution.

Thus, French's idea of finding a connection between individual actions and collective outcomes via the concept of power, and his implicit application of α-*effectivity* and MWCs, has its limitations. It suffers a drawback in that it pardons people of moral and legal responsibility when there are reasons to believe that they are responsible and should be held to be so. The allocation of moral responsibility for powerless complicity and the attendant social dynamics that come with it is one of our political instruments to control the abuse of power by others: we can dirty our hands without having or having exercised any power. To keep our hands clean may mean that we have to resist, even ineffectually, those who are exercising their power.

The uses of power

That a power ascription may prove too narrow for allocating responsibility does not imply that we should throw the concept overboard for the purposes of allocating moral and legal responsibility. It does have fundamental importance. There are two generic cases to discuss.

The first case is when causal contribution and a belief that a person is morally responsible for an outcome bifurcate. An example of such a case is a committee with a weighted voting rule. Consider a set of voters $N=\{a,b,c,d,e\}$ and a vector of weights $w=(35, 20, 15, 15,1\ 5)$ in alphabetical order and a quota of 51 for some proposal, i.e. a proposal passes if, and only if, at least 51 votes are obtained in its favour. The set of players could be the secured creditors in a bankruptcy proceeding with the weights representing the monetary value of claims and the proposal to be voted on is either to re-organize or to liquidate the bankrupt firm.[17] Now suppose $T=\{a,b,c\}$ formed and was in favour of the proposal. Who was responsible for the approval of the proposal? Before answering the question, it should be noted that in such a voting game causality and power will perfectly overlap, because each voter has only two actions (voting 'yes' or 'no') so that the MSCs are the MWCs.

Now the answer. Clearly voters d and e, both of whom voted against the proposal, cannot be causally responsible because not only did they vote against it, neither alone nor together are they α-*effective* for proposal. If we examine $T=\{a,b,c\}$ we find that a and b satisfy the NESS test and are therefore causally responsible and by the same token can be ascribed power for this particular contingency. But what of c? Clearly this voter does not satisfy the NESS test. But does this absolve him or her of moral responsibility for the outcome?

If there is any moral content to the outcome and c's decision to vote in favour of the proposal, then this seems to be a case of moral (good) luck. Player c is relieved of moral responsibility for the proposal passing thanks to some circumstance obtaining that is beyond his control, the forming of coalition $\{a,b,c\}$, although in other circumstances the forming of $\{a,b,c,d\}$ for instance, the same action (voting in favour of the proposal) is conducive to the same outcome obtaining because this coalition can be decomposed into MSCs/MWCs that contain c. If we are unprepared to accept this as a genuine case of moral luck, then we can either invoke the concept of collective responsibility and its various refinements or apply the concept of power. As we stated at the outset, the concept of collective responsibility is not without its problems. The advantage of using the concept of power is that it still keeps us within an individualistic framework and therefore within the bounds of personal responsibility.

How will power work in this case given that in this instance c's causal contribution and power in T overlap? The idea is that, instead of examining the *actual* coalition that came into being, we examine the game as such. That is, we ask if the rules of the game allocate power to c and not if c had power in a particular play of the game. The answer to this question is given by the existence of an MWC that contains c and in this case it is 'yes': $\{a,b,c\}$ and $\{a,c,e\}$ are both MWCs. We can now say that in virtue of this power *and* c's membership of an α-*effective* coalition in favour of *the proposal*, c bears moral (and maybe legal) responsibility for the proposal being passed. We can connect c's action of voting for the proposal with the outcome via c's *potential* to be a causal condition (power) for x. Hence c is not absolved of his moral (or legal) responsibility as a matter of fortune.

The second case we need to discuss concerns those circumstances that call for remedial action or punishment (i.e. we do not just want to attribute blame) but we find that the causal criterion spreads responsibility too widely and that the determination of a threshold of causal responsibility is arbitrary. Here we can apply the concept of power to narrow down the set of agents that are to be called to account. This is precisely the problem of war crimes. The weakness of the causal criterion is that in most cases almost anyone can be implicated. The concept of power is more useful here because it singles out not merely those agents who made a causal contribution, but those agents who by acting in concert had the potential to *guarantee* an alternative outcome.

In a similar fashion, power appears to be the key concept if remedial responsibility is unhinged from actual or past causal contributions. For instance, when we want to put right bad situations we may have reason to allocate the responsibility to do this to those who are best placed to do the remedying. In this case we would only look at those agents who have the *capacity*, either alone or in concert, to guarantee an end to the bad state of affairs.[18] If we believe in the capacity principle we would not assign the responsibility to those who could make a mere causal contribution. In this case power can be used to identify the boundaries of the moral community, and a measure of power can be used to discriminate among those members.[19]

Taking stock

We can now draw together the main threads of our analysis. First, we have provided a much needed synthesis of the literature on causality, power and responsibility in collectivities and placed this in a formal structure.[20]

Second, and quite specifically, we have shown that it is possible to reconcile the role of individual acts with overdetermined collective outcomes. On the present plan, this means that we can strengthen French's (1984: 72) conclusion that causal responsibility in collective undertakings such as the Canby Saloon brawl is 'not necessarily nondistributive' (French was challenging a claim by Feinberg (1968) that it is non-distributive).[21] If the story we have told is true, then we can say that, for the class of outcomes that can be modelled in a game-theoretic framework (which we glossed over above), causal responsibility in a collectivity is *necessarily* distributive (although this leaves open the practical matter of defining the game form). The crucial point is that, for *any* profile of actions that is sufficient for an outcome, by definition either that profile is an MSC for the outcome or there is a subset of players that have actions that can form a profile that is an MSC for the outcome. Thus we can *always* identify a set of individuals each of whom can be said to have causally contributed to the outcome.[22] The NESS test is, then, a very effective way of rebutting causal excuses and avoiding the escape into the confusions of collective responsibility. Although this last implication may be attractive it does come at a cost: the weakness of the NESS test means that for moral responsibility other criteria (such as volition) have to do more work; the question of 'whose hands' is logically distinct from the question of 'whose hands were dirty'. Causal analysis answers the first question, moral appraisal the second.

Third, the class of outcomes for which causal responsibility is necessarily distributive is large. As long as the situation can be modelled as a game form, the NESS test can be used to analyse three generic classes of collective action. In the first class of collective action we have what is called *unwitting co-action*. This is the case in which a collectivity of individuals act to common effect without anyone necessarily being aware of the contributions of others, or even of the effect that they produce together. In the second kind we have *witting co-action*. This is the case in which a collectivity of individuals act to common effect and in which everyone is aware of one another but not necessarily aware of the effect that they produce together (market activity is such an instance). And in the third kind of collectivity we have *joint action*. This is the case in which all members of a collectivity are aware of each other and their contributions to the joint effect, i.e. coordinated collective action. It is what we usually mean by cooperative or team activity in which each member of a collectivity does his or her bit to realize a common aim.[23]

In this regard, the game-theoretic framework that we have pointed to can take in cases that are less obvious than an unruly crowd, a committee or a corporation. It can also be used to distribute causal responsibility among national or cultural groups. A good example is Feinberg's (1968) discussion of racism in the postbellum American South. Acts of violence against blacks, Feinberg suggests, were carried out in a context in which Southern whites in general passively sympathized with such acts, even if they were not actively involved in perpetrating them, as a result of a widely shared culture of racial inequality or 'folkways'. Feinberg says that each of the Southern whites who approved of these folkways on the grounds of their strong (and hardly avoidable) solidarity with the majority was implicated in each of the acts of violence against the blacks and therefore can be burdened with moral responsibility for the brutalities of the racial system. Our analysis says it is unnecessary to invoke solidarity to distribute moral responsibility because we can do the trick with the concept of causality. Those people who, at any given time, contributed an action to an MSC that could have brought the folkways to an end bear such responsibility (supposing, of course, that the coalition of people who did not support the folkway were powerless and that other conditions for moral responsibility are fulfilled). The postbellum social system is nothing other than the Canby Saloon brawl writ large. This appears correct because it locates responsibility not in some vague system of norms or in people's attitudes but clearly in the hands of those with greater or lesser degrees of political power.

Fourth, the NESS test outlines a structure for *quantifying* our responsibility judgments in circumstances of collective action. That is, if we believe that it makes sense to say that, given an outcome x and the actions that i and j performed, i is more responsible than j, such that for some given threshold level of importance i is to be held accountable and j not, then we require a method of quantifying such a judgment.[24] We cannot enlarge on it here, but the natural way to construct a ranking of causal responsibility for a given outcome is to count up and compare the number of MSCs that an agent contributes to. This would seem to be particularly apt and plausible for committee structures that have well-defined sets of players, actions, outcomes and outcome functions.[25]

Fifth, by systematically investigating the NESS test we have shown that a person can be held causally responsible for an outcome even though he or she is not directly indispensable for the emergence of that outcome and can even be so if he or she is entirely powerless to prevent that outcome. Whereas the first of these results has already been recognized in the literature (D. Miller 2001; Miller and Makela 2005), the second is new.

Finally, by defusing the 'many hands problem' one of the traditional justifications for a theory of collective responsibility evaporates. This is not to say that such a theory is superfluous; rather it merely says that a theory of collective responsibility that is dependant on, but not reducible to, the members of the collectivity is not required to mop up the problem of causal responsibility. Such a theory must, therefore, find its justification elsewhere. There are clearly cases in which such a theory is necessary, such as when the members of a collectivity change over time and a particular effect manifests itself only once the causal agents have long departed from the collectivity. We also may need it for handling the legal problems of compensation. But these are questions that are indeed separate from the questions about factual judgments concerning the connection of a person to a certain state of affairs.

Notes

1 We would like to thank René van den Brink, Frank Hindriks, Hartmut Kliemt, Matthew Kramer, Vincent Merlin, Hannu Nurmi, Philip Pettit, Clemens Puppe, Frank Steffen, Mark Siebel, Dennis Thompson, Wolfgang Weigel, and seminar and workshop audiences in Caen, Groningen, Helsinki, Galway and Turku, for comments and suggestions. Martin van Hees deserves special thanks for the many hours he has contributed in discussing the main ideas of this chapter.

2 By 'collectivity' we mean an arbitrary collection or set of individuals that may or may not have some minimal coherence or structure. Some authors refer to this as a mere 'collection' or 'aggregate collectivity' and reserve the term 'collectivity' for groups with some minimal structure and coherence (or 'identity'). As there is no standard usage we have chosen 'collectivity' for stylistic reasons. We are also aware that there are many different types of such collectivities, e.g. a 'corporation' is different from a 'crowd' and different still from a 'nation', but for our purpose we need not make these types of distinctions because we are not concerned with the question of which types of collectivities can be held morally responsible as opposed to merely causally responsible. The importance of the distinctions is discussed in French (1984: 1–18) and Sverdlik (1987).

3 Although we use the term 'causal responsibility' we are aware that for a broad class of cases it is conceptually more precise to use the term '*contributory* responsibility' or speak of *conventional* causality or conventional generation because 'causality' refers to the connection between two events which are related by empirically ascertainable 'laws of nature'. The outcomes of collective decisions and actions are governed by law and convention and not merely by laws of nature as such. For example, that a house burns down following the outbreak of a fire of a certain size follows from laws of nature; that a particular policy is implemented following the agreement of a certain number of people follows from legal rules and conventions. The distinction is discussed in more detail in Kramer (2003: 280). However, to use the term 'contributory responsibility' or 'conventional causal responsibility' would unnecessarily burden the discussion with new terminology without adding any clarity given the common usage of causal responsibility to account for relations between events that are governed either by laws of nature or by law and convention.

4 A catalogue of real cases can be found in Bovens (1998).

5 See for example the collection of papers in May and Hoffman (1991). Very recent examples can be found in Miller (2004) and Pettit (2007).

6 For a recent treatment of the metaphysical problems see List and Pettit (2006) and Pettit (2007). For an overview of different legal doctrines of collective identity see French (1984) and Colvin (1995).

7 This section is summarized from Hart and Honoré (1959), Honoré (1995), Kramer (2003), Mackie (1965, 1974), Pearl (2000: 313–315) and Wright (1985, 1988).

8 Note that for the NESS test to be non-trivial certain background conditions are taken as given. If it were not the case then the presence of air would be a cause of a car accident, a rape, etc.

9 There is a formal difference in Mackie's (1965) initial formulation of INUS and Wright's formulation of NESS in that in the original formulation of INUS Mackie includes a condition that rules out over-determination (condition 4). Mackie required that to qualify as a cause a condition must be a necessary member of the single sufficient set that was present on the occasion or if more such sets were present the condition was a necessary member of each such set. This restriction in fact makes INUS equivalent to strong necessity. It is noteworthy that in his later formulation of INUS Mackie (1974) dropped this condition, and also argued in favour of strong necessity as a better description of what we mean by 'cause'.

10 NESS is not entirely immune from other problems from which but-for causality also suffers, such as the problem of collateral effects and the problem of causal priority. Kramer (2003: 285–295) provides a succinct overview of the problems. Further, there are additional objections to NESS on the grounds that the inclusion of a sufficiency condition apparently implies that there is no causation without determinism. As many writers note, causation can take place in a probabilistic environment. For a discussion see Suppes (1970). We grant that NESS is not the complete story of causation, but it would seem to apply to most social outcomes that we are discussing and therefore we need not be too concerned about this issue here. Here it is worth remarking that Vallentyne's (2008) proposal that a cause of an outcome is a prior event that increases the probability of an outcome presupposes the NESS test. We cannot go into detail here, but if an event increases the probability of an outcome then that event must be a NESS condition.

11 In fact the NESS test is a framework for evaluating excuses that are based on 'alternative cause'.

12 Thompson (1987: 47), for instance, writes that his use of the 'but-for' test for causal responsibility is 'deliberately weak'. However, in an earlier contribution Thompson (1983) approvingly cites Feinberg's (1970: 202n) acceptance of the even weaker concept of 'weak necessity'. Yet, despite Thompson's approval of 'weak necessity', and the exception to be found in D. Miller (2001), the NESS test has up to now not found its way into discussions of responsibility in collectivities. In a sense our current contribution is only one of making explicit what is latent in the literature.

13 The relationship between social power and social causality is analysed in Braham (2008).

14 Goldman does not actually use this definition of 'social power', but it is implied in his whole analysis.

15 Note that Goldman's definition does not actually state that S must be minimally sufficient, but this is assumed in his definition of collective power. This is important because obviously the fact that i is a necessary member of S does not imply all other members are necessary. Moreover, he discusses the minimality requirement prior to his definition of social power (Goldman 1972: 240).

16 The claim that an ascription of social power requires reference to resistance or opposition is not undisputed (see Dowding 2003). For a full exposition of need for the resistance criterion see Braham (2008).

17 See Braham and Steffen (2002) for the analysis of voting rules in bankruptcy law.

18 The capacity principle for remedial responsibility is discussed in S. Miller (2001).

19 Clearly this opens up a new area of the application for power indices based on simple games: the analysis and discussion of the moral responsibility of political decision-makers (see Holler 2007).
20 Much confusion still abounds. For instance, in a recent analysis, Sartorio (2004) purports to show how we can be responsible for something without causing it. Her examples are nothing other than duplicative causal over-determination and her solution for 'being responsible for something that causes an event', or 'causation as the vehicle of responsibility', is a re-invention of the NESS test.
21 By 'distributive' Feinberg means that it can be allocated. He is not assuming, however, that there is a fixed pie of responsibility to be distributed.
22 It should be noted that this also defuses Pettit's (2007: 198n) recently identified 'no hands problem'. In fact, a close inspection of this problem, which is based on the 'discursive dilemma', shows that it can even be defused with the standard 'but-for' test. Note that the determination of 'whose hands' should not be conflated with 'whose dirty hands'. It is quite possible that morally bad outcomes can be brought about by agents who are morally blameless. The 'no hands problem' is more properly a 'no dirty hands' problem. Pettit did not actually demonstrate that the agents in his example are morally blameless. For a discussion of this issue see Braham and Hindriks (2008a,b).
23 For a different classification, see French (1984: 1–18).
24 Note that Parfit (1984) has forcefully argued that as far as moral responsibility is concerned this is mistaken 'moral mathematics' because the size of a contribution to an outcome is morally irrelevant. But there evidently are cases in which it ostensibly makes sense to form such judgments. Put another way, we often do engage in the practice of holding this or that person to account based upon a scalar judgment of his or her causal responsibility for the mere reason that justice considerations may require that we assign remedial responsibility or punishment or reward.
25 For a proposal how to construct a power index based on the NESS test, see Braham (2005).

References

Bovens, M. (1998) *The Quest for Responsibility*, Cambridge: Cambridge University Press.
Braham, M. (2005) 'Causation and the measurement of power', *Homo Oeconomicus*, 22: 645–652.
—— (2008) 'Social power and social causation: towards a formal synthesis', in M. Braham and F. Steffan (eds), *Power, Freedom, and Voting*, Heidelberg: Springer.
Braham, M. and Hindriks, F.A. (2008a) 'Judgement aggregation and moral repsonsibility', mimeo, Faculty of Philosophy, University of Groningen.
—— (2008b) 'Corporate responsibility and the discursive dilemma', mimeo, Faculty of Philosophy, University of Groningen.
Braham, M. and Steffen, F. (2002) 'Voting rules in insolvency law: a simple-game theoretic approach', *International Review of Law and Economics*, 22: 421–442.
Colvin, E. (1995) 'Corporate personality and criminal liability', *Criminal Law Forum*, 6: 3–44.
Dowding, K. (2003) 'Resources, power, and systematic luck: a response to Barry', *Politics, Philosophy and Economics*, 2: 305–322.
Feinberg, J. (1968) 'Collective responsibility', *Journal of Philosophy*, 65: 674–688.
—— (1970) *Doing and Deserving*, Princeton, NJ: Princeton University Press.
French, P.A. (1984) *Collective and Corporate Responsibility*, New York: Columbia University Press.

Goldman, A. I. (1972) 'Toward a theory of social power', *Philosophical Studies*, 23: 221–68.

——— (1974) 'On the measurement of power', *Journal of Philosophy*, 71: 231–52.

Hardin, R. (1988) *Morality within the Limits of Reason*, Chicago: Chicago University Press.

Hart, H. L. A. and Honoré, A. M. (1959) *Causation in the Law*, Oxford: Oxford University Press.

Holler, M.J. (2007) 'Freedom of choice, power, and the responsibility of decision makers', in A. Marciano and J.-M. Josselin (eds), *Democracy, Freedom and Coercion: A Law and Economics Approach*, Cheltenham: Eward Elgar.

Honoré, A. M. (1995) 'Necessary and sufficient conditions in tort law', in D. Owen (ed.), *Philosophical Foundations of Tort Law*, Oxford: Oxford University Press.

Kramer, M. H. (2003) *The Quality of Freedom*, Oxford: Oxford University Press.

Ladd, J. (1970) 'Morality and the idea of rationality in formal organizations', *Monist*, 54: 488–516.

Lewis, H. D. (1948) 'Collective responsibility', *Philosophy*, 24: 3–18.

List, C. and Pettit, P. (2006) 'Group agency and supervenience', *Southern Journal of Philosophy*, 44: 85–105.

Mackie, J. L. (1965) 'Causes and conditions', *American Philosophical Quarterly*, 2: 245–264.

——— (1974) *The Cement of the Universe*, Oxford: Oxford University Press.

May, L. and Hoffman, S. (eds) (1991) *Collective Responsibility: Five Decades of Debate in Theoretical and Applied Ethics*, Lanham, MD: Rowman and Littlefield.

Miller, D. (2001) 'Distributing responsibilities', *Journal of Political Philosophy*, 9: 453–471.

Miller, S. (2001) *Social Action: A Teleological Account*, Cambridge: Cambridge University Press.

——— (2004) 'Holding nations responsible', *Ethics*, 114: 240–268.

Miller, S. and Makela, P. (2005) 'The collectivist approach to collective moral responsibility', *Metaphilosophy*, 36: 634–651.

Parfit, D. (1984) *Reasons and Persons*, Oxford: Oxford University Press.

Pearl, J. (2000) *Causality: Models, Reasoning, Inference*, Cambridge: Cambridge University Press.

Pettit, P. (2007) 'Responsibility incorporated', *Ethics*, 117: 171–201.

Sartorio, C. (2004) 'How to be responsible for something without causing it', *Philosophical Perspectives*, 18: 315–336.

Suppes, P. (1970) *A Probabalistic Theory of Causality*, Amsterdam: North Holland.

Sverdlik, S. (1987) 'Collective responsibility', *Philosophical Studies*, 51: 61–76.

Thompson, D. F. (1980) 'Moral responsibility of public officials: the problem of many hands', *American Political Science Review*, 74: 905–916.

——— (1983) 'Ascribing responsibility to advisors in government', *Ethics*, 93: 546–560.

——— (1987) *Political Ethics and Public Office*, Cambridge, MA: Harvard University Press.

Vallentyne, P. (2008) 'Brute luck and responsibility', *Politics, Philosophy and Economics* (forthcoming).

Wright, R. (1985) 'Causation in tort law', *California Law Review*, 73: 1735–1828.

——— (1988) 'Causation, responsibility, risk, probability, naked statistics, and proof: pruning the bramble bush by clarifying the concepts', *Iowa Law Review*, 73: 1001–1077.

9   The logic of valuing

Boudewijn de Bruin

Introduction

The aim of this chapter is to analyse the logical form of valuing. I will argue that valuing a concept or property, such as gold, is a universal statement qua logical form, that valuing an object, such as a soccer ball, is an existential statement qua logical form, and, furthermore, that a correct analysis of the logical form of valuing contains doxastic operators. I will show that these ingredients give rise to an interesting interplay between uniform and non-uniform quantification, on the one hand, and *de dicto* and *de re* beliefs, on the other.

This project contrasts with two other projects traditionally referred to by the terms 'logic of value' and 'logic of valuation'. I am not concerned with logical principles governing propositions involving value modalities, logics of value. And I am not interested in the validity, or lack of validity, of arguments on the border of the fact–value dichotomy, logics of valuation.[1]

Adopting a doxastic outlook on valuing, the proffered analysis remains none-theless neutral with respect to many issues from meta-ethics. As Michael Smith (2002) has persuasively argued, to say that valuing is a form of believing is not to exclude non-cognitivism, non-relativism or irrealism. Nor is the analysis particu-larly narrow. Although for the sake of argument I take the bearers of value to be concepts and objects, exactly the same structural observations can be made if you attach value to events, propositions or even possible worlds.

I will stress one area of application, the value of political freedom. The received view is that the value of freedom lies in the value of the specific things one is free to do. But Ian Carter (1999) has recently shown that freedom has irreduc-ible, 'non-specific' value, too. I will show that underlying the debate between the proponents of the received view and their critics is a disagreement about logical form: non-uniform *de dicto* beliefs about freedom as a concept, for the received view, and uniform half *de dicto*, half *de re* beliefs about freedom as an object, for its critics.[2]

The structure of the chapter is as follows. In the next section we defend the analysis in terms of universal and existential quantifiers and doxastic operators, while the following section brings it all together in a two-dimensional typology of uniform–non-uniform and *de dicto*–*de re* beliefs. This is followed by a section on freedom, and the final section provides a brief conclusion.

Quantification and beliefs

Valuing concepts

Smith values gold. When he visited the Egyptian Museum in Cairo he was struck by the beauty of Tutankhamen's death mask, the way gold is combined there with lapis lazuli and turquoise to give the Pharaoh his proud yet mild and gentle look. So, Smith says, he values gold because he values Tutankhamen's death mask. But Smith does not show any particular interest in other objects of gold. He ignores, at the exhibition, the other golden masks, the bracelets, the necklaces, the emblems. He wears a silver wedding ring because he does not like the colour of gold. He has never bought any gold plates or cutlery or sculptures for himself.

Smith, I would say, is mistaken about what he really values. He does not value gold. Indeed, he values some particular object (partly) made of gold. To value gold he would have to value more golden things. The logical form of valuing gold G is

$$\forall x \, (G(x) \supset \text{Value } x),$$

'Smith values all golden objects', rather than

$$\exists x \, (G(x) \,\&\, \text{Value } x),$$

'There exists a golden object Smith values'.

This may seem to put excessive demands on Smith. Of course, to value gold, Smith has to think highly of more than one golden object; but can't he value gold without having to treasure all objects made of gold? As it stands, the universal reading sounds too strong. But we will see that it all depends on how to analyse 'Value x' in this context. It is appropriate to suspend criticism for a moment.

Valuing objects

Smithies values the official soccer ball signed by 1999 US World Cup team star Brandi Chastain. Although she bought it at an auction herself, the soccer player Chastain does not matter much to her. Actually, she has not even watched the match with China in 1999. In addition, she does not like Chastain's extravagant style of playing soccer. And she finds the $195 she spent on the ball quite excessive. But she does not regret having bought it because it adds to her collection of celebrity autographs the signature of a sportswoman.

Does Smithies value the soccer ball? Shouldn't she place a value on other aspects of the ball as well? Shouldn't she appreciate everything, or almost everything, about the ball? Of course not. To value the ball it is sufficient for her that some aspect of the ball strikes her as valuable. She may not have a high opinion of

Chastain, she may not like playing soccer at all, she may think the colours of the ball are awful and Chastain's handwriting childish; as long as there is one thing about the ball she delights in, it would be wrong to deny that she values the ball. It would be wrong to analyse valuing the soccer ball b as:

$$\forall C \ (C(b) \supset \text{Value } C),$$

'Every property C of the soccer ball b is valuable'. It suffices that

$$\exists C \ (C(b) \ \& \ \text{Value } C),$$

'At least one property C of the ball b is valuable'.

Beliefs

Smithson values Vermeer's *View of Delft*. He really got infatuated with the canvas when he first visited the Mauritshuis in The Netherlands, and he has been interested in it ever since. He has bought numerous books on Vermeer and on Dutch seventeenth-century art and culture. He has learned all kinds of oil painting techniques to be able to study the painting the old-fashioned way by copying it. But, when prompted, he doesn't know just how to explain what it is that makes *View of Delft* dear to him. Yet he knows that there is something that appeals to him, something hard or impossible for him to describe, but still something that somehow explains why he values it. He values the painting not for a specific characteristic, but just so. That is, the logical form of his valuing is:

$$\text{Believe } \exists C \ (C(d) \ \& \ \text{Value } C),$$

'Smithson believes that there exists a valuable concept C that is true of *View of Delft*'.

Now suppose Smithson learns a lot about aesthetics and theories of perception, and, thinking harder, comes to realize that what strikes him most in the oil painting is quite simply the warm red and brownish tones of the roofs of some of the houses on the left of the canvas. He values the painting for some very specific characteristics. The logical form of his valuing correspondingly changes to:

$$\exists C \text{ Believe } (C(d) \ \& \ \text{Value } C),$$

'Of some particular C, Smithson believes that it applies to *View of Delft*, and that it is valuable'.

I believe that this is quite a general phenomenon. To develop a taste for French cheese, to learn to like Charles Ives's *Concord Sonata*, to become aware of the benefits of political freedom after the fall of the Berlin Wall, there will rather often be a moment where your state of mind or attitude is best described as involving *de dicto* beliefs about value that are not *de re*. You do not know what you like about the cheese and you do not have beliefs about what you specifically value in the music or the freedom, but all the same you do value something.

The same is true of the logical form of valuing concepts. Smiths values gold. She values all instances of gold without being familiar with all these instances of course. It would be presumptuous to analyse her valuing as

$$\forall x \text{ Believe } (G(x) \supset \text{Value } x),$$

ascribing to her precisely this kind of familiarity *de re*. Rather, Smiths's state of mind should be phrased as:

$$\text{Believe } \forall x \ (G(x) \supset \text{Value } x).^{[3]}$$

Typology

The logical form of valuing a concept is a universal statement about valuing objects. The logical form of valuing an object is an existential statement about valuing concepts. Combined, this means that the logical form of valuing a concept is a universal statement in which somewhere an existential statement about valuing an object comes in, and that the logical form of valuing an object is a existential statement in which somewhere a universal statement about valuing a concept comes in. Where is this 'somewhere'?[4]

Ignoring for a moment the second dimension, the doxastic operator, there are two ways to combine: a uniform and a non-uniform one. Plugging in existential quantification in universal quantification yields, for valuing gold G,

$$\forall x \ (G(x) \supset \exists C \ (C(x) \& \text{Value } C)),$$

'Every golden object has a property I value'. The verbal rendering is intentionally opaque. Does it mean that different golden objects may have different valuable properties for me? Or is there one single property that applies to all golden things? To sort things out, let us rewrite the above sentence as:

$$\forall x \exists C \ ((G(x) \supset C(x)) \& \text{Value } C),$$

'For every object x there is a valuable concept C such that if x is gold it is also C'. Clearly, this says that different objects may have different valuable properties. Very different is what we get when we swap the quantifiers:

$$\exists C\, \forall x\, ((G(x) \supset C(x))\, \&\, \text{Value } C),$$

'There is some valuable concept C such that all golden objects x fall under it'. It is crucial to be aware of the differences between the two kinds of valuing. Let us use the term 'uniform' for the latter variety, and the slightly artificial 'non-uniform' for the former. You value the concept gold non-uniformly if you find something valuable in every single instance: you take the golden ring as only a traditional symbol of marriage, you use a golden plate to show off, you dote upon a golden sculpture because of its florid kitsch, and so on, but there is nothing valuable that all golden objects share. You would value gold uniformly if, for instance, you were to value gold's resistance to corrosion or its malleability and ductility, or if you were to love the fact that even the tiniest pieces of gold can be exchanged on the gold market for money, or if you liked its olive-brown or yellow colour, its lustrous sheen.

Let us turn to valuing objects, and let us start with the uniform way of valuing object b taking the form:

$$\exists C\, \forall x\, (C(b)\, \&\, (C(x) \supset \text{Value } x)).$$

You value a soccer ball signed by Brandi Chastain because you are fond of women's sports memorabilia. And you value it uniformly because you value all other women's sports memorabilia, too.

Non-uniformly valuing an object b is of the form

$$\forall x\, \exists C\, (C(b)\, \&\, (C(x) \supset \text{Value } x)),$$

You value the soccer ball, but you are unable to specify one single valuable concept. You would say you are fond of women's sports memorabilia. But at the same time there are women's sports memorabilia you do not value such as the hockey stick of Nadine Ernsting, Germany's 2004 Olympic top scorer. You would say you like soccer, not hockey. But at the same time you do not value the shirt worn by Pele in the 1958 World Cup final against Sweden. You would say Pele is a man not a woman. You value the soccer ball nonetheless, and what makes it valuable is that it has two properties that are valued only when combined, not in isolation, women's sports and soccer.[5]

Having set apart uniform and non-uniform valuing, we have lost track of the doxastic dimension. So where to place the doxastic operator? Given two quantifiers, there are, in principle, three possible positions for the operator: a purely *de dicto* prefix, a purely *de re* suffix, and a half-and-half infix. Table 9.1 displays the resulting typology. It works for concepts and objects, for it shows the quantifiers and the doxastic modality only.[6]

Application to political freedom

If speaking of value in relation to Tutankhamen's death mask sounds hyperbolic, and attaching value to Brandi Chastain's autograph vulgar and tasteless, if differences between *de dicto* and *de re* valuing Vermeer's *View of Delft* seem snobbish or *outré*, the value of political freedom provides a more serious and significant illustration of the different kinds of valuing.

As stated in the beginning of this chapter, the received view of Ronald Dworkin and Will Kymlicka reduces the value of freedom to the value of the specific things one is free to do. This view, however, has undergone vehement criticism. Its critics point to its failure to account for the fact that often a decrease of our overall freedom is experienced as showing no 'respect for [our] autonomy and discretion' or for our capacity to make responsible decisions.[7] Even if my actual desires are not frustrated at all by removing one of my liberties, say the liberty to read a novel I definitely do not want to read, I will attach less value to my overall freedom after the censor has banned the book. The value of my overall freedom, then, cannot be reduced to the value of all specific liberties from which it is made up. Or in the words of Ian Carter:

> The difference between my view and that of Dworkin and Kymlicka … is that their view entails denying that our freedoms have value *independently of the value we attach to the specific things they leave us free to do* … To say that freedom is non-specifically valuable is to say that it is valuable 'as such'.[8]
>
> (Carter 1999: 33–34)

I will not take a stand in this debate. But I will demonstrate that underlying the debate is a difference in logical form of valuing: proponents of the received view value freedom as an object, and they value it in a non-uniform *de dicto* fashion; the critics value freedom as a concept, and they value it in a uniform half-and-half way.

The received view, first. The concept freedom F is valuable whenever all its instances, which I call 'liberties', are valuable:

$$\forall x \, (F(x) \supset \text{Value } x)$$

Table 9.1 Typology

	non-uniform	uniform
de dict	Believe $\forall x \, \exists C$	Believe $\exists C \, \forall x$
half-and-half	$\forall x$ Believe $\exists C$	$\exists C$ Believe $\forall x$
de re	$\forall x \, \exists C$ Believe	$\exists C \, \forall x$ Believe

But this is only a rough indication of how I interpret the proponents of the received view. First, all uniform ways of valuing freedom (of the form $\exists C\ \forall x$, with a Believe-operator affixed at one of three positions) can be ruled out. For it is definitely not the point of the received view to ascribe one and the same valuable property to all liberties. Freedom of speech is valuable because, say, it gives you the opportunity to write the kind of novels you want to write, whereas the value of freedom of worship has to do with what is demanded by your religion. On the other hand, purely *de re* non-uniform valuing (that is, $\forall x\ \exists C$ Believe) would ask too much of the received view. For every single liberty its champions would have to have in mind a specific property making it valuable. And, unless this case reduces to uniform valuing, more than one valuable property would have to be provided. Half-and-half ($\forall x$ Believe $\exists C$) is possible, but still requires some specific *de re* familiarity with all liberties. Purely *de dicto* (Believe $\forall x\ \exists C$), then, is the most plausible phrasing of the position. The received view, then, comes down to the belief that any liberty has some valuable property.

Second, the critics of the received view. As I said, my claim is that the critics value freedom *f* as an object. Valuing freedom as a *concept* would imply valuing freedom's specific instantiations, the liberties, and this is precisely what the critics of the received view reject. So their valuing is roughly of the form

$$\exists C\ (C(f)\ \&\ \text{Value } C)$$

Uniform, non-uniform, *de dicto*, *de re*? A rendering of the critics' position in terms of the non-uniform variety ($\forall x\ \exists C$) would force them to admit to being unable to identify a unique valuable property of freedom. This is a coherent position, but except in the form of the purely *de re* version it is a relatively weak one. Moreover, to some extent the critics do mention concrete valuable properties. Ian Carter describes a connection between freedom's value and the value of human agency. Matthew H. Kramer asserts that freedom is an indicator of respect for a person's autonomy or rationality. And Martin van Hees emphasizes human responsibility. The critics of the received view, then, value freedom uniformly, and they value it purely *de re*.

Conclusion

The purpose of this chapter was to analyse the logical form of valuing concepts or properties and objects. I argued that valuing a concept is a belief about a universal statement, and that valuing an object is a belief about an existential statement. Exploiting the differences between *de dicto* and *de re* beliefs, and the differences between uniform and 'non-uniform' quantification, a two-dimensional typology of six types of valuing was obtained. An application to valuing political freedom sketched an example of the use of the analysis.

Notes

1   Early references are Hartmann (1961) and Chisholm and Sosa (1966) for logics of
    value, and Perry (1957) for a logic of valuation.
2   The received view is found in the writings of Ronald Dworkin and Will Kymlicka.
    See, for instance, Dworkin (1979) and Kymlicka (1988). Carter (1999), Ch. 2, is the
    fullest expression of the criticism. Others siding with Carter include Matthew H.
    Kramer (2003), Serena Olsaretti (1999), and Martin van Hees (2000). The 'half-and-
    half' variety will be explained below.
3   One may ask whether the beliefs have to be true. Can I value water for its soporific
    qualities? If you answer affirmatively, I may object that it does not have these quali-
    ties. If you answer negatively, I may object that I may believe that water has these
    qualities. The present analysis can accommodate plain and possibly false beliefs as
    well as true beliefs and even knowledge by adjusting the intended interpretation of the
    Believe-operator.
4   Valuing a concept because of its objects, valuing the objects because of certain
    concepts, and so on *ad infinitum* or not? Whether this regress stops, and where, and
    whether this happens because of a *summum bonum* or because of a vicious circle, is
    up to the individual whose valuing is analysed and not for us to decide. There is no
    infinite regress in my proposal itself.
5   The question whether non-uniformity implies uniformity (for concepts as well as
    objects) will depend on the extent to which combining concepts by (possibly infi-
    nite) disjunction results in concepts. This may seem a bit of formal cheese-paring,
    because in ordinary second-order logic the biconditional $\forall x \exists C \varphi(x, C) \equiv \exists C \forall x \varphi(x, C)$
    is a tautology (the union of the non-uniformly obtained *sets* from the left hand side
    unproblematically serves the uniform right hand side). For *concepts* this is far from
    obvious.
6   The framework can also be applied to valuing other bearers of value, such as events,
    propositions and even possible worlds. First, observe that as soon as the uniform–non-
    uniform dimension is ignored, valuing a concept C is of the form

    $\exists C$ (C is contained in D & Value D).

    To analyse valuing events, for instance, the only question to be answered is what is
    the analogue of the relation 'is contained in'. A possible answer is 'is caused by',
    which yields

    $\exists C$ (C causes D & Value D)

    as the logic of valuing events. Prefix or suffix the existential quantifier with the
    Believe-operator, and you are done.
7   Kramer (2003: 241). For responsibility, see van Hees (2000: 154).
8   Given the overall claim of the book, Carter should have spoken about the value of 'our
    freedom' rather than of 'our freedoms'. The next sentence in the quote corrects the
    mistake.

References

Carter, I. (1999) *A Measure of Freedom*, Oxford: Oxford University Press.
Chisholm, R. and Sosa, E. (1966) 'On the logic of "intrinsically better"', *American
    Philosophical Quarterly*, 3: 244–249.
Dworkin, R. (1979) 'We do not have a right to liberty', in R. L. Cunningham (ed.), *Liberty
    and the Rule of Law*, College Station: Texas A&M University Press.
Hartman, R. S. (1961) 'The logic of value', *Review of Metaphysics*, 14: 389–432.

Kramer, M. H. (2003) *The Quality of Freedom*, Oxford: Oxford University Press

Kymlicka, W. (1988) 'Liberalism and communitarianism', *Canadian Journal of Philosophy*, 18: 181–204.

Olsaretti, S. (1999) 'The value of freedom and freedom of choice', *Notizie di Politeia*, 56: 114–121.

Perry, O. L. (1957) 'The logic of moral valuation', *Mind*, 66: 42–62.

Smith, M. (2002) 'Exploring the implications of the dispositional theory of value', *Philosophical Issues: Realism and Relativism*, 12: 329–347.

van Hees, M. (2000) *Legal Reductionism and Freedom*, Dordrecht: Kluwer Academic Publishers.

10 Holistic defences of rational choice theory

A critique of Davidson and Pettit

Thomas A. Boylan and Paschal F. O'Gorman

Introduction

The history of philosophy and the history of the mathematical sciences are inextricably linked. For instance, from Aristotle to Frege, Russell and Whitehead we witness the mathematico-logical clarification and axiomatization of deductive reasoning. Moreover, in the early decades of the twentieth century the axiomatization of probability occurred. For numerous philosophers, many of the domains of rational decision-making appear to resist mathematical analysis. This also changed during the course of the twentieth century. Analytic-minded philosophers and social scientists saw in what Pettit and others call *Homo economicus* the fundamental principles of rational decision-making that apply or should apply across the whole social spectrum.

In its historical development in the early decades of the twentieth century, *Homo economicus* was developed in the linguistic context of what philosophers call logical atomism and methodological individualism (Livingston 2001). However the 'ordinary language' paradigm shift in philosophy, initiated by the later Wittgenstein, resulted in the philosophical rejection, in large parts of the philosophical community, of logical atomism on the one hand and methodological individualism on the other. In their place, philosophers, such as Quine and Davidson, developed holistic approaches to philosophy of language in general and to philosophy of mind in particular (Quine 1960; Davidson 2001a,b,c).

Because of its historico-philosophical links to logical atomism and methodological individualism, a new philosophical case had to be made for *Homo economicus* in this holistic setting. Donald Davidson took up this challenge and developed a novel defence of *Homo economicus* within this holistic context. Moreover, in parallel and in sympathy with the spirit of the holistic linguistic turn, Philip Pettit also developed what he calls 'a conciliationist position', which reconciles *Homo economicus* with the common sense belief that *Homo economicus* principles are in fact not used by ordinary people arriving at their own decisions in their own unique cultural settings (Pettit 2002).

In this chapter we critically engage the approaches of Davidson and Pettit, fully accepting the paradigm shift to holism. Arising from our critique we suggest, contrary to the assumption of Davidson and Pettit, that rationality as such is not rule-governed in the sense of being definable by a finite set of precise rules or algorithms. Rather, in the spirit of the later Wittgenstein, we explore the possibility that, in the phrase of van Fraassen, rationality is 'bridled irrationality' and, in particular, that irrationality is constrained in divergent ways in different language-games or forms of life (van Fraassen 1989). In this conception, rationality is a family resemblance term, which has no common essence. In this setting, we argue for an empirical rather than an a priori approach to economic rationality. A central task is to identify in which domains *Homo economicus* principles apply and also to identify domains in which they do not apply. In the latter case, for instance in cases of economic decisions working in conditions of radical uncertainty as distinct from conditions of risk, the challenge is to develop models of rationality that are descriptively adequate to reality. In short, in the holistic turn, *Homo economicus* does not furnish us with the essence of human rationality.

The chapter is structured as follows. In the next section we outline Davidson's defence of *Homo economicus*. This is followed by the introduction of an alternative model of rationality, which is followed in turn by a critical engagement with Pettit's conciliationist position. After that we outline how economics may become more empirical. The final section provides a brief conclusion.

Davidson's defence of *Homo economicus*

The late Donald Davidson ranks among the leading and most influential American philosophers of the closing decades of the twentieth century. He developed 'a thoroughgoing holism' (Davidson 2004: 191) of the broad categories of meaning, belief, intention and desire. The philosophical context of his holism at the level of meaning was inspired by Quine's rejection of the empiricist dogma of the analytic–synthetic distinction (Quine 1951). However, Davidson's holism is much more radical and extensive than that of Quine. In Davidsonian holism 'states of mind we call propositional attitudes are identified and individuated by their relations to other states of mind' (Davidson 2004: 11). More generally and more extensively, 'there are no beliefs without many related beliefs, no beliefs without desires, no desires without beliefs, no intentions without both beliefs and desires' (Davidson 2001c: 126).

In this radically holistic framework Davidson constructs a novel defence of *Homo economicus*. Based on Davidson's own account, we reconstruct Davidson's defence in the context of a Socratic dialogue between HE (the *Homo economicus* rational agent) and NHE (the non *Homo economicus* agent).

NHE is faced with the following choices:

(i)   a large house at rent €1,000 a month;
(ii) a medium house at rent €800 a month;
(iii) a small house at rent €600 a month.

NHE prefers the large house to the medium; the difference in price is small for him. NHE prefers the medium to the small; here also the difference in price is small for him. But NHE prefers the small house to the large; in this case the difference in price is enough to outweigh consideration of size. HE points out to NHE that his preferences form an inconsistent triad and hence are irrational:

NHE: So what? Those are your standards of rationality, not mine.

HE: Decision theory says you must choose an option available to you such that none is preferred to it. In your case whatever option you choose there is another you like better.

NHE: If my option is between the large and the medium I choose the large; if it is between the medium and the small I take the medium; if my option is between the large and the small I take the small.

HE: Suppose I offer you all three, then what?

NHE: I take the large!

HE: But you prefer the small to the large!

NHE: Only if my choice is between the large and the small; if the medium is available I prefer the large.

To draw the dialogue to a conclusion HE points out to NHE that, by his own lights, he is sabotaging himself: a Dutch-book (sets a wagers such that under all circumstances the total pay-off is negative) can be made out against him.

According to Davidson, HE made a grave mistake at the beginning of the dialogue. HE is trying to pin down NHE to admit that he ought to subscribe to the principles of the *Homo economicus* model. The dialogue is conducted on the assumption that NHE has a choice. According to Davidson, 'this is a mistake.' For Davidson, NHE has no choice: 'he can't decide whether or not to accept the fundamental attributes of rationality' (Davidson 2004: 196). Rather 'these are principles shared by all creatures that have propositional attitudes or act intentionally' (ibid.: 194). 'Everyone does subscribe to those principles whether he knows it or not' (ibid.). Why? In the context of the holism of meaning, belief and desire 'it is a condition of having thoughts, judgments and intentions that the basic standards of rationality have application' (ibid.: 196).

Clearly Davidson is in the Kantian tradition. He is asking the philosophical question: what are the conditions of the possibility of a holistic state of mind in which the holism is one of meaning, belief, intention and desire? His answer is that any agent with holistic beliefs, intentions and desires 'cannot fail to comport *most of the time* with the basic norms of rationality' (Davidson 2004: 197, our italics). Thus he insists that whether a human agent subscribes to the principles of rationality 'is not an empirical question. Rather to identify irrationality, an agent must comport most of the time with the basic norms of rationality' (ibid.).

This may be illustrated by Davidson's analysis of the irrationality of an agent who acts contrary to his own best evaluation of the situation. The agent has a choice between two options, A and B. He weighs up the evidence on both sides and, after comparing these, he judges A is preferable to B. However, contrary to his own evaluation, the agent does B. The agent has reasons for doing both A and B but, according to his own lights, he has better reasons for doing A. According to Davidson, what needs explanation is not why the agent did B – we know why – but rather why he didn't do A, given his analysis of the situation. The irrationality of the choice of B lies in the fact that the agent 'goes against his second-order principle that he ought to act on what he holds to be best, everything considered' (Davidson 2004: 177). In light of this principle the irrationality of the agent's choice is exposed. The irrationality entered when the agents' desire to do B 'made him ignore or override his principle' (ibid.: 178).

An alternative model of rationality

It should be noted that this Davidsonian defence of the *Homo economicus* model is totally independent of various versions of methodological individualism, frequently associated with methodological defences of *Homo economicus*. On the contrary, an integral part of its originality lies in the fact that it is a radically holistic defence of that model. By virtue of the holism of meaning, located in our natural languages, the Davidsonian *Homo economicus* agent is first and foremost a social being. There are no traces of the individualism that haunts modern philosophy either in a Cartesian rationalist or in a Humean empiricist sense. As Davidson succinctly puts it: 'a condition for being a speaker is that there must be others enough like oneself' (Davidson 2001c: 120).

In this holistic social setting, Davidson concurs that the *Homo economicus* model has a strong normative element (Davidson 2004: 153). This normativity has two sources: the Dutch-book argument and Davidson's Kantian-type argument. The logic of the Dutch-book argument is impeccable. The issue is what are we to take from it about rationality? Van Fraassen's thesis is that, if and when we commit ourselves to a rule for the revision of opinion it must be via the *Homo economicus* model (van Fraassen 1989: 173). In other words the Dutch-book argument for *defining* rationality in terms of the *Homo economicus* model assumes that all rational decisions are rule-governed. However, there is another view of rationality that is not so limiting, in which the boundaries of rationality are much wider and more fluid. This is the case when 'rationality is only bridled irrationality' (ibid.: 172). We call this the socio-historical learning feedback model, or the SHLF model of rationality. We connect this to our Wittgensteinian analysis of rationality (Boylan and O'Gorman 2003).

In this analysis we invoked Wittgenstein's later work, particularly *On Certainty* (1969) and the *Philosophical Investigations* (1953), to demonstrate that the concept of rationality underlying orthodox economics is unduly restrictive and ultimately incompatible with the later Wittgenstein's contribution on rationality. Fundamental to Wittgenstein in this context were his concepts of 'the form of life' and the 'language-game' along with the centrality of acting as the generative basis of these concepts. In *On Certainty*, Wittgenstein argued that certain dispositions are so basic to our everyday forms of life that there is no reasonable way in which they could be doubted. For Wittgenstein, according to Kenny (1973), many types of doubt are ruled out. There are some propositions about which we cannot doubt, but neither are we mistaken about them. However, for Wittgenstein, 'to say that something cannot be doubted, or cannot be the subject of a mistake, is not the same as to say it can be *known*' (ibid.: 211, our italics). For Wittgenstein, according to Kenny, 'I know that p' makes sense only when we can claim 'I do not know' or 'I doubt' or 'I will check up that ...' also makes sense (ibid.: 214). Wittgenstein was in general not prepared to agree with G. E. Moore, in response to whose work *On Certainty* was written, that there were certain propositions that he *knew* and that provided the existence of the external world. However, he did agree with Moore that there were particular empirical-type propositions that had a special status and the status of these propositions he described as 'solid' or that 'stand fast' for us (Wittgenstein 1969: 112, 116, 151). Wittgenstein is clear that the role of these propositions is quite different from that of axioms in a deductive system, i.e. they are not axioms in the sense of being the starting point of a deductive chain of reasoning. Rather he links them to his concept of 'world-picture', which he argues is not learned by experience, but is in fact 'the inherited background against which I distinguish between true and false' (ibid.: 94). Nor are these propositions the *basis* for our language-games. However, they are integral to our actions, and 'it is our acting which lies at the bottom of the language-game' (ibid.: 204).

Lionel Robbins in his celebrated essay, *An Essay on the Nature and Significance of Economic Science* (1932), defended the postulates of orthodox economics along lines that could be construed as distinctly Wittgensteinian. For Robbins these

> are not postulates the existence of whose counterpart in reality admits of extensive dispute once their nature is fully realized ... they are so much the stuff of everyday experience that they have only to be stated to be recognized as obvious.
>
> (Robbins 1932: 79)

On this interpretation, the neoclassical principles of rationality cannot be doubted, though technically they are not known. They are basic in that they are rooted in our social actions, which create our forms of life. Alternatively stated, the hard core of the rationality principles of orthodox neoclassical microeconomics inform the basis of human action in the economic world and consequently it is either impossible or unreasonable to doubt these postulates. The philosophy of the later Wittgenstein could arguably be viewed as providing a philosophical defence of an unchanging set of principles that constitute the core of orthodox neoclassical rationality.

However, on closer examination this position is neither defensible nor justifiable. In the *Philosophical Investigations*, Wittgenstein argues that a principle cause of philosophical error is the over-use of a particular diet of examples. Rather than settling for a narrow or overly restricted set of examples, we should seek the widest range of pertinent examples to establish whether or not there is a common core emerging. The issue of a common core is central to Wittgenstein's thinking and he is adamant that we should not commit to the idea that there must be some common core to rationality. When we encounter the axioms of orthodox rationality theory, which assumes that each economic agent has, among other characteristics, a complete and transitive preference ordering of all possible choices, we do well to remember that this holds only for simple problems in the context of decision-making. We know, as Savage pointed out over 50 years ago, that 'the behaviour of people is often at variance with the theory. The departure is sometimes flagrant' (Savage 1954: 20). Within the Wittgensteinian framework, if behaviour is *often* at variance with orthodox theory, then the theory is not 'basic' in his sense of that term. Wittgenstein, as we have pointed out, gives priority to 'forms of life', and in prioritizing forms of life he looked to what was basic to human action. Savage's position is not compatible with Robbins's claim that the standard axioms of choice are 'the stuff of everyday experience', and for Wittgenstein are therefore not basic in his sense of that term. In Boylan and O'Gorman (2003) we argued more generally that the philosophy of the later Wittgenstein was totally incompatible with the orthodox economic position on rationality, and went on to critically examine the philosophical basis for this argument. We do not propose to rehearse these arguments here. Suffice it to say that, for the purposes of our argument in this chapter, our Wittgensteinian analysis complements, we believe, our argument for the SHLF model of rationality, which is central to our position here.

The SHLF model is diametrically opposed to the notion of rationality adopted by Davidson. As we saw above, Davidson starts with the assumption that rationality is rule-governed and subsequently uses these normative rules to identify irrationality. The SHLF model is based on our interpretation of a later Wittgensteinian approach to rationality. Briefly, in the SHLF model the human agent has a store of wisdom built up over a period of time in specific socio-cultural contexts. Through learning feedback mechanisms, similar to the Popperian quadruple of problem–tentative solution–error elimination–new problems, the SHLF model updates or modifies this store of wisdom (Boylan and O'Gorman, 2008). This dynamic store of wisdom does not exist in a non-historical, Platonic world. Rather it is embedded in Wittgensteinian language-games or forms of life. In this way, divergent rational traditions emerge and there is no common rule-governed core to these traditions. Rather than saying, with Davidson, the *Homo economicus* model must apply for the most part, we propose empirical investigations to ascertain when, how and to what extent the model or its parameters apply. For instance, as pointed out by Pettit, a number of rational decisions are culturally framed in such a way that the *Homo economicus* model does not apply (Pettit 2002).

The SHLF model of rationality includes theory choice in the sciences in periods of revolutionary science. In these periods, scientists creatively invented new hypotheses and theories going way beyond what is permissable in the *Homo economicus* model. As van Fraassen points out, 'when I say rationality does not require conditionalization ... I have not implied that standards of criticism do not exist, but only that they are not a matter of logic' (van Fraassen 1989: 175). The SHLF notion of rationality would also include what Keynes called decision-making under radical uncertainty, as distinct from decision-making under conditions of risk, for which the *Homo economicus* model applies. Such decisions occur today in such areas as high-technology research and development, where the past is no guide for the future.

So much for the Dutch-book argument for defining rationality in terms of the *Homo economicus* model. As we already noted, Davidson also offers a different defence; the operability of the *Homo economicus* principles is a *sine qua non* for the existence of our holistic web of meaning, belief, intention and desire. In the language of possible worlds, Davidson's thesis is as follows: the *Homo economicus* principles of rationality are for the most part operable in any and every possible linguistic world of the holism of meaning, belief, intention and desire. A significant question here is how are we to understand Davidson's qualification, which is conveyed in the Aristotelian terminology for the most part? Clearly irrationality exists in our holistic world of meaning, belief, intention and desire; some of the time intentional agents make irrational decisions. In this connection, Davidson maintains that we could not identify such irrational decisions if we did not use the *Homo economicus* principles. In so far as irrationality exists, then the *Homo economicus* principles hold only for the most part. Clearly this sense of 'for the most part' is compatible with the *Homo economicus* definition of rationality. However, is it compatible with the SHLF notion of rationality? From the SHLF point of view one could read Davidson as follows. Normal rationality is governed by the *Homo economicus* model in that its principles apply to normal decision-making. However, in a small number of exceptional cases, such as decisions in revolutionary periods of science or decisions under Keynesian uncertainty, other rational considerations apply. Thus the *Homo economicus* model would be a necessary condition for normal rationality. We now turn to the thesis that the *Homo economicus* model holds for the most part in normal situations and on how this impacts on the possibility that this model is a necessary condition of normal rationality.

Pettit's conciliationist thesis

Davidson's Kantian defense of the *Homo economicus* model extends the domain of application of this model from the relatively narrow domain of economic transactions to the vast range of non-economic choices. The focus of his Kantian argument is not just a rational economic agent operating in a market economy. Rather it is any rational, linguistic agent with a holistic web of meanings, beliefs, intentions and desires, which of course includes rational economic agents. Any such rational agent must, for the most part, operate the principles of the *Homo economicus* model.

As we already noted, Davidson maintains that it is not an empirical issue whether or not a person subscribes to these principles. However, if the principles hold for the most part in every possible holistic world of meaning, intention, belief and desire, then they hold also in our world and thus may be discovered or seen to operate for the most part in our world. The *prima facie* evidence, however, is to the contrary. As Pettit and others point out, the *Homo economicus* model 'clearly does not apply across the broad range of human interaction' (Pettit 2002: 209). Rather, according to Pettit, the normal mode under which people interact with one another 'is closer to the model of a debate than the model of a bargain' (ibid.: 229). Pettit sums this up in the apt phrase of the 'cultural framing of a situation'. In this terminology people 'let their actions (in non-market contexts) be dictated in what we might call cultural framing of the situation in which they find themselves' (ibid.: 233). This cultural framing is a vast network connecting politeness, honesty, fair play, friendship, kindness, commitment to ideals, membership of certain groups and so on. Contrary to Davidson, it would appear that this cultural framework, and not the *Homo economicus* model, is the cement of human rationality. The *Homo economicus* model simply does not, contrary to Davidson, operate for the most part in culturally framed decisions.

Pettit fully endorses the thesis of cultural framing, yet he wants to develop 'a conciliationist position' that reconciles the cultural framework insight with the *Homo economicus* model (Pettit 2002: 222). Pettit rejects any effort to reconcile both by maintaining that the *Homo economicus* model is implicitly present in cultural framing situations, when 'implicitly present' is taken to mean that, in acting, 'agents conduct some peripheral scanning of what their own advantage dictates that they should do' (ibid.: 231). This line of approach would locate this peripheral scanning in the Sartrean distinction between conscience de and conscience (de) – the tram driver is explicitly conscious of the line in front of him but, while aware of, is less explicitly conscious of the surrounding area. The reconciliation affected by Pettit is by deploying 'the virtual–actual model' (ibid.: 232). The *Homo economicus* model is virtual in the sense of being 'non actual' but 'hovering on the edge of realization', rather than being 'realized in some sub-articulate fashion' (ibid.: 232). He spells this out as follows. Let us suppose 'the hegemony of cultural framing holds in everyday decision making. In this sense people may proceed under more or less automatic cultural pilot in most cases' (ibid.: 233). However, 'at any point where a decision is liable to cost them dearly in self-regarding terms the alarm bells ring and prompt them to consider personal advantage' (ibid.: 233). In this way

> the homo economicus model has no actual presence in dictating what people do; it will not be present in deliberation and will make no impact on decisions. But it will always be virtually present in deliberation ... The agent will run under cultural pilot, provided the pilot does not lead into terrain that is too dangerous from a self-interested point of view. Let such a terrain come into view, and the agent will quickly return to manual, beginning to count the more personal losses and benefits that are at stake in the decision at hand.
>
> (Pettit 2002: 233–234)

Clearly a Pettit-type argument may be applied to our SHLF model in that it is subject to 'the hegemony of cultural framing'.

In our opinion Pettit's virtual–actual distinction is analogous to J.S. Mill's distinction between secondary or conventional principles of morality and the fundamental utilitarian principle, i.e. the so-called greatest happiness principle (Mill 1838). In everyday life people use conventional morality to guide their actions. However, it can happen that these secondary conventional principles conflict. To resolve this conflict, one has recourse to the fundamental principle. In this sense the fundamental utilitarian principle is not present in normal moral deliberation. However, it virtually exists in that, at times of difficulty, one can have recourse to it. This analogy to Mill will be used to explore the implications of Pettit's conciliationist position.

In particular, our question is whether Pettit's approach falls within the SHLF model of rationality, or ultimately within rationality as defined by the *Homo economicus* model. The *prima facie* answer is that Pettit's position falls within the SHLF model of rationality. There is more to rationality than what is prescribed by the *Homo economicus* model: culturally framed decisions are rational but beyond the scope of the model. Let us scrutinize the case a little more thoroughly. When does the *Homo economicus* model come into operation and what are the implications of its use in these circumstances? Two sets of circumstances were envisaged above. First, following Davidson, the model is used to identify the irrationality of some choices. In these cases, the principles of the model appear to function as necessary criteria of rationality. However, if we accept the SHLF model of rationality, these criteria cannot be necessary conditions of rationality. If they were, then culturally framed decisions would be irrational. Rather in the SHLF model one would point out that in the case of culturally framed decisions the fundamental parameters of the *Homo economicus* model do not apply.

The second scenario in which the *Homo economicus* model becomes actual is, following Pettit, when alarm bells ring for individuals using culturally framed considerations. In this scenario, in response to these alarm bells, the agent switches to the parameters of the *Homo economicus* model. This switch can be read in two different ways, depending on how far one exploits the analogy to Mill's distinction between secondary and primary principles. If one accepts Pettit's distinction between virtual and actual, *without* assuming that the *Homo economicus* model is *fundamental or core,* then one is operating within the SHLF model of rationality. At times, there is a conflict between the self-regarding principles of the *Homo economicus* model and some of the values of our cultural framework. In the SHLF approach to rationality, priority is not necessarily given to the *Homo economicus* model: if conflict emerges then this conflict at times is resolved in favour of the values of our cultural framework. Thus the *Homo economicus* model is not the ultimate or fundamental bedrock of rationality.

On the other hand, one could agree that the *Homo economicus* model is virtual, while insisting that it *constitutes the fundamental basis of rationality.* In this reading, though the model is virtual, it is strongly prescriptive in the sense of summing up the fundamental or foundational principles of rationality. Thus the model, which exists in virtual reality, is the ultimate bedrock of rationality. It is to rationality what the utilitarian principle is to the Millean reading of conventional morality. It, as it were, sums up the first principles of rationality. The SHLF model of rationality would find this virtual, foundational reading of the *Homo economicus* model unacceptable. For instance, if alarm bells were to ring with a decision in conditions of radical uncertainty, recourse to the *Homo economicus* model in its foundational reading would reduce the parameters of the decision to one of risk, thereby abstracting away the uncertainty, which is core to the decision process. In short, if the *Homo economicus* model is taken as the ultimate but virtual ground of rationality, then *fundamentally* human rationality is rule-bound. This clearly conflicts with the SHLF model of rationality.

Economic rationality: empirical challenges of the SHLF model

Thus far our case has been largely negative. We have outlined some reasons why we are not convinced by Davidson's holistic, Kantian-type defence of the *Homo economicus* model. Positively, we briefly outlined a *prima facie* case for the SHLF model of rationality, whereby, in van Fraassen's phrase, human rationality is seen as bridled irrationality. This model sets the boundaries of rationality much wider than those of the *Homo economicus* model and would include culturally framed decisions. But what of specific economic decisions? Perhaps these are defined by the *Homo economicus* model? We already acknowledged that the logic of the Dutch-book argument is impeccable. Thus it could be argued that, whatever about human rationality in general, the *Homo economicus* model provides the necessary logical framework for economic decision-making.

Indeed one might plausibly buttress this position by exploiting a Pettit-type thesis of the virtual reality of this model along the following lines. In their normal, non-economic lives, consumers make rational choices in the context of their cultural frameworks. However, when it comes to consumer choice of goods and services, alarm bells begin to ring when they apply their non-economic, cultural frames to these economic decisions. As consumers they do not wish to sabotage their own economic interests. Thus the *Homo economicus* model becomes active in their consumer choice. In a similar fashion, producers also quickly learn the indispensability of this model. In this fashion both producers and consumers become rational maximizers and, thus the *Homo economicus* model becomes normative.

As with the Dutch-book argument outlined earlier it seems to us that a negative response is still possible. The Dutch-book argument in this specific case is assuming that *economic* rationality is rule-bound. An alternative is to maintain that the SHLF theory of rationality also applies to economic rational decision-making. In this SHLF approach, the economic choices that are rule-governed are subject to the logic of the *Homo economicus* model. However, some rational economic decisions fall outside the boundary set by the *Homo economicus* model. We now briefly sketch some possible lines of enquiry that could be followed in the SHLF approach to this range of economic rational decision-making processes.

Initially, one could make a *prima facie* case for the SHLF model of economic rationality by specifying some clear examples of rational economic decision-making that are not subject to the *Homo economicus* model. We have already noted one: economic decisions under conditions of radical uncertainty. Another interesting example is suggested in the history of economic thought. The famous Irish philosopher, Berkeley, in his *Querist*, advocated the choice of a currency not backed by gold/silver bullion. It could be argued that his mode of argumentation represented advocacy for a model of a more exchange-based economy to facilitate development in seventeenth-century Ireland, which arguably went far outside the axiomatized parameters set by the *Homo economicus* model. So-called 'forced' economic decisions may constitute another counterexample. Certainly the choices of very poor consumers, contrary to revealed preference theory, do not show their actual preferences.

As we already noted, the SHLF approach to economic rationality is imbued by the spirit of the later Wittgenstein as he advises us to ignore prescriptions, and in their place to look and see (Boylan and O'Gorman 2003). This empirical approach gives rise to various research programmes in economics, unconstrained by the parameters of the *Homo economicus* model. One such research programme would exploit the use of computer simulation studies of complex systems to develop alternative models of economic rationality to the *Homo economicus* one. For instance, these computer simulations could be used to invent hypotheses about economic decision-making, whereby so-called basic principles of the *Homo economicus* model of rationality are rejected. Such a rejection would be analogous to an attack on a hub in a complex network of nodes, in which a hub has greater weight than other nodes in the network. Moreover, such studies would be wholly compatible with a holistic approach to economic rationality. Other empirical research programmes would have recourse to decisions trees, expert systems and other techniques to study economic rationality in different domains (e.g. health) or by specific kinds of economic agents (e.g. entrepreneurs, investors, venture capitalists, etc).

The general attitude of this SHLF empirical programme is not to prescribe in advance the extensiveness of the *Homo economicus* model. Only after detailed empirical research can this issue be answered. In short, in the SHLF framework the *Homo economicus* model is but one among others and, although its domain of application may elucidate the domain of economic decision-making in the case of risk as distinct from uncertainty and other non-probability choices, its extensiveness in the real social world of economic rational choice is a matter of empirical research.

Conclusion

We have argued that Davidson's holistic defense of *Homo economicus* presupposes that there is an essential core to human rationality that is rule-governed. In the spirit of the later Wittgenstein we maintain that human rationality is historically contextualized and dynamic with no common core. In this context we expose an ambiguity in Pettit's conciliationist position: on one reading the principles of *Homo economicus* are fundamental whereas on another reading they are not. Moreover, in our SHLF conception of rationality, we do not in an a priori manner prescribe any particular model of rationality. Rather, by carrying out detailed empirical research in different economic domains, the economist is challenged to construct a variety of models of rational decision-making that are descriptively adequate to their specific domains.

References

Boylan, T. A. and O'Gorman, F. P. (2003) 'Economic theory and rationality: a Wittgensteinian interpretation', *Review of Political Economy*, 15: 231–244.

—— (eds) (2008) *Popper and Economic Methodology: Contemporary Challenges*, London: Routledge.

Davidson, D. (2001a) *Essays on Actions and Events*, 2nd edn, Oxford: Clarendon Press.

—— (2001b) *Inquiries into Truth and Interpretation*, 2nd edn, Oxford: Clarendon Press.

—— (2001c) *Subjective, Intersubjective, Objective*, Oxford: Clarendon Press.

—— (2004) *Problems of Rationality*, Oxford: Clarendon Press.

Kenny, A. (1973) *Wittgenstein*, Harmondsworth: Penguin.

Livingston, P. M. (2001) 'Russellian and Wittgensteinian atomism,' *Philosophical Investigations*, 24: 30–54.

Mill, J. S. (1838) 'Bentham', *London and Westminister Review*, August 1838; reprinted in A. Ryan (ed.) *Utilitarianism and Other Essay: John Stuart Mill and Jeremy Bentham*, Harmondsworth: Penguin, 1987.

Pettit, P. (2002) *Rules, Reasons, and Norms*, Oxford: Clarendon Press.

Quine, W. V. O. (1951) 'Two dogmas of empiricism', *Philosophical Review*, 60: 20–43; reprinted in *From a Logical Point of View*, Cambridge, MA: Harvard University Press, 1961.

—— (1960) *Word and Object*, Cambridge, MA: MIT Press.

Robbins, L. (1932) *An Essay on the Nature and Significance of Economic Science*, London: Macmillan.

Savage, L. (1954) *The Foundations of Statistics*, New York: Wiley.

van Fraassen, B. (1989) *Laws and Symmetry*, Oxford: Clarendon Press.

Wittgenstein, L. (1953) *Philosophical Investigations*, Oxford: Blackwell.

—— (1969) *On Certainty*, Oxford: Blackwell.

Index